When Paddy Met Geordie
The Irish in County Durham and Newcastle
1840-1880

Roger Cooter

**University of
Sunderland Press**

© Roger Cooter

ISBN 1 873757 65 4

First published 2005

We are very grateful to *The Ireland Fund of Great Britain* for a generous grant in aid of publication

Cover Design by Murphy Creative Ltd
Copy edited by Felicity Hepburn

Published in Great Britain by
The University of Sunderland Press
in association with Business Education Publishers Limited
The Teleport
Doxford International
Sunderland
SR3 3XD

Tel: 0191 5252410
Fax: 0191 5201815

All rights reserved. No part of this publication, may be reproduced, stored in a retrieval system, or transmitted, in any form or by any means, electronic, mechanical, photocopying, recording or otherwise, without the prior permission of the University of Sunderland Press.

British Cataloguing-in-Publications Data
A catalogue record for this book is available from the British Library

Printed in Great Britain by the Alden Group, Oxford.

*In Memory of Heinrich Speetzen
(1938-1990)*

Contents

List of Maps and Tables

Foreword by Donald MacRaild

Author's Preface

Introduction   1

Chapter 1
    Enumerations   7

Chapter 2
    Living Conditions and Social Place   21

Chapter 3
    The Catholic Church   45

Chapter 4
    Anti-Catholicism   73

Chapter 5
    Occupational Place and Labour Relations   111

Chapter 6
    Political Awakenings   143

Conclusion 173

Appendix 175

References 187

Bibliography 245

Index 263

List of Maps and Tables

Maps

1.1-1.4 Percentage and Density of Irish-born Population in England and Wales, 1841, 1861.

3.1 Catholic Churches and Missions of Co. Durham and Newcastle, 1846.

3.2 Catholic Churches and Missions of Co. Durham and Newcastle, 1876.

4.1 Distribution of Roman Catholics in England, 1851, by Census.

4.2 Distribution of Roman Catholics in England, 1851, by Marriages in Roman Catholic Churches.

4.3. Distribution of Roman Catholics in Co. Durham and Newcastle, 1851, by Census.

Tables

1.1 Population of Durham and Newcastle, 1841-81.

1.2 Immigrant Population in Durham and Newcastle, 1841-1881.

1.3 Irish-born Population in Durham and Newcastle, 1841-1881.

1.4 Distribution of Irish-born in County Durham, 1851-61.

1.5 Approximate Growth of Irish Population in Durham and Newcastle, 1841-71

3.1 Estimated Roman Catholic Population of Durham and Newcastle, 1847-82

3.2 Easter Communicants in Durham and Newcastle, 1847-82

4.1 Places of Worship and Seating Accommodation in Durham and Newcastle

4.2 Relative Position of Church of England, National and Local, 1851

Foreword

The publication of Roger Cooter's study of the Irish in the North-east more than thirty years after it was submitted as a Durham University thesis is testament to a work of scholarship that was ahead of its time. The work remains important and is deserving of a wider audience than it has so far enjoyed.

Cooter's research offered a revisionist perspective at a time when revisionism was not even remotely fashionable among scholars and students of the Irish in Britain.[1] His examination of the Irish in the North-east was among the first to question the general tendency among historians to focus on social dislocation, isolation and, in particular, violent reprisal against the migrants. Classical studies had concentrated upon Irish Catholics as victims of indigenous hatred, an out-group at the bottom of the social scale: indeed, these themes remained constants until the 1990s. But Cooter took an essentially integrationist approach to the Irish experience. The inspiration for his position came from E.P. Thompson who, in his famous account of class development in early industrial England, pointed to the ease not the difficulty with which the Irish had established themselves within the wider working class. Other writers, such as the sociologist John Rex, also point to this ease of passage into the mainstream – a journey made easier by many shared customs, an essentially permeable culture and shared skin colour.[2]

For Roger Cooter, as for these other pioneers, the Irish experience in the North-east was relatively (if not absolutely) tranquil and stood in marked contrast to the studies of Irish settlement in the archetypal migrant towns of south Lancashire and the west of

Scotland. Cooter noted a number of specific characteristics of the northern region that prevented anti-Irishness and sectarianism building up the same head of steam as it did in the North-west. In particular, he noticed traditions of religious toleration and low levels of Anglicanism; a liberal political culture; and an expanding labour-hungry economy which aided Irish integration. Cooter's original thesis was tacitly comparative in that his understanding of the toleration shown towards Irish settlers and Catholics in the North-east was measured against a backdrop of fierce religious rivalry and regular communal violence in parts of Lancashire, notably Liverpool, and in the towns of Scotland's central belt.

When Cooter first conducted his research, the supporting literature was relatively sparse. Only one national study of the Irish in this period had been completed, whereas today there are three.[3] Although much new research has been conducted into the Irish in Britain since he first worked on this subject, the core elements of his work remain intact, providing a viable starting point for further research. In some senses this is a surprising claim, because the decades since he first wrote this work have witnessed a huge body of new literature. But echoes of Cooter remain. The wider historiography continues to stress the importance of regions and localities in the way that he did. The exhortation can be seen quite clearly in the collections of pioneering essays edited by Roger Swift and Sheridan Gilley, which point out the shifting perspectives on the subject matter, with case studies and regional analyses providing a particularly fruitful way forward.[4] Moreover, a host of journal articles, far too numerous to cite here, have since borne witness to the scholarly industry that has built up in specific localities in the wake of the pioneering exertions of these scholars of the 1960s and 1970s.

******

Despite Roger Cooter's work, the North-east region remains relatively under-emphasised by historians of Irish migration. Even now, a bibliography of the Irish in the North-east barely runs to double figures.[5] Why is this the case? The issue of timing is important for several reasons. First, the North-east was a late arrival on the industrial scene and so missed out in the wave upon wave of social reportage that accompanied the Irish elsewhere. In the generation after Napoleon, when great tides of Irish settlers were washing into the ports of western Britain, little mention was made of a similar presence entering the North-east. A particular example is most important: the accounts of Irish settlement in Britain which accompanied the larger investigations of the case for a poor law in Ireland in the 1830s. Whilst Cumberland merited mention in George Cornewall Lewis's important parliamentary report of 1834 (published in 1836), the limited scale of the North-east's Irish 'problem' is hinted at by the range of his survey, for apart from Edinburgh, it was restricted mainly to the west coast between Glasgow and Liverpool. Lewis's decision to overlook what was, in the North-east, a growing Catholic Irish population is mirrored by similar omissions on the part of later historians.[6]

The contemporary perception was to impact upon what historians would later write. Cooter's thesis noted with some frustration the fact that works such as J.H. Treble's thesis on the Irish in the north contained precious little information about the North-east dimension.[7] Treble's omission was governed partly by the lack of markers laid down in the social reportage of the period in question. But it was also governed by chronology. Indeed, this question of timing is also one of emphasis on the development of regional culture. It is inconceivable that, by the later nineteenth century, any social survey of Irish migration or of urban and industrial growth, would have neglected the North-east as Lewis did with his survey in the 1830s. But we must remember that what came after the 1830s, in terms of economic development, totally outstripped previous experience. Whilst the nature of development may not have changed – coal, minerals and ships remained staples in the region – the scales of production were vastly expanded. Most of the great names of the Tyneside region were products of the post-1850 period. The shipbuilding districts north and south of the Tyne, including Jarrow and Hebburn, Howdon, Wallsend, Willington and Walker, were hamlets in the 1840s; but by the 1880s they had become major towns and large centres of

Irish settlement. The growth in the local economy created a demand for labour, and a commensurate expansion in the opportunities for migrants, which is central to Cooter's emphasis on industrial and social quiescence rather than sectarianism.

If the question of timing helped to explain the academic neglect of the North-east's Irish communities, the same issue also played out with respect to sources, in particular the absence of necessary demographic data. At the time of Cooter's research, census-based analysis was in its infancy. Today's culture of analysing massive quantities of machine-readable census data was much slower and more expensive in the 1970s. Moreover, pioneering work of this sort was only coming to press as Cooter's research came to an end. The most notable case was Michael Anderson's pathbreaking research on the 1851 census, which appeared in 1971.[8] Anderson's work soon inspired many others to examine the census as a source for examining the Irish 'on the ground', albeit within the constraints of decennial 'snapshot' data.[9] Liverpool University's Department of Geography was in the process of producing major large-scale analyses of a similar type – including the works of Papworth and Pooley on Liverpool.[10] These evaluations of the census enumerators' handbooks, using techniques which are now common, were rare in those days. In the intervening years, technology and access to data have resulted in a number of book-length studies of the Irish which make use of detailed census schedules.[11] In parallel to these British-based studies, other pioneering works have been undertaken in Ireland with respect to Irish occupation data, neighbourhood formation, and sectarian socio-economic profiling.[12]

Although these works of census analysis, with their sociological and geographical approach, would become enormously influential as templates for future study, they remained infant projects in the early 1970s and even beyond. Aside from technological restrictions, there was a more important reason why this is so: the hundred-year closure ruling on those same manuscript sources. In the early twenty-first century, historians can access all census scripts from 1841 to 1901; in the 1960s, the furthest forward an English historian could scan was 1861. Clearly, this not only impacted upon the scale of operations *per se*, but also had a particularly acute effect on the North-east, where pre-1860s censuses were likely to reveal less about the region's mass Irish community than studies which looked beyond that date.

Cooter addressed these difficulties by concentrating on the tabulated census overviews which enabled him to sketch out the main centres of Irish settlement. But certain parts of his thesis, not least contentions about the nature of Irish work, could not be followed up in a systematic way without access to enumerators' handbooks. Since the 1990s Frank Neal's ongoing large-scale analysis of the manuscript censuses for the North-east has begun to yield important findings about the structure of the Irish populace. Another recent major census-based analysis, which also derives inspiration from the Liverpool school, is Mike Barke's study of Newcastle's nineteenth-century population history.[13] Whilst works such as Neal's and Barke's are beginning to reveal much more about patterns and changes in Irish household size, marital patterns, birthplaces, and occupations, it remains to be seen whether these will support or undermine Cooter's original notions with respect to the socio-economic position of the Irish.

Beyond these more technical works of census analysis, a number of subsequent works have been produced to shed new light on the Irish in the North-east. But none of them has attempted the kind of broad social, economic and political coverage offered in Cooter's study. Much of this new work has examined new themes, and some significant contributions have been made to our knowledge of the region's political and religious cultures, and of the Irish within such cultures. Doherty's study of the pre-famine period, which concentrates on Northumberland and Newcastle, offers a complement to Cooter's study of the post-Famine decades. Caroline Scott's important PhD thesis picks up Cooter's theme of tolerance and relative quietude and explores it with respect to anti-Catholicism and no-popery traditions in Newcastle, Manchester and Liverpool. Like Cooter, she promotes a model of North-east society in which intolerance is much less pronounced than in Lancashire. And a host of local studies has added to our knowledge without changing the way we think about the region or its Irish. It is certainly clear that the North-east's tolerant Liberal culture aided Irish settlement: Cooter is correct on that score and no amount of revision is likely to undermine the core idea. The North-east returned very few Tory MPs in the period 1880-1914 and supported Irish Nationalist claims to Home Rule with a gusto unparalleled elsewhere. The extent of Tyneside's approbation for the Irish cause is often characterised by the support which Joseph Cowen, Radical MP for Newcastle and owner of the *Chronicle*, showed for the cause. But it ran deeper than that – despite important Tory grandees, such as Londonderry, and the solid bloc of Unionist votes throughout the region, men such as Cowen, the shipbuilding entrepreneur Charles Mark Palmer of Jarrow, and the largest body of employees, the miners, supported Liberalism and, in turn, were at least were not hostile to the political cause of nationalist Ireland.[14]

Whilst Cooter's analysis of the political culture of the Irish Northeast is undoubtedly correct, some other elements of his work have been challenged. Whether such contestation will result in falsification, adaptation or revision is not yet clear. The argument that a key factor in the relative absence of ethnic conflict in the North-east was full employment has been called into question because both Lancashire and western Scotland had labour-hungry economies, yet animosity there was rife. It was a concern with this question that led Neal to test Cooter's assumptions by examining levels of anti-Irish violence in the North-east region. Drawing upon extensive press sources for a wide array of fights, assaults and beatings, and covering much of the Northeast from Morpeth to Middlesbrough, Neal concluded that the region was far less free of sectarian violence than had been suggested.[15] Cooter himself had acknowledged this fact, but whether he did underestimate the levels of violence will depend on further research.

In part, a tendency towards violence is explained by the character of the Irish communities themselves. It is highly possible that new research will reveal a higher proportion of Protestants and a higher proportion of Ulster-derived migrants in the western sector of Northeast England from where much of Neal's evidence of violence – some of it serious – is derived. A high Irish Protestant presence alongside a sizeable Catholic population may account for higher levels of violence. Cooter points to the relative scarcity of Orange lodges in the North-east as proof of the low incidence of sectarian disharmony in the region; but new evidence has shown that there was a rather stronger Orange presence at certain times. The lodge system in those parts of west Durham where Irish Protestants settled was very strong, lasting continuously for more than a hundred years from the 1860s. Whilst the lodges in towns such as Consett, Crook and Chopwell were not as numerous as in Barrow-in-Furness or Preston, and were not individually as powerful as in Jarrow or Hebburn, they were important. New research also suggests that the Miners' Strike (1844), which Cooter looks at in terms of violent reprisals against Irish 'knobsticks' brought in to break the conflict, was part of this general drift of Irish Protestants to the North-east. These men whom Londonderry brought over were the same individuals who propagated what was for a while a powerful, if small, coterie of lodges in east Durham, especially Rainton and Murton in the 1850s and 1860s.[16] But the key point is that Cooter acknowledges focal points of anti-Irish violence but denies that such violence was as common or intense as, later on, Neal would argue. Whilst Cooter's thesis and Neal's essay stand in opposition awaiting further contributions to the debate, there is, as yet, no resolution to the issue.

The discussion of violence illustrates that Cooter's work remains important. It advances a strong thesis about the nature of the North-east, backed by a cogent and coherent argument. This continuing sense of relevance explains why it is now being brought to the press. With a wider circulation we hope the work will promote further consideration of the key issues raised. Roger Cooter never intended his study to constitute the final word on the subject. I sincerely hope that, by producing the work in book form, we will ensure that this is not so.

Donald M. MacRaild
Professor of History
Victoria University of Wellington, New Zealand

Author's Preface

It is not very often that one has the chance to publish the fruits of research conducted some three decades before. A rare opportunity, it's also a surprise. Having long since abandoned the Irish and the North-east for a career in the history of science and medicine, I had assumed that this, my first post-graduate product, was still in the company of other bound Masters' theses, gathering dust in a university library. It was hugely flattering to learn otherwise: that for some time been it had been taking on thumb-prints instead – those tread marks of scholars chasing sources and resources for debate. I'd forgotten that I had intended it to be so; indeed, to that end, had submitted parts of it to print.[1] My central argument – that the social, economic, political and religious state of mid-nineteenth century North-east England was such as to render the immigration of poverty-stricken Irish Catholics unusually pacific – ran counter to popular academic belief at the time, as well as, somewhat, to the historical fashion for social narratives of struggling underdogs. If my calculations were right and the ratio of Irish-to-English in the North-east was the fourth highest in the England by the 1860s (surpassed only by their numbers in London, Manchester and Liverpool) then – presuming other historical accounts were not wildly mistaken – the relatively tolerant reception of the Irish in the North-east was in need of explanation. All the more so in view of my finding that Irish blacklegging in the local coal industry was not only rare but opposed by the Irish themselves and, further, that these nationalist-minded immigrants had slid into local politics with remarkable ease. Perhaps, then, more than I appreciated at the time, there *was* reason for others to be interested.

I'm delighted that it should have turned out so. And it seems all the more fortuitous that this study should be published now – at a time when asylum seeking in Britain is back in the news big time and is commonly cast (as with the Irish in the nineteenth century) in terms of welfare scroungers and burdens on the rates. Reminiscent, too, are the alleged connections between 'illegal immigrants' and (Fenian-like) 'terrorists', to say nothing of the explosive power of ethnic and religious differences currently fanned furious in political rhetoric. Thus the moment would seem propitious for telling this rather different, altogether more salutary tale.

I can hardly recollect the exact circumstances of my becoming interested in it. The topic was suggested to me by the supervisor to whom I was assigned by the History Department at the University of Durham, Alan Heesom (as it happened, a most knowledgeable and tolerant mentor). Whether he registered a connection between my own immigrant status and that of the migrants to Durham and Newcastle a century before, I do not know. Superficially, at least, my arrival – peachy-keen from undergraduate history in my home town of Vancouver – had little in common with that of the poor Irish Catholics who sought refuge from their blighted homeland (despite the resemblances there sometimes seemed between the hovels of mid-nineteenth century Sandgate that many of them came to occupy and the communal student digs that my wife and I were allotted in Gilesgate). Still, somewhere in my brain I must have made those connections. Like all immigrants I was impressed by the 'foreignness' of my new residence – the smells (not least of pubs, coal fires, and car fumes), the tiny (generally grubby) local shops, the currency, the cobbled streets, the regional Geordie accent too thick for me to understand, the warm beer, the tobacco shag, the style of dress, the women, and the appalling food. As an immigrant from civilisation's last and latest stop before its (Turner-thesis like) return across the Pacific, I was acutely aware of having turned back in historical time, that I was now in the very thick of the thing I'd thought to build a career on. Here, history was omnipresent and inescapable, from the Castle Keep and the towering Cathedral, to the town square market and the Miners' Gala (the annual knees-up for the hard-fought and, until the 1980s, seemingly imperishable unionisation).

So here, far from my own origins, I was choosing to study the social embedding of a cruelly dispossessed and uprooted population of nineteenth century asylum seekers. Their's was a struggle that I could only picture from the outside. Yet – although I don't recall thinking it at the time – these Irish immigrants and I were bonded in various ways. Beyond merely our foreign status – our 'otherness' by virtue of speech and dress[2] – we had in common our different non-indigeneous constructions of the past and identity. Of course the particulars of mine were a far cry from the nationalist, ethnic and religious ones that operated for the nineteenth-century Irish Catholic immigrants to the North-east. As a west-coast Anglo-Canadian I was motivated less by my sense of absence of identifiable roots than by a resistance to the prospect of having any such politically-constructed identity imposed upon me. Was I supposed to find my identity in a past of French and British imperialism and a present of economic and cultural domination by Washington? 'Canadian' is at best an ambiguous national identity. But this consciousness (itself an 'identity' of sorts) has always seemed to me a good thing, keeping one alert to the potential mindlessness of historically constructed identities, be they national, regional, religious, or ethnic, or a mix of them all. Too, it strikes me now as Whiggish to cast upon past populations what is a distinctly twentieth-century psychological configuration of 'the self' and identity, and I am relieved that I did not attempt to do this in my study. But I stray from the point, which is simply that there was more going on in my take-up of this local research than I was probably aware of at the time. From a safe historical haven (made all the safer through my then unquestioned faith in history as an exercise in objective truth seeking) I was, I suspect, gazing obliquely at myself, at the same time as I was vicariously envying those 'others' whose pasts were apparently so much richer and (re)rooted than my own. In retrospect at least, it seems no accident that I began my apprenticeship in history-writing mapping the social conditions of these other immigrant 'others'.

It is impossible not to have some intellectual reservations about bringing the work to print now. Methodologically, the discipline of history has changed enormously since the early 1970s when my research was undertaken. Indeed, in many ways history-writing has been revolutionised. Although my thesis challenged conventional accounts of Irish immigration into Victorian Britain, its approach was well within the firmament of the then 'new social history', as brilliantly illuminated for us by E.P. Thompson's *The Making of the English Working Class*. (My thinking was in fact directly inspired by Thompson's claim in *The Making* that 'it is not the friction but the relative ease with which the Irish were absorbed into the working-class communities which is remarkable'.)[3]

Doubtless it would have been a very different study had it been written later, in the wake of 'new cultural history' with its attentions to gender and ethnicity. And it would have been different again had it followed the deconstructionist and discursive turnings opened out through the work of Michel Foucault.[4] Yet other possibilities suggest themselves through the current trend in history towards the study of material cultures, the visual, and visualisation.

Of course, just as methodological approaches have changed along with the kind of stories that historians seek to tell, so too empirical research has widened and deepened. This is as true for Irish and 'migrant studies' as it is for almost everything else in history. Donald MacRaild's *Foreword* makes this clear, and fortunately spares me the otherwise now near-impossible task of reviewing the relevant literature of the past three decades and revising the dissertation accordingly. I bask in his accomplishments and that of fellow toilers in the field. It means that I have been able to confine myself merely to tampering with some of the infelicities of style in the original text, leaving in aspic, as it were, the notes, sources, and underlying historiography that were appropriate to the moment of study's creation – never mind that several of the unpublished sources I cite are no longer so, that characters on the margins of the text (such as the colourful No-Popery fanatic William Murphy) have long since become the subject of serious scholarship,[5] or that the Public Record

Office is now the 'National Archives', and the 'British Museum' is no longer the common-name for the Library that has moved. Overall, it seemed best to leave well enough alone.

I am enormously grateful to Tony Hepburn for inviting the project, and for helping to make it possible through a grant from The Ireland Fund for Great Britain. To this Fund we are both deeply obliged. I'm also indebted to my colleague Adam Wilkinson for expertly digitising what was hammered out on my much-loved Imperial typewriter; and to Sharon Messenger and Caroline Overy for their expertise with the proofs.

This is also an opportunity to express more publicly my gratitude to those who were responsible for the original endeavour. First and foremost, I must thank my ex-Geordie history teacher at Simon Fraser University, David Huitson, who wisely advised me to start my career in British history in the North-east. Alan Heesom, now Dean of Arts and Humanities at the University of Durham, was, as I have said, responsible for putting me on to the topic, and for acting as a model supervisor throughout its research and writing. Many libraries and archives were as tolerant and obliging. The staff at the University of Durham's Palace Green Library were unstinting in their help, and Dr Doyle, in particular, established many fruitful connections on my behalf. At Ushaw College, the rich archival pickings were matched by abundant good food and company; there, Father Payne, the Librarian, was helpfulness beyond the call of Christian duty. So, too, from his rectory was Father W. Vincent Smith, who generously shared with me his font of knowledge and wealth of archives on the history of local Catholicism. Robin Gard, historian doyen of North-eastern Catholicism was similarly unstinting with his knowledge and encouragement.

Fortunately, during the course of my writing I never suffered from any of the wants of the people I was studying. My then wife Margaret was an abundant source of moral and domestic support, as well as literary good sense, for which I remain lastingly indebted. Good friends were never in short supply either, during the study's preparation. Some, alas, are now gone. I dedicate this book to one of them – a fellow immigrant, who first befriended me in Durham and helped turn my short time there into the very best of memories.

Roger Cooter

Professorial Fellow
Wellcome Trust Centre for the History of Medicine
at UCL London

May 2005

Introduction

Innocuous beginnings can often have unexpected ends. This study set out to chart the record of the Irish in the North-east of England as a chapter in the social history of Irish immigration into nineteenth-century Britain. It seemed an appropriate and promising task in view of the relative historical neglect of the North-east, and the absolute neglect of the region's Irish population.[1] A cursory survey of the resources – largely from the annals of the miners' unions – suggested that the Irish had been of some importance in the area and that their role had probably been overlooked in the rush to explore broader themes in northern, if not north-eastern history. The first task, therefore, was to provide a statistical backdrop: to reveal the extent of the Irish population and compare this to their numbers elsewhere in the country. This was an arithmetic job with precedents more in demography than in social history. However, the results substantiated that the Irish had indeed composed a numerically significant substratum of the society, comprising roughly the fourth-largest such population in England. Legitimacy was thus given to a two-part undertaking: first, to delineate the life and livelihood of these immigrants and, second, to assess their impact on, and interactions with, the host population.

The first task was tougher than expected and not a little dispiriting. Government Blue Books, fulsome on other nineteenth-century centres of Irish population, contain surprisingly little information on the Irish in the North-east. General histories, too, were mum, as were standard works on English Catholicism. Randomly combing the pages of the local press for a forty-year period turned up few articles on Irish Catholics. Labour histories of the North-east, while sometimes confirming that the Irish were an important sector of the workforce, were not very helpful in indicating specific areas of Irish participation, other than – famously – their use as blacklegs in the miners' strike of 1844. Nevertheless, some information contained in the Londonderry Papers on the Irish in that strike, as well as on the Irish Catholics in Seaham Harbour was encouraging. And the Catholic *Tablet*, which intermittently had a correspondent in Newcastle, proffered a good deal of further information. Two collections of Catholic papers at Ushaw College and Seminary,[2] a collection of cuttings and miscellany at the North of England Institute of Mining and Mechanical Engineers,[3] the records of the Durham Miners' Association, and several volumes of transcriptions in the Catholic Diocesan Archives, eventually brought together enough material to make the study feasible. From these and many lesser sources — none of which dealt exclusively with the Irish in the North-east[4] — it was possible to compose a historical collage, the value of the scattered details and fragmentary items emerging the more clearly after they had been pieced together.

The second task, the nature of the interaction of the Irish with their host community, proved challenging in a slightly different way. The more gobbets of information that I gathered, the more it became apparent that the Irish were seldom an issue of any local importance. There was no point in kidding myself into believing that their significance had simply been overlooked by previous historians. From a wide reading of contemporary literature, history, private letters and newspapers the uncomfortable truth emerged that the Irish in the region were almost invisible.

While historians of other Anglo-Irish communities have noted that the English generally had little every-day awareness of the Irish in their midst, the lack of commentary in the North-east seemed peculiar. On the rare occasions when the Irish *were* mentioned, the comments were singularly lacking in extremes of ethnic and religious bigotry. Evidence of the Irish serving as scapegoats for social or economic ills were almost non-existent. The further the research proceeded, the greater became my suspicion that the Irish in the

North-east bore a relation to the indigenous population that was quite different from that recorded for other areas of Britain. I soon reached the conclusion that the seemingly unobtrusive nature of the Irish in the region was not attributable to them as such, but rather, to the relatively unique social, religious, economic and political fabric of the North-east into which they moved.

To a degree, then, this is a negative study explaining why the Irish were *seldom* a subject of public discussion relative to other areas; why, as Catholics, they suffered *less* for their religion; why as labourers, they inspired *little* antagonism; and why, as Irish Nationalists, they provoked only *minimal* hostility. But it is positive as well. Before reactions can be analyzed, it is necessary fully to depict the entry of the Irish into the local community and their subsequent role within it. The thesis thus weaves throughout, being explicit at some points and implicit at others. But it has not been my intention to use the interpretation as a Procrustean table for every piece of evidence. In aiming at generalization, I have felt no compunction in including contradictory evidence where such would enlarge on the general conditions and social relations of the Irish immigrants.

In concentrating on County Durham and Newcastle, rather than on the whole of the North-east or on a more specific locale, my purpose has been two-fold. First, the area is small enough that it has been possible to concentrate on specific incidents in considerable detail. At the same time, the area contains enough of the geographic region of the North-east to facilitate broader generalizations. The scarcity of Irish in the interior of Northumberland accounts for my not including the whole of that County in the study. Certain towns to the west and east of Newcastle on the north bank of the Tyne did have sizeable Irish populations, as did Middlesbrough across the River Tees in Yorkshire. My only excuse for not attending to them in detail is that of space in a work already overlong.

My further purpose in dealing with this specific locale is that of bringing to light differences between the Irish in urban and rural contexts. Irish immigration into England after 1840 has been viewed, quite rightly, as primarily an urban phenomenon. Of this, the Irish quarter in Newcastle provides good illustration. Durham, on the other hand (by which, throughout this study, is meant the County not the City) had a considerable Irish population scattered about the various iron works and, to a lesser extent, in colliery villages. In this respect the area had some parallels with rural Wales. While it might be argued that company towns like Consett, built around the iron works, were simply small urban environments imposed on rural landscapes, the position of the Irish in these places was significantly different from that in urban ghettos. The stereotyped 'Paddy' which has emerged from the London sketches of Henry Mayhew or Charles Booth requires a degree of revision when set next to these 'rural' Irish. Moreover, the Catholic Church in attempting to deal with these scattered groups of Irish faced problems unlike those it encountered in cities. Thus, in dealing with Durham, I have tended to avoid the major centres and concentrate more on outlying communities, though the degree of concentration has had to be decided by the availability of source material.

It is, of course, impossible to focus on an area like Durham and Newcastle without being parochial. Asa Briggs has written that 'outward-looking rather than inward ... looking Northern history is what is most needed, the kind of history which sets out to compare.'[5] While this study did not 'set out' to compare, it became fundamentally comparative. For in postulating that the North-east had a distinctive identity and that this uniqueness was responsible for the different set of attitudes towards the Irish, the comparative basis is explicit. In most cases the regional peculiarities are sufficiently obvious to require no further comment, but in exposing how this regionalism affected the Irish, I have drawn upon many alternative examples. Published sources, dissertations, and conference papers on the Irish in London, Cardiff, Bradford, Salford, Liverpool and Scotland have been augmented by various contemporary reports.

What was begun as a straightforward study of an immigrant population in a relatively unobserved locality, then, burgeoned through the course of research into something more ambitious. The Irish of Durham and Newcastle became not only a study in themselves, but a lens for viewing the wider society, and a platform for questioning fundamental assumptions about Victorian attitudes towards Irish immigrants.

Chapter 1

Enumerations

> ...a little Irish blood, with its electric vitality, goes a great way in leavening the *mass* of other races, and is often apparent, even after many generations.
> John Denvir, *The Brandons: A Story of Irish Life in England* (London, 1903), p. 13.

When the government's Committee on Emigration expressed its fear in 1827 of 'the wheat-fed population of Great Britain ... [being] supplanted by the potato-fed population of Ireland', they were thinking least of all of the North-east of England.[1] The labour-hungry revolution in industry that was under way elsewhere in the country had barely touched Durham and Newcastle. Agriculture, mining, some metal industry and a small localised shipbuilding industry provided little incentive to job-hunting Irish. A decade later the area still signalled few opportunities to unskilled migrants. Sunderland, a town that would later bustle with industry, was so stagnant that its population declined.[2] To an Irish emigrant disembarking at a thriving west-coast port, a journey to the North-east was not promising.

Circumstances greatly changed, however, when industrial capital washed over the area after 1840. Once opened, the flood gates permitted an inflow of labour that was unprecedented elsewhere in England. Particularly through the rapid expansion of the railways and ports, the major industries of coal, iron, and shipbuilding entered a golden age of expansion and profits. As the historian David Dougan puts it, 'The labour flowed in and the work flowed out and the

North-east became just about the richest part of the richest country in the world. If you wanted coal you came to the North-east, if you wanted engineering goods you came, or if you wanted armaments or chemicals, iron or machinery. And in particular after 1850, you came if you wanted ships.'[3]

The still largely rural North-east of 1831 was transformed into an industrial beehive, much of its serene landscape defiled by slag heaps from collieries and smoke from iron works. By 1851 the urban population of Durham had already reached 42 percent.[4] Barren moors became the victims of 'progress' as industrial-company towns like Tow Law and Consett established themselves in virtually unpopulated areas and, forty years later, were boasting populations of 3,978 and 7,708 respectively.[5] Another company town, Jarrow, was raised by the investments of the shipbuilder Charles Palmer from 3,500 in 1841 to 25,000 in 1881.[6] While the township of Seaham, owned by the Marquis of Londonderry, increased in the single decade 1841-51 from 173 souls to 729,[7] the port of West Hartlepool in the same decade jumped from 2,079 to 11,736.[8] In older more established towns there were similar, albeit less dramatic, increases.

Table 1.1:   *Population of Durham and Newcastle, 1841-1881*

	1841	1851	1861	1871	1881
Newcastle*	49,860	89,156	109,108	128,443	147,359
Co Durham	324,284	411,679	508,666	685,058	867,258
Total	374,144	500,805	617,774	813,501	1,014,617

*The figures for 1841 and 1851 are those for the District of Newcastle; for 1861 and 1871, Newcastle Municipal and Parliamentary Borough; and for 1881, Newcastle Urban Sanitary District.
Source: *Population Census*, 1841-81; *Kelly's Directory of Newcastle*, 1886.

Between 1841 and 1881 the population of Durham and Newcastle rose by over 180 percent. Newcastle's percentage increase was slightly greater at 190 percent. Nowhere else in England was there such a marked rate of growth, at times even double that of the national rate. In the decade 1861-71, for instance, the population of the North-east grew by 26.5 percent, as compared to the national average of 13.2 percent.[9]

Table 1.2: *Immigrant Population in Durham and Newcastle, 1841-1881*

	Newcastle	Percent of Newcastle Population not born in Northumberland	Co. Durham	Per cent of Durham Population not born in Durham	Total Immigrants	Percent of Total Population
1841	16,622	34.0	65,216	20.0	81,838	21.9
1851	59,819	67.4	132,067	32.5	191,886	38.3
1861	40,935	37.6	164,980	32.4	205,915	33.3
1871	36,149	30.5	236,452	34.4	272,601	33.9
1881	51,304	34.7	279,490	32.1	330,794	32.6

Source: *Population Census: Enumeration Abstracts on Place of Birth*, 1841 (PP, 1843, XXII, p.223); 1851 (PP, 1852-3, LXXXVIII, Pt. II, p.303); 1861 (PP, 1863, LIII, Pt. II, p.485); 1871 (PP, 1873, LXXI, Pt. I, p.541); 1881 (PP, 1883, LXXX, p.454).

As Table 1.2 reveals, by 1851 as much as 38 percent of the booming population were born outside the respective counties of Durham and Northumberland. This was an increase of 134 percent over 1841. For the District of Newcastle, the immigrant population was a staggering 67.4 percent.[10]

Although the population continued to increase over the next decades, 1851 represents the apogee of immigration. Thereafter the immigrant population rose by only 7 percent in 1861, 33 percent in 1871, and 21 percent increase in 1881. After 1851 the population 'matured' and stabilised, growing more through its own volition than by immigration.[11] By 1861 it was beginning to furnish a large proportion of youths for industry, thought even in 1881 immigrant supplement was still required.[12]

Other than those who emigrated from neighbouring English counties, the Irish comprised the largest proportion of the incomers. This was the case for each inter-censal period except 1841, when the Scots outnumbered the Irish in both Durham and Newcastle, and for 1881 in Newcastle only. In both cases the difference was marginal.[13] As with the immigrant population as a whole, the greatest percentage increase of Irish was over the decade 1841-51.

Table 1.3: *Irish-Born Population in Durham and Newcastle, 1841-1881*

	Newcastle	% Irish	Co. Durham	% Irish	Total	% Total Population
1841	2,857	5.7	5,407	1.6	8,264	2.2
1851	7,152	7.9	18,501	4.4	25,653	5.1
1861	6,596 [7,518]*	6.0 [6.7]	27,719	5.4	34,315 [35,237]	5.5 [5.6]
1871	6,904	5.4	37,515	5.5	44,419	5.5
1881	5,495	3.0	36,794	4.2	42,289	4.1

*The bracketed numbers are those in the official census reports. Other discrepancies between the Enumeration Abstracts and the official census are minor and have not been entered here since they do not affect the percentages.

Sources: *Population Census: Enumeration Abstracts on Place of Birth, 1841-1881.*

Comprising only 2.2 percent of the total population of Durham and Newcastle in 1841, the Irish increased their numbers by 209 percent to become 5.1 percent of the total population in 1851. In Newcastle the Irish-born made up 8 percent of its 'cosmopolitan' population.

The potato blight was largely accountable for the increase – not only in its effects upon Ireland, but upon Scotland as well. It is evident from the ages of the Scottish children of Irish parents listed in the enumerators' manuscripts for 1851 that a significant proportion of the Irish immigrants had migrated from Scotland. From the numbers of children listed as having been born in Ireland, however, it is clear that the majority had come directly from there.[14] On Wall Knoll Street, Newcastle, for example, where the Irish and their progeny made up 41.1 percent of the population, sixty children, or twenty-nine percent of the accountable Irish community, were born in Ireland, as compared to forty children within these families who had been born in England or Scotland.[15] Again, an examination of the Ecclesiastical District of Thornley, containing the iron works at Tow Law and Dan's Castle and having an Irish community of 228 or 17 percent of the total population in 1851, shows that forty children were born in Ireland while thirty-six were born elsewhere.[16]

Maps 1.1-1.4 **Percentage and Density of Irish-born Population in England and Wales, 1841, 1861***

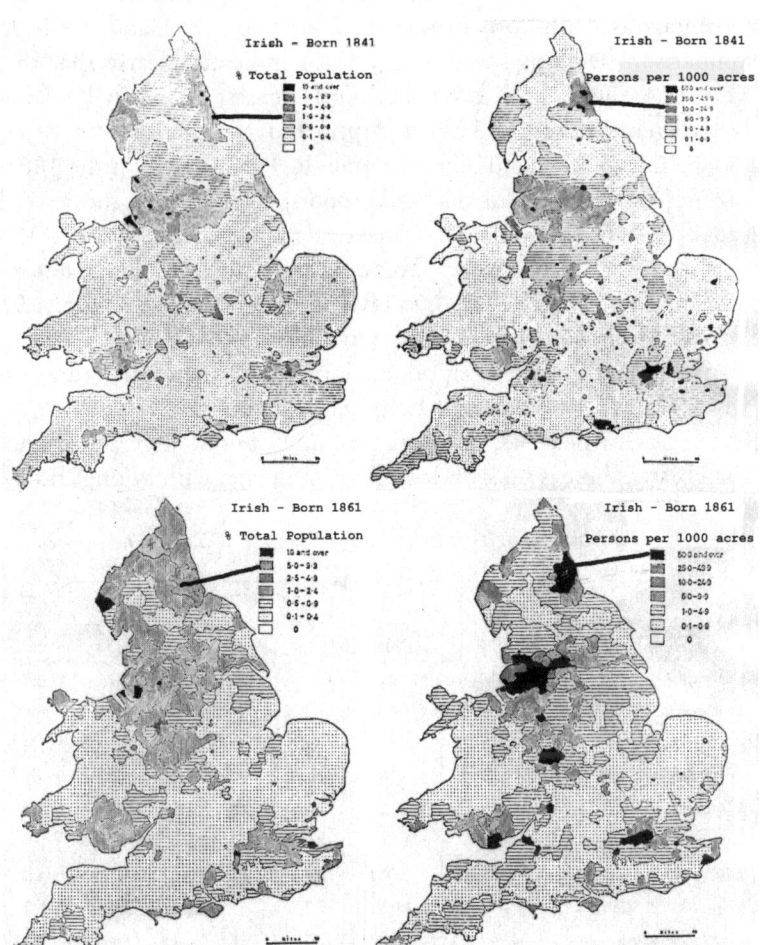

*R. Lawton, 'Irish Immigration to England and Wales in the mid-nineteenth century,' *Irish Geography*, IV (1959-1963), pp.42-47.

By 1861 the number of Irish-born had risen by an additional 10,000, a 30 percent increase over 1851, to comprise 16.6 percent of the immigrant population and 5.5 percent of the population as a whole. In only three other counties in England and Wales was this last figure matched: Cumberland, Lancashire and Cheshire.[17] Maps 1.1 to 1.4 give a rough idea of the relative density and percentage of Irish-born in the North-east for 1841 and 1861. A comparison between Maps 1.2 and 1.4 indicates clearly that the North-east came to be about the fourth densest region in England for Irish immigrants. This is supported though the statistics presented to Sunderland Town Council in 1867, based on the 1861 statistics, which revealed that the proportion of Irish to the rest of the population in Sunderland, Newcastle and Gateshead was 1:19, 1:16, and 1:15 respectively.[18] This compares (for the same date) to Preston, 1:14, Manchester, 1:7, Liverpool, 1:5 and Stockport, 1:9. For the whole of Lancashire the ratio was 1:10. Testimony to the relative strength of the Irish population within a ten-mile radius of Newcastle was also recorded by a special correspondent to *The Nation* in 1872 who observed that 'except in London, Liverpool, and Manchester, there is no such Irish force to be met with in England'.[19]

Table 1.4: **Distribution of Irish-born in Co. Durham, 1851-1861**

Poor Law District	1851 Total Population	Irish Born	%	1861 Total Population	Irish Born	%
Darlington	21,618	539	2.5	26,122	975	3.8
Stockton	36,866	1,868	3.5	57,099	3,478	6.1
Auckland	30,083	1,222	4.1	50,491	3,196	6.3
Teesdale	19,813	228	1.2	20,880	272	1.3
Weardale	14,567	272	1.9	16,418	314	1.9
Durham	55,951	3,920	7.0	70,274	5,746	8.2
Easington	21,795	506	2.8	27,293	1,325	4.8
Houghton-le-Spring	19,564	1,058	5.2	21,713	1,119	5.2
Chester-le-Street	20,907	584	2.8	27,660	1,172	4.2
Sunderland	70,576	4,103	5.8	90,704	4,901	5.5
South Shields	35,790	1,164	3.3	44,849	1,943	4.3
Gateshead	48,081	3,028	6.3	59,409	4,306	7.2
Hartlepool	16,068	ng	ng	29,153	1,184	3.7

Source: *Population Census: Abstracts on Place of Birth*, 1851, pp. 280-82; 1861 pp. 543-44.

Table 1.4 reveals how the Irish-born population were distributed in County Durham. Although the more restricted information on the 'Irish-born' given in the censuses of 1871 and 1881 frustrates efforts to expand the table, the relative distribution exhibited in 1851 and 1861 remained much the same over the following two decades. While the Poor Law District of Durham appears highest, the majority of these Irish were scattered over the large area of the District and not in the City itself, which, in 1871, showed only five percent Irish-born. The densest Irish-born area in County Durham was the borough of Gateshead, which still had 6.7 percent Irish-born in 1871.

Despite mortality and emigration after 1861, the Irish-born still made up 5.5 percent of the population of Durham and Newcastle in 1871, suggesting considerable immigration over the period. Not surprisingly there was a decrease in the Irish-born population between 1871-81, yet they still made up 12.8 percent of all immigrants and 4.1 percent of the total population. As we approach 1881, however, the figures for Irish-born become increasingly misleading as to the actual size of the Irish community. As indicated by the examples of Wall Knoll Street and the village of Thornley cited above, by 1851 a considerable proportion of these communities were already second-generation and therefore not included as 'Irish' in the census abstracts. To arrive at anything like the actual size of these communities it is necessary to first examine the extent of the Irish community prior to 1841 and then to approximate its decennial expansion.

From at least the beginning of the century the Irish had been present in Durham and Newcastle, though they constituted no significant proportion of the population prior to *c.*1838. Seasonal migrations of Irish agricultural labourers occurred annually and, each year a few more remained behind.[20] While this annual tide was of little significance in itself, it did establish connections that developed and attracted larger numbers in the years that followed. The failure of the Irish potato crop in 1821-22 gave impetus to emigration and added to the number of agricultural labourers seeking employment, some of whom probably ended up in the agricultural North-east. On the other hand, it is unlikely that the decimation of the Irish textile industry in 1825-26 contributed many hands to the rural farms and even fewer to the collieries.

Well into the 1830s the relative positioning of the Irish was west of an imaginary line from Glasgow to London. Although they would comprise nearly six percent of Newcastle's population in 1841, a decade earlier it was only their dearth that merited comment. In a letter of November 1831 to Lord Brougham from the knowledgeable local judge and Whig reformer, James Losh, it was noted in passing that the Irish 'are not numerous here'.[21] Certainly they were not evident in the collieries at this time for, besides the lack of Irish familiarity with the hewing of coal, the colliers formed inbred and exclusive communities to which strangers were unwelcome. The idea that the pitman had to be bred to his work from childhood was popular among both owners and pitmen.[22] In 1831 only eight Irish children were to be found in the pits of south Durham,[23] a clear indication of the scarcity of Irish adults in the trade. Although on northern railway construction in the 1840s, the Irish made up 'perhaps one-half of the navigators',[24] in the 1830s they had been resented in this trade as much as they were in the collieries. The 'serious riot [which] took place at Hartlepool, between the Irish and English labourers employed on the railway', in which 'the English party searched the town, and drove out every Irishman they could find',[25] was typical of early railway construction throughout England and was a major reason why some employers were reluctant to hire the Irish. They were confined, therefore, to the traditional agricultural roles, to miscellaneous factory jobs and, as often as not, to such self-employed trades as rag-picking, clothes dealing, tinkering, hawking, and the handling of junk. Such 'crowds of miserable Irish', as Thomas Carlyle called them, with 'their rags and laughing savagery' were largely to be found hidden in small pockets of destitution primarily within urban centres.[26]

Throughout the 1830s the Irish increased their numbers in England and, concomitantly, the concerns of their often reluctant hosts. The 1841 enumeration of those born in Ireland was itself one manifestation of this heightened concern. Another indication was the government commission appointed to enquire into the poor of Ireland in 1836 – a commission which included a lengthy appendix on the state of the Irish in Great Britain. But 'Appendix G', like its predecessors, concentrated on the west coast immigration ports – on Glasgow and Liverpool, in particular – and gave no mention of the Irish in Durham or Newcastle.[27] Its author, G. Cornewall Lewis, made no claims to comprehensiveness, however, and admitted that

> Upon the whole ... the *general diffusion* of the Irish over Scotland and England is more remarkable than their *numbers*. They are to be found, in greater or less strength, in every manufacturing and commercial town, from Aberdeen, Dundee, and Greenock, to the central counties of England and the metropolis. ... Their roaming and restless habits appear to have carried them to every place where there was any prospect of obtaining profitable employment.[28]

The first real signs of these 'restless habits' in the North-east were witnessed in the late 1830s. This had less to do with the expansion in the major industries (which, with the exception of coal, did not get under way until the 1840s), than with the commencement of the famine conditions in Ireland. As more than one Irish historian has pointed out, the 'hungry forties' began as early as 1838 with the first of five calamitous harvests, both of grain and potatoes. The sheer impossibility of making ends meet in a year of bad potato yields produced a staggering increase in emigration figures'.[29] One of the effects of this wave of immigration into England was to force the Irish further afield in search of employment. Because of the Poor Law Removal Acts, new immigrants in England were denied parish relief and hence had a freedom of mobility that allowed them to flood into areas where jobs were available. According to Lewis, they therefore had advantages over the unemployed English who were restricted by the '*operation, of the poor laws*, by which the unemployed poor has been chained to the soil, and confined within the narrow limits of his own parish'.[30] Thus, from the late 1830s, increasing numbers of Irish in the North-east went unopposed into the tertiary chemical, earthenware, and glass industries, while others moved into the developing iron works and the numerous quarries throughout the area. As well, to a limited extent, they made inroads into the coal trade, though primarily in new pits and then mainly as surface labourers. In 1841 in Bishop Auckland, for example, there were 'not less than 400 Catholic souls', the result 'of the numerous coal mines opened in this neighbourhood, and the establishment of several public works', according to the *Catholic Directory*.[31] At the same time 'scattered over a wide extent of country' in the Stockton-upon-Tees area, remarked Vicar Apostolic Mostyn in the same source, Irish Catholics were 'employed in the coal mines', sufficient to 'attempt the establishment of a resident priest in the locality'.[32] Both of these areas contained pits and both of these entries in the *Catholic Directory* were the first to make appeals on behalf of new immigrant congregations in Durham and Newcastle.[33]

The Irish, then, had not been long resident in the North-east.[34] Thus the 1841 census figures for Irish-born come closer to the *actual* numbers of Irish than those recorded for Irish populations elsewhere in England, Scotland or Wales. Detailed sampling suggests that the birthrate among the Irish in the early decades of emigration was, contrary to popular belief, slightly lower than that of the population as a whole.[35] Hence the total for the first and second generation Irish in our study area for 1841 amounted to about 9,000 (that is, the total Irish population for that date plus 9 percent, the average natural increase for the North-east). If we do a similar calculation projected over the next thirty-year period it is possible to ascertain an estimate of the total size of the Irish community.

Table 1.5: **Approximate Growth of Irish Population in Durham and Newcastle**

	A Increase of Irish-born	B % Natural Increase	C Population Available for Increase	D Natural Increase	E Growth	F Total Irish Population
1841		9.0	8,264	744	744	9,000
1851	17,389	14.7	26,397	3,880	21,269	30,227
1861	9,584	15.0	39,811	5,972	15,556	45,783
1871	9,172	15.0	54,955	8,243	17,415	63,198

Source: Column A is derived from Table 3; column B is calculated from J.W. House, *North Eastern England Population Movements* (Newcastle, 1954) Table 1, p.56; column C is calculated from 'F' of previous line plus 'A'. The figures here are based on the assumption that 'the typical age of [Irish] emigrants at all periods was 20-25 years of age' (John A. Jackson, *The Irish in Britain* (London, 1963), p.19). Hence the majority of those immigrants who were capable of reproduction in 1841 (assuming that they had not long been resident) were not able to reproduce in 1871, if they were still living. The figures given for 1871 take this into account. Column D is 'B' multiplied by 'C', and column 'F' is 'E' plus 'F' of previous decade.

Several assumptions are implicit in these estimates, however, which require further explanation. First, they make no allowance for Irish *emigration* from Durham and Newcastle. 'All along', as one well-informed Catholic remarked of the national scene in 1892, 'there has been more or less of emigration at the same time with immigration ... and for some years past, many of the Irish have left and are leaving England.'[36] However, there is little evidence to suggest that in the North-east Irish emigration prior to 1881 was of any significance compared to other Irish centres in England. Although Britain was often regarded by the Irish as a stopgap before departure to the American 'promised land', those who came to the North-east relinquished convenient access to the emigration ports of the west coast. Thus notices such as that in the *Newcastle Courant* in 1850 of Irishmen 'making good' in America – the 'land of plenty where ... the meanest labourer has beef and mutton, with bread, bacon, tea, coffee, sugar, and even pies, the whole year round'[37] – tended to be less enticing for the Irish in South Shields than those in Liverpool. And despite the lure of the El Dorado, which caused a 'great tide of emigration from Durham to Australia' in 1854-

55,[38] there were few Irish in the region at the time who could afford to avail themselves of the opportunity. Financial limitations also prevented the Irish from emigrating during the many local strikes and lock-outs – an alternative that was taken up by many skilled workers.[39] In the late 1870s, during the recession in the coal trade, various emigration schemes were set up by the Durham Miners' Association, which by then contained several hundreds of first and second generation Irish. While among the indigenous workforce these schemes met with some success,[40] the Irish took little part in them; instead they acquiesced in wage cuts. Indeed, as we shall see later, during the depression of the late 1870s many Irish entered pit employment for the first time, replacing the locals lost to emigration. Geographic isolation, then, combined with poverty at one moment in time and economic security at another, meant that few Irish left the area in the period under study.

Secondly, Table 1.5 fails to indicate the number of Irish paupers deported to Ireland in accordance with the numerous Poor Law Removal Acts. Here, as elsewhere, the available evidence is not definitive. Although some contradictory estimates of removals were recorded in 1854,[41] no complete national tabulations were undertaken until 1861. However, the extant records reveal that removals had only the slightest effect upon the numbers of Irish in the North-east. Of those who approached the formidable doors of the Poor House without the five-year residency requirements (as specified by the 1834 Act) few appear to have been shipped back to Ireland. Perhaps, in all, as many as 1,000 Irish in our study area were returned to Ireland before 1863 – the last date for the listing of poor removals – the great majority of these being evicted from Stockton, Sunderland and Newcastle.[42] Thereafter, Irish removals petered out, the removal legislation relaxing more or less in line with the diminishing of the earlier emigration from Ireland of hordes of paupers.

Thirdly, and finally, Table 1.5 supposes that successive generations of Irish remained within a social and cultural milieu that was predominately Irish. While this is not strictly the case, it is sufficiently so for the forty-year period of this study. The Catholic Church lamented a degree of Irish leakage from the faith, but there was less comparable leakage of Irish sons and daughters from the community. Religious beliefs could be dropped or discarded or even expropriated, as we shall see, but the habits and customs of living, the accents and manners of speaking, and the strength of nationalist pride were far harder to shed. Nor did many wish to leave the security afforded by the community – a security usually enhanced by the embrace of Catholicism and the Irish public-house. It is clear from the census enumerators' manuscripts that in areas where the Irish resided, they did so in close proximity. Presumably, to face the Anglo-Saxon majority alone was to encounter alienation, at the very least. As for assimilation, the majority of Irish immigrants seem to have had neither the desire nor the inclination. Irish Catholicism and Irish nationalism (particularly after 1865) gave the Irish a religious and political distinctiveness that they were keen to sustain.

Sheer necessity also kept the Irish together. Throughout our period they depended mostly on one another, and largely assumed that no one else had an interest in their welfare. When the Methodist Rev. Hardcastle took a 'soulful' interest in some local Irish harvesters, they were convinced that he must be Irish. When Hardcastle inquired into why this was so, he was told by one of the harvesters 'we never saw English people take any interest in us'.[43] Later, when the English did take an interest, the motivation was often fear or anger, or at best a bigoted solicitude for the evils of the Irishman's faith. The net result was that by the 1870s the immigrants and their progeny had coalesced into fairly tight-knit communities. Places like Ushaw Moor and Framwellgate in Durham were visibly Irish, while Wall Knoll Street, Newcastle, which in 1851 was 41 percent Irish, by 1871 was almost 100 percent so.[44] It would be wrong, therefore, to conclude that before 1880 there was any significant diminution of 'Irishness' on the part of those who had not been born in Ireland. As Raphael Samuel has pointed out with regard to later generations of Irish in London, they 'shared a good deal of the belligerent fidelity of the first generation. The walls of the Irish home continued to be adorned by a free intermixture of sacred and patriotic subjects, as they had been when Mayhew described them in the middle of the century'.[45] It could scarcely have been otherwise, for not only did new immigrants preserve direct links with the homeland, but, increasingly, their ethnicity was reinforced by religious pressures and nationalistic movements.

Although the statistics presented here are not absolute, we can fairly safely postulate that by 1881 from 65,000 to 70,000, or about 6.5 percent of Durham and Newcastle's population, were Irish immigrants from the late 1830s onwards and their descendants. In certain areas the percentage was much higher. Contemporary estimates of the Irish-to-non-Irish populations in 1872 put the ratio in South Shields at 1:9, in Hebburn and Jarrow at 1:3 and in Gateshead at 1:4.[46] Here, then, was a numerically significant proportion of the population. That it was acknowledged as such is evident from *Kelly's Directory of Durham* for 1890 where, for the first time, the not unguarded compilers admitted that 'the population is chiefly of Northumbrian descent ... there are a few Welsh; but there is a large body of Celts from Ireland'.[47]

So if the relations between the Irish and non-Irish in the North-east were more relaxed than in other areas of Britain, it was not because the Irish were proportionately less numerous or socially visible. In view of their relatively later and more sudden inundation of the North-east, and their heavy concentration in certain areas, one might well have expected the reaction from the host community to have been all the sharper and more forceful than in other areas of heavy Irish immigration in Britain. That this was not the case requires explanation.

Chapter 2
Living Conditions and Social Place

> In the storey above, which I got at by a staircase, in the most shameful condition, I found in one room two families. 'How many are there of you?' 'Only nine of us!' There were three beds. An old man lay ill on one, another man on the second, and a woman on the third. They had no blankets. 'Devil a stitch', they said. They were Irish. Rent 1s.
> *Inquiry into the Condition of the Poor of Newcastle-Upon-Tyne* (Newcastle, 1850), p.17.
>
> Of the many asylums to which the Irish fled after the great exodus of the forties, there was none in which, owing to many circumstances, they were able ultimately to find more favourable surroundings than the Tyneside'.
> T.P. O'Connor, 'The Irish in Great Britain', in Felix Lavery (ed.), *Irish Heroes in the War* (London, 1917), p. 21.

The living conditions of any immigrant population depend in some measure on their state antecedent to emigration. The famine conditions which motivated Irish emigration to England need not long detain us here for as a modern 'Diaspora' the records are abundant and familiar. The stark reality facing the Irish peasantry in the 1840s – starvation, disease, and death – was so pervasive that few of those who came to England could anywhere approach even the limited respectability of the earlier Irish peasantry. As the local press described them coming into Glasgow in 1847:

> The last arrivals of Irish with which we have been afflicted are quite different from all previous importations. Formerly men came who could work, but now we see only squalid and debilitated lads,

accompanied by frail old men and women, and young children, reduced to the last stage of sickness and misery.[1]

Those who made their way to Durham and Newcastle were in no less a decrepit condition, the bulk of them coming from the most depressed western counties of Ireland. While no official records of their place of origin were kept, in the Irish quarter of Newcastle the Census Enumerators often exceeded their duty by entering the county of birth. Incomplete as these records are, Counties Mayo and Sligo clearly predominate. The Assistant Overseer of Newcastle Poor Law, George Grey, hesitated to be precise, admitting, 'I think they are just as frequently from the southern and western parts of Ireland as from the north'.[2] However, a correspondent to *The Tablet* in 1851 confidently referred to the Irish in Sandgate as 'Connoughtmen [sic]'.[3] The same correspondent (who was by no means unsympathetic to the Irish) spoke with equal authority when he stated that 'the Gateshead Irishmen are chiefly from Ulster'[4] But if Ulstermen, they displayed no more affluence than their brethren from further south. By all reports the Irish of Gateshead were some of the most impoverished in the North-east.[5] Further evidence of origins was given by the Assistant Overseer for Sunderland who stated that the Irish in his area came 'out of the interior of Ireland and not from Dublin'. He singled out Roscommon as 'a very fruitful source'.[6] For the other Irish in Durham there are no testimonials of birthplace. However, the comments upon their general condition strongly suggest that those who came to Durham were rural in background and unfamiliar with urban industrial life.

The largest proportion found their way to Newcastle, a town not well equipped to receive them. The slums of Newcastle in the nineteenth century, including the notorious Sandgate area, existed as they had for hundreds of years, except that the squalor had increased.[7] In 1850 the 3,000 souls of Sandgate Street were 'crammed into a space which, if properly laid out, would be four or five times as extensive. There are about twenty-five entries on each side of the street, with from eight to ten houses in each, containing on an average, eight rooms in each house ... From ten to twenty people are very often to be found in one room'.[8] When the staff of the architectural magazine, *The Builder*, visited in 1861 they were appalled: 'Cologne has a bad name, Cairo has a worse reputation, but that part of Newcastle called Sandgate, must be allowed to exceed either city in stenches, filth, overcrowding, and pestilential ills'.[9] Conditions were so bad that even in newer clusters of tenements the death-rate reached 47.7 per 1,000 souls,[10] permitting Newcastle to compete with Liverpool and Manchester for the 'unenviable notoriety'[11] of the highest mortality rate in England.[12] Little wonder that after the great fire of 1854 there were silent regrets that not more of the slum area had been razed. The chroniclers of the conflagration noted that 'if it were not for the fearful loss of life, and large amount of personal suffering, which it has occasioned, it might be regarded as a public benefit'.[13]

Irish immigrants by no means eased the slum conditions of Newcastle, but they were hardly responsible for them. It was into a situation of unmitigated filth that they brought their rural habits and contributed to the already existing squalor and disease. Nor were they wholly responsible for the overcrowding at mid-century. A chronic housing shortage pre-existed, compelling native and non-Irish labourers and their families to share some of the worst living conditions. 'The dwelling for the working classes are not much better than those for the poor', it was reported, 'single rooms ... are charged £5 per annum. Few mechanics can afford to pay for more than one room'.[14] Not surprisingly, the place that became the Irish ghetto was that which drove sanitary reporters to despair. The keeping of pigs, in particular, a habit allegedly peculiar to the Irish,[15] was the bane of every inspector. Indeed, an indirect measure of the Irish presence in Newcastle by 1848 was a City Council by-law 'that swine shall not be kept within any dwelling-house. or in any room or building occupied by man'.[16] It is indicative of the Irish indifference to the law that some twenty years later the Inspector of Nuisances was still reporting numerous cases of infringement of the swine law.[17]

While the extent of urban slums was greatest in Newcastle, the city was not untypical of surrounding towns. Dr. Reid's report for the *Royal Commission on the Health of Towns* (1845) was emphatic that it not be supposed 'that such lodging-houses exist only in the metropolis or in the manufacturing towns'.[18] In Durham City he found them 'not greatly different from those in other places'.[19] In the Pipewellgate and Barn Close areas of Gateshead he found an average mortality rate exceeding that in Newcastle;[20] in Sunderland he cited even worse conditions with 'one room generally containing a whole family, consisting in many cases, of seven, or even more individuals, and not unfrequently pigs are admitted within the houses.[21] In south Durham, an area not included in Reid's report, town conditions were much the same and, as elsewhere in Victorian England, the Irish inhabited the worst housing with the least sanitation. The Medical Officer of Health for Darlington in 1851 spoke of the colony of Irish there as 'existing in low, crowded and ill-ventilated hovels'.[22]

But the Irish in Durham (as shown in Table 1.4) were not all confined to the slums of the larger towns. Some found refuge in colliery villages, sometimes in the clusters of small houses that were provided by employers. In the annals of the local coal trade these pit-houses are often pictured as bastions of 'homey comfort', equipped with a red-knuckled wife, a good coal grate, and a plot out back for growing leeks. Reports from Medical Officers of Health and others paint a rather different picture. John Holland, writing in 1835, commented that the pitmen's dwellings are 'often more remarkable for the amount of population, than the neatness or cleanness of their domestic arrangements'.[23] The *Durham Directory* of 1856 was more precise, stating that 'the space between the fronts of the houses, forming the street, is unpaved and undrained, but that between the backs of the houses not unfrequently exhibits a joint-stock dust-heap and dung-hill running along the avenue, flanked here and there by pig-sties and heaps of coal'.[24] Later, when the Irish became more numerous in the trade, improvements in housing were not as universal as panegyrists claimed. A miner's letter to the editor of the *Durham Chronicle* in 1865 shows just how much 'improvement' was met through rebuilding:

at the village of Byers Green they recently built 80 new houses, without showing the least thought for the comfort of the pitmen. There are neither public nor private refuges or ashpits, but stinking muck-heaps are lying within six feet of a man's fireside .... One single room is the sole habitation of men, women, and five or six children.[25]

As late as 1882 at Ushaw Moor, a predominantly Irish colliery, it came as a surprise to those who had not before witnessed the interior of the 'huts' or the 'stables', as the miners dubbed them, to see 'the most wretched dwellings it is possible to conceive'.[26]

There can be little doubt that the Irish in the colliery towns, as in the urban slums, did little to enhance the conditions they found. But as in Newcastle, factors either preceding the Irish influx or totally outside their control were at the root of the problem. Among those factors operating to worsen conditions was the emergence of trade unions, which tended to weaken paternalist 'improvements' on the part of coal owners. Another source was the instability of the coal market, which tightened expenditure on housing and such like. A further contributing factor was the habit of annual migrations by labourers, which left little room for the exercise of domestic pride. As 'foreigners', the Irish were generally placed in the most run-down accommodation, a fact that often served to heighten the impression that they were the instigators of poor conditions rather than the victims.

In company towns, like Jarrow (run by Palmers, the shipbuilding firm) or Consett (controlled by the Derwent-Consett iron plant), conditions were much the same as in the colliery towns. The houses – chiefly cottages – were either owned or leased by the works, and a rigid hierarchy pertained in their allocation, with the least-skilled workers and their families at the bottom in the poorest housing. Lodging houses in South Shields were reported in January 1853 as containing 499 English persons and 375 Scots, but 803 Irish.[27] Nearby in Jarrow, it was noted in the *Newcastle Daily Chronicle* that:

the substratum of society ... is composed of Irish. These inhabit the old pit houses ... consist[ing] mostly of one room. In these rows there is overcrowding of the most frightful character, and every condition essential to producing a pestilence exist .... Many of these cottages lodge from 15 to 19 people in one night. There is no regard to sex .... Many of the beds in these cottages are never cold, for as soon as they are vacated by the men who are going on the day shift they are occupied by the men who have come off the night shift.[28]

In Consett there was an 'immense number of our brethren from the "Sister Isle"[29] who were 'made to have about half a dozen more representatives in that neighbourhood than all the rest [of the inhabitants] put together'.[30] Although this 'rough census of the population' was dismissed as unreliable, there is no doubt that the Irish formed a large proportion of Consett's population and comprised the bulk of its common labourers. As in Jarrow, the living conditions were far from ideal. Because Irish labourers were contracted (usually in gangs), little effort was made to house them since they were not considered company employees. Some were allocated decrepit and well-used cottages, but the majority fended for themselves, sleeping in overcrowded lodging houses or barrack-like tenements. While company spokesmen wrote eulogies on the 'good life' of Consett,[31] inspectors of nuisances were applying to the justices to close houses down, and complaining of the mess and stench 'created by piggeries in the main street'.[32]

There were, however, differences in Irish living conditions between the outlying districts of Durham and the region's urban centres. In the small towns, the Irish usually had some means of sustenance, whereas in Newcastle, Gateshead and Sunderland there was a much higher proportion of destitute poor without any such means. In the terms of the early social scientist, Seebohm Rowntree, the latter exemplified 'primary poverty', where a family's total earnings were below a level necessary 'for the maintenance of merely physical efficiency'.[33] As epitomised in Newcastle, there were a great many Irish who by their employment were unable to procure a subsistence income. Among them were the seasonal harvesters who remained behind, and the 'lodgers, prostitutes and vendors of fish and all classes of goods', which the Census enumerator found inhabiting that part of Sandgate from the Trolley to the Blue Bell Entry.[34] It was to this group that George Grey referred when he spoke of those 'Irish poor who do not seem to settle down to any kind of labour – not fixedly – but who move about from one kind of labour to another'.[35] A local report had earlier designated these Irish as 'the vagrant class – half mendicant, half hawkers'.[36] However there were as many 'Irish who are very industrious, who are employed as labourers about manufactories, foundries, glass-houses, and in labour generally'.[37] Typical of this group was John Galliger of 'Cox Entry', described in the Enumerator's manuscript as a fifty-four year old labourer born in Ireland, with his wife Bridget and their nineteen year old son who worked on the docks.[38] The Irish in the industrial towns of Durham were primarily of this order, or 'secondary poor' as Rowntree classed them, with family earnings sufficient to maintain physical efficiency ('were it not that some portion of [the income] is absorbed by other expenditure, either useful or wasteful').

A further quantitative difference between the Irish in County Durham and Newcastle was the greater propensity of those in the latter place to coalesce into ghettos.[39] In part this was simply the difference between a larger population in the city as opposed to a more dispersed population in the county. In part, too, it was a reflection of differences in degrees of poverty. But the number and the relative poverty of the Irish in Newcastle did not in themselves account for the Sandgate ghetto. Nor wholly fitting would be the standard interpretation for this coalescing, that of religious and racial intolerance toward the Irish.[40] As we shall see later, there does not appear to have been any deliberate or intended action by the indigenous population that would have initially pressed the Irish into a confined area, or would have forced them to draw closer together and thus, perhaps, accentuate their Irishness. The explanation for the ghetto would seem to lie not in any single cause, but in a combination of these and other factors.

In the first place the general overcrowding in Newcastle, together with the poverty of the Irish, necessitated their occupying the cheapest and least salubrious parts of the town. Once thus grouped, they themselves created enough pull to attract increasing numbers of their kinsmen. The critic of industrialism, Thomas Carlyle, pointed to this causation of Irish ghettos in 1840; and Engels, similarly critical of the society that tolerated and perpetuated such appalling living conditions, agreed that the Irishman 'drives the Saxon native out'.[41] Increasingly, the Irish poured into the slum for nowhere else could they find to the same extent the common bonds of language, background and occupation. Hence their take-over of pubs, shops, and lodging houses until certain areas were dominated by them. In 1874 Newcastle's Medical Officer of Health reported that in only three other provincial towns – Liverpool, Manchester and Bradford – was there a higher proportion of Irish.[42] And of the over 7,000 Irish in Newcastle by that date, the greatest number were within the labyrinth of alleys and closes that made up Sandgate. Just as Henry Mayhew and his imitators had depicted 'Little Irelands' in England, so in Newcastle there came to be preserved a viable and distinctive way of life in the heart of the slum. 'Why if you go there', exclaimed one interloper, 'you will find yourselves almost in a strange land. A language is spoken you hardly know; habits are in operation unfamiliar to you; work is done you know not of. Verily, it seems like another nation'.[43] As the correspondent to *The Tablet* declared in 1852, 'Sandgate, the scene of crime, of misery and poverty, of filth and pestilence' is the 'one spot, one locality in Newcastle, which may be emphatically termed the St. Giles' of the north'.[44]

The Catholic church, although unconnected with the actual formation of the ghetto, exerted a disproportionate influence on its subsequent development, inasmuch as the overwhelming majority of the immigrants were of that faith.[45] Since the first Irish Catholics took up residence in the parish of All Saints the slums had been served by priests, though it is doubtful that they exerted much influence on the actual place of Irish settlement. But in 1846 the Brotherhood of St. Vincent de Paul was introduced into the area, and in 1851 a Catholic chapel-of-ease was established in the heart of Sandgate in a disused Presbyterian Church on Wall Knoll Street. By the 1840s, then, and especially after 1851, the church might have served as one of the incentives for Irish settlement.

The Church also played an important role in the coalescence of the ghetto through the use of priests who 'speak the Gaelic'.[46] Thus were bonds of kinship among the Irish strengthened and, allegedly, 'a means of self-identification with the larger society' made.[47] In that Catholicism was inextricably woven with Irish nationality, the church further served as 'a nexus of communal solidarity'[48] by the negative forces it generated in the English community. The amount of this reaction will be the subject of later discussion; the point here is simply that the ghetto *preceded* any hostility, rather than being the product of any local hostility to nationalist and religious sentiment.

In Durham, in such large villages such as Thornley, Wolsingham, and Tow Law, much the same pattern can be witnessed in the congregating of the Irish, with Catholic missions arriving later to solidify the communities. The chief difference between the Irish in these towns and those in the larger urban centres might be described as the difference between 'social association' on the one hand, and 'socio-economic community' on the other. In Newcastle the ghetto was sufficiently independent that many of its inhabitants could pursue their meagre livelihoods with little or no contact with the larger society. But in the coal and iron towns, the Irish were united with all the inhabitants by virtue of common occupation. By their employment, therefore, the Irish in the small towns of Durham were in greater contact with their non-Irish neighbours. Thus the segregation of the Irish in the single-industry towns was dependent more purely on social and religious factors than on the economic pressures determining the ghetto.

Social Life

The unprecedented influx of labourers to meet the economic expansion of the North-east in the mid-century resulted in considerable social upheaval. Quiet rural parishes awoke to find their pasts shattered and their presents uncertain. 'Shifting, continually shifting ... [was] the order of the day', moaned an incumbent in the diocese of Durham.[49]

With so large a part of the population without native roots, social order was hard pressed. Contributing to it were the rural, ill-educated and un-skilled Irish: predominantly young, predominantly male, and given more to violence and pleasure than thrift, sobriety and domesticity. Court proceedings in the local press abound with Irish names in incidences of riotous behaviour. Unsurprisingly, after the initial influx of Irish, the press tended to place such incidents in small type, as if acknowledging them as commonplace. A two-hour riot involving over 50 Irishmen in Durham City in 1865, for example, was relegated to an obscure corner of the *Durham Chronicle* and entitled 'A Sunday Scene in Framwellgate'.[50] This particular riot, like innumerable others, began in the local public house and was terminated only by the intervention of a priest.

In the industrial frontier of the North-east, drink was not merely a fortification against the strains of labour, it was also one of the very few recreations available. It was observed in the slums of Newcastle that there were 'no open places or recreation, no playgrounds, no clubs, no means of amusement; but there were public-houses and beer-houses in great abundance. There was music in them; here perhaps only a barrel-organ, there simply a fiddler screaming out his Irish jigs'.[51] In every town with over a dozen Irish there was at least one beer house that was Irish by occupation if not by ownership. In 1865, Hartlepool (typical of older established towns) had thirty-two public houses for a population of 12,000; Tow Law (site of new iron works and many Irish labourers) had seventeen beer houses for a population of 2,500.[52] The Irish public house served as a club, immigrant information centre and clearing house and, all too often, an arena for battles among the clientele.

Little was done to curb the excesses of Irish drinking other than punitive action by the law. Although there were priests who sought to contend with the drinking – including the use of a 'stout blackthorn' every pay-night to keep the flock in check[53] – until the mid-1860s priests were relatively few and far between and heavily overworked. Not every priest could devote himself to discovering the Irish drinking haunts and policing them 'as late as 12 at night', as Bishop Hogarth is reputed to have done in Darlington.[54] As *The Rambler* pointed out in 1854, 'our clergy ... have such an enormous amount to work, both present and prospective, before them, in the discharge of their ordinary and purely clerical duties, that it is impossible to expect from them any thing more than an encouragement and supervision of those other works of charity'.[55]

There were also problems with some of the English priests, who tended to be over-sympathetic to the Irish, pointing to 'the agony which pierces the soul of every priest, when he sees any of his sheep or lambs ... [in] the public-house in place of God's service'.[56] Further, some of the Irish priests – themselves often not without intemperate yearnings – were too familiar with Irish habits to be over bothered by them. Not only was the 'Apostle of Temperance', Father Theobald Mathew, barely supported by the Catholic Church in the North-east and his influence weakest there, but the famine influx had largely undone his work throughout England.[57] Long before Mathew's death in 1856, temperance work among Irish Catholics had fallen neglected beside the more determined effort to build churches for the new congregations.[58] Occasional 'retreats' by visiting priests often devoted a portion of their time to administering the abstinence pledge to the flocks, but the results were seldom lasting.[59] While the terrorisation of towns by gangs of inebriate Irishmen, such as that which occurred in Southwick in 1867,[60] or that which is reputed to have resulted in a white line being painted across the main street of Thornley to divide the nationalities,[61] were not entirely representative of Irish drinking habits, the number of smaller drunken affrays involving the Irish were all too numerous.

In the 1860s some efforts were made to broaden Irish social life in order that the drinking might be reduced. Appropriately, St. Patrick's Day was often seized upon as the moment for action. For example, in 1865 Bishop Hogarth:

seriously exerted himself to inaugurate something like decency and order among that unruly portion of his flock; and without in the least interfering with their national hilarity, has organised from year to year something new in the shape of rational amusement, inculcating also, in every possible way, the virtue of sobriety.[62]

Reporting this, the *Durham Chronicle* commented that such an effort was necessary because 'for years in Darlington the anniversary taking place on the 17th of March was one continual orgy [sic] and row amongst the low Irish of both sexes'. The Bishop's directive was followed, and only a year later the *Chronicle* was reporting that 'St. Patrick's Day in Durham passed off very quietly; and people were congratulating themselves on the fact'.[63] By 1875, St. Patrick's Day had become anodyne in Durham and Newcastle, noted only for the abundance of amateur concerts in the schools and peaceful Irish political meetings. By 1883 the 'festival of the Shamrock Saint' was being looked upon, in West Cornforth at least, 'as a red-letter day'.[64]

But if St. Patrick's Day was taken in hand and held as a model of what *could* be achieved, it remained until the 1870s untypical of the other 364 days of the year. To judge from press coverage of events generally, the Irish appear to be noted above all for murders, secondly for brutal assaults, thirdly for petty thefts, and fourth for drunken behaviour. However, if one reads the court columns, it is clear that this ordering should be reversed.[65] Police statistics, too, tell a different story; those released by the Newcastle police in 1861 (which for the first time specified 'Irish-born' criminals) indicate that the type of offences committed could not easily be linked to nationalities. The figures do reveal, though, that 18.5 percent of those apprehended were born in Ireland (or three times the proportion of Irish to English in Newcastle).[66] By 1869 this figure had risen to 21.3 percent of those taken into custody (or nearly four times their proportion in the city).[67] Available statistics for Roman Catholic prisoners in Durham on January 1st, 1862 and 1864, also depict an increase from 17 percent to 26 percent of all prisoners.[68] Throughout England police statistics showed similar increases in the number of Irish-born criminals,[69] with alcohol usually being cited as the predisposing cause. It thus became increasingly obvious to the Catholic Church that action was necessary to alleviate what *The Tablet* called 'the disproportionate space they [the Irish] fill upon the prison register'.[70]

The work of reform lent itself to the strong social conscience of Archbishop Manning. He first became interested in the temperance movement in 1867 through the agency of the United Kingdom Alliance (founded in 1856). This forced him, he declared in Newcastle in 1882, 'to a knowledge of the real demoralising power of this drink traffic'.[71] Unlike earlier temperance interventions, Manning's was not only to reform habits, but to create a powerful body of dedicated total abstainers who would be able to exert political pressure. With this in mind he formed the League of the Cross in 1872. From the outset it was clear that the League was directed at Irish Catholics. At the first convention in London in 1875 Father Nugent presented Manning with a cross made of Irish marble, declaring that:

> the next generation of Irish people in this country, would be different to what they were at present. He understood well the influences that had led their people into intemperance and moral degradation. The tide which flowed into this country from 1847 to 1856 was so overwhelming that they had neither churches, schools, nor pastors to look after the people ...[72]

Although there was no representation from the North-east at this conference nor at the following one in Manchester, Manning kept the Catholic hierarchy well informed on the League's progress. Few branches of it were set up in Durham or Newcastle, but the impetus for Catholic temperance resulted in the establishment of many similar bodies. In the colliery town of Sacriston, for example, Father Lescher began a temperance association in 1876 under the patronage of St. John the Baptist. Unable to attract enough total abstainers, 'it was thought best to include all who were willing to take any kind of pledge, of Total or Partial Abstinence', and children were admitted as half-members.[73] In South Shields a temperance 'Confraternity of the Holy Cross' was in business by 1874,[74] while in Consett sobriety was sought though the Society of the Holy Family.[75] It was not until Manning's 'Northern Crusade of the

League of the Cross' between 1880 and 1882 that the League became more active in the north, and not until March 1885 that a branch was established in Newcastle.[76] By then concerts, annual picnics and various outings were replacing the exclusive dependence on the public house. The press were sensitive to the change, noting in 1887 for example, that the most striking features of the Irish on a local outing to Holy Island was 'their appearance, their going and coming, their decorous but cheerful bearing, their comportment from first to last'.[77]

A narrower facet of Irish social life, which also came to be supervised by the Church, was the Irish club, particularly Ribbon lodges and Hibernian societies. While the Ribbon lodges have a clear place in the history of Ireland as secret, agrarian, anti-Protestant, anti-landlord societies, the nature and extent of their operations in England remains obscure. In the North-east there is no evidence from either Irish or English sources to substantiate their existence. References to Ribbonmen come mainly from the Catholic Church, which lingered under the impression that any group of Irishmen not directly under its control were probably Ribbonmen or Ribbon-like in composition and intent. The Ancient Order of Hibernians,[78] a vigilantly Catholic society that could trace its origins to as far back as 1565, did not long escape the church's condemnation as a dangerous 'secret society' with Ribbon connections.[79]

To be a Hibernian one had to be Catholic, 'Irish or of Irish decent,... of good moral character', and *not* belong to any secret societies. At all times their motto was to be 'Friendship, Unity, and True Christian Charity'.[80] The Order played an important role in organising and leading poor Irish Catholics in industrial centres of England and Wales, and basically fulfilled, as it did in America, 'that desire in human nature, and especially in Celtic nature, to belong to some guild, confraternity, or other society'.[81] A branch of the Order was in existence in Newcastle in 1844, for, as we shall see, it conducted negotiations with the miners' unions to prevent importations of Irish strike-breakers. But in 1838, according to one author, Hibernians were accused of being 'secret' and condemned by the Church, the authorities having been alerted through a letter from the General Secretary of the Ribbonmen in Dublin to the Liverpool Hibernians.[82] Some Hibernian Societies therefore reformed themselves into sick and burial clubs, and upon these Vicar Apostolic Briggs of the Northern District consented to bestow his blessings as long as they were approved by the Bishops of Ireland.[83] Yet the relationship between the Church and the Hibernians was never very stable, for the Church was never wholly convinced that Hibernians were not Ribbonmen by another name. The Church also disliked the fact that the Society was independent and outside its control.

What exactly prompted Bishop Hogarth to renew the attack on the Hibernians in 1852 is not clear. During the St. Patrick' Day proceedings they had played their usual conspicuous part after attending Divine Service at the respective churches of St. Andrew and St. Mary'.[84] The church attendance bears noting, for only five days later Bishop Hogarth accused the Hibernians of secrecy and wrote to his clergy:

> We know that many of the worst crimes, which disgrace human nature, have been the offspring of SECRET SOCIETIES, to which many misguided men have associated themselves ... We are moreover informed that, for some time past, a very considerable section of one of the secret Societies has assumed the fictitious name of the HIBERNIAN SICK-CLUB, in order to conceal their identity with the HIBERNIAN SOCIETY ... and we once more repeat ... THAT ALL THE MEMBERS OF SECRET SOCIETIES, AMONG WHICH WE NUMBER THE HIBERNIAN SOCIETIES ... ARE NOT TO BE ADMITTED TO A PARTICIPATION IN THE HOLY SACRAMENTS.[85]

Yet on St. Patrick's Day, 1854, the Hibernian Society again paraded through the streets of Gateshead and Newcastle and 'made a collection at the close of their festivities, and presented the proceeds £8 to the Infirmary of Newcastle, through the Mayor, accompanied by a letter of thanks from his worship'.[86] In July of that year the priests at South Shields made 'a strong but affectionate appeal ... to the "Hibernians", or "Ribbonmen" to withdraw themselves from those illegal "secret societies", so strongly condemned by the Church'.[87] The Bishop repeated his charge in April 1857 and drew up a 'Declaration to be Made By Members of the Hibernian and other Secret Societies Before They Are Admitted to the Sacraments'.[88] But it was initially a losing battle; less than a year later the Bishop was lamenting that 'the Hibernian Society, We regret to find, is too widely spread among the industrious poor of our Diocese'.[89] In May of 1858 he was again compelled to speak out, for, the notion 'that We ... *shall finally be compelled to yield to their urgent and often repeated demands* ... has so far prevailed as to induce some to retrace their steps and return to that Society which they had lately renounced'.[90] He ended his address by reminding the clergy that the church required 'the most perfect obedience and submission'. Not until 1859 was the situation almost in hand, and in February of that year the Bishop was at last able to express his pleasure that there had been a 'gradual decrease ... of unlawful and secret societies, effected under the blessing of God, by the zeal and preserving energies of our Clergy'.[91]

As with intemperance, the Church ultimately thwarted a 'dangerous' social activity. In its stead, Holy Guilds,[92] branches of the Catholic Institute, Catholic Friendly Societies, Catholic Young Men's Societies, Catholic Orders of Odd Fellows, and innumerable other confraternities and benefit societies were promoted to provide harmless amusements and instruction, and to maintain the church at the centre of Irish social life. As one member of the Newcastle branch of the Young Men's Society wrote to the editor of *The Tablet*, 'What Sir, has the heart-broken, expatriated Celt, to console him in his myriad woes? Nothing but God and the Church, burning love for Eternal Rome, and undying affection for the *Soggarth Aroon*'.[93] Although in 1880 the new Bishop of the diocese in his first Pastoral spoke of 'the besetting sin of drunkenness, and the seduction of secret societies' as the two 'arch-enemies, against whom we must wage implacable war',[94] he was only echoing the concerns of the past and attempting to retain the amount of control which the church had by then obtained.

Local Reactions

English responses to the Irish in England ranged from outright hostility to apologetic eulogy. At one extreme were bigoted and condescending expostulations:

> the influx of starving exiles from Ireland who were so unprepared for superior civilisation that they could not carry beer with propriety and good fellowship; so ready to fight as to add largely to the statistics of crime, yet, poor souls, seldom able to fight with the success that earns at least the consideration of fellow roughs.[95]

From a wealth of such statements it was not difficult for Irish Catholic writers to infer that 'the lower class of Irish are to the rest of the population of England what the Hebrews were to the Egyptians'.[96] This, it was claimed, was the product of racial discrimination that the 'Catholicity of the Irish, no doubt, magnifies and increases'.[97] At the other extreme were exalted views of Irish 'willingness, alacrity, and perseverance',[98] of their 'superior steadiness and docility',[99] and of modesty so great that they 'frequently made excuses for themselves or their children, for not attending chapel or school, on the ground of want of proper clothing'.[100] This sympathetic approach was a favourite among investigators like Mayhew or Booth who preferred to call Irish sins 'frailties' and Irish crime 'disorder'.[101]

To a degree this same spectrum of attitudes could be found in Durham and Newcastle. Stephen Edward Piper, Medical Officer for Darlington in 1851, singled out the Irish as the principal culprits in the housing shortage, employing the adjectives: 'dirty ragged', 'swarming vagrant', 'squalid half clad', and 'deplorably ignorant'.[102] An investigator of Sandgate in 1850 was of the opinion 'that the influx of Irish into our large towns has had the most deteriorating influence both upon themselves and the native population with which they have come in contact'.[103] On the other hand, some sympathy could be evoked even for an Irishman who had murdered his wife when it was considered that the couple lived in 'underground rooms 'in Blandford-street' and that they were surrounded by the 'evil of poverty'.[104] There are also numerous accounts that point to

Irish wit, conviviality and simple-mindedness. Such was the Irish Paddy, long a favorite fictional character.[105] In local accounts like 'An Irishman's Revenge on his Pig', this stereotype was reinforced, while it was humorously suggested that perhaps 'the household affections of the Irish people – which all travelers agree contain many traits of excellent character – become warped and distorted during their voluntary exile from the land of birth'.[106]

On the whole, however, commentary on the Irish in the Northeast tended to be less hostile than that which has been recorded of other Irish populations in England. One aspect of the more tolerant attitude can be seen in the singular lack of references to them. Whereas in other areas there was little hesitation in calling an Irishman an Irishman, or in denouncing the Irish for anything that faintly suggested their culpability, in Durham and Newcastle there a reticence in implicating them. When they were mentioned it was frequently as 'from the Sister Isle' or 'Hibernian friend' or 'Celtic Cousins'.

In English Catholic circles the lack of reference to the Irish was often attributed to a certain hesitation in admitting that the growth of Catholicism in a particular parish was the result of an influx of 'low Irish'. More important is the fact that 'Irish' and 'Catholic' became increasingly synonymous terms, making it fatuous for Catholic leaders to qualify their flocks as 'Irish Catholics'. But from Protestants, too, there was a lack of outspokenness on the Irish and, when referred to at all, it was often with surprising levels of toleration. This can be illustrated through the record of epidemics in the area in comparison to commentary on the Irish in epidemics elsewhere in England.

Between 1846 and 1849 there were several virulent outbreaks of typhus, scarlatina and cholera, and it was commonplace to blame the generation and the communication of these diseases on Irish immigrants. The cause of typhus being unknown, the disease was commonly referred to as 'Irish fever'. A writer in Leeds bitterly reflected that the swarms of Irish who arrived in that city 'famished, in rags and without money and ... with no thought of the decencies of life', had caused 'a terrible outbreak of typhus fever'.[107] The president of the Manchester Statistical Society commented after the epidemic there that 'its dissemination and virulence were coextensive, not with the prevalence of nuisances, but rather with the current of Irish immigration so remarkable in that year [1846-47]'.[108] But contemporary observers in Newcastle made no such accusations, even though the number of deaths from the fever was highest in Sandgate. Dr. Robinson, after making a thorough investigation of the epidemic's causes in Newcastle, failed even to mention the Irish.[109] Another doctor investigating the fever-dens blamed the epidemic on the overcrowding and lack of ventilation and drainage, but not specifically on the Irish.[110] Whereas in other areas the outbreaks allegedly 'earned the Irish the prejudice of the contemporary press',[111] in Newcastle and Durham the press duly reported the deaths without any mention of the Irish – this, despite the fact that the Catholic Bishop of the diocese (William Riddell) lost his life in administering to Irish Catholic victims.[112]

When the cholera raged in the summer and autumn of 1853 the local press again referred to it as an issue of public health of which 'neither the causes which produce the malady, its diagnosis, or the antidote are known'.[113] Although the Newcastle Corporation 'voted the Catholic priests £10 for cab hire' to administer to stricken Catholics, the Irish were not held up to public execration.[114] By the Anglican incumbent of St. Mary's, Gateshead, where over 350 lives were lost in a single month, the outbreak was described as God's wrath for the sins of the 'Infidels, Sabbath breakers, drunkards and blasphemers'.[115] It is significant that the only body which attempted to implicate the Irish in this epidemic was the visiting Commission for the Board of Health's 1854 *Report ... to Inquire into the Causes which have led to ... the Late Outbreak of Cholera in the Towns of Newcastle-Upon-Tyne, Gateshead, and Tynemouth.* The Commissioners referred back to the 'Irish fever epidemic' in Newcastle of 1846-8, and made plain that the Irish and their hovels were the seedbed of the city's ill-health.[116] Dr. Thomas Headlam of Newcastle in giving evidence before the Commissioners was forced to admit that the epidemic of 1847 'prevailed chiefly from the immigration of Irish trampers who had been suffering from famine'.[117] But when the Commissioners attempted to attribute the cholera of 1852-3 to 'the old seats of Irish fever', Headlam replied that this was not so, for the cholera 'extended over the whole town, and to places usually considered healthy'.[118] It is also worthy of note that when the *Sunderland Herald* printed that 'English dogs were cleaner than Irish people' they were quoting the Commissioners' *Report*.[119] But the local press, irrespective of political creed, did not attempt to use the Irish as a scapegoat for the sanitary neglect of the Newcastle Corporation; relative to other areas of Irish habitation, public and private statements (so far as they can be determined) were decidedly lacking in conventional anti-Irishness.

Earlier local sanitary reports also bear witness to the lack of any specific castigation of the Irish. When Alderman Dunn headed the sanitation committee in 1844-45, for example, he was adamant that if you give the poor better housing 'they will turn it into a noisome hovel'.[120] He cited the Irish on Wall Knoll and Sandgate Streets, but noticeably did not single them out as the instigators of the insalubrious conditions. Like James Losh before him, Dunn merely grouped the Irish with the 'low lodging-house keepers, prostitutes, thieves, and vagrants'.[121] Indeed, almost all of the available evidence on the Irish in the North-east fails to point to any consensus of opinion that the Irish lowered the Englishman's 'superior prudence', morals, drinking habits or living conditions. While the Irish were forced to exist at a lower standard, were more given to strong drink and rowdy behaviour, and lived in more slovenly conditions, their influx was not regarded as having a 'disastrous social effect' on the wider community – 'always tending to drag down their neighbours to a lower level of living'.[122] Looking back on the famine influx some years later, the *Newcastle Daily Chronicle* could only remark, 'their invasion, peaceful and industrious, brought no cause for alarm'.[123]

A further example of local attitudes toward the Irish lies in the behaviour of Poor Law Officials with regard to Irish removals. According to one Poor Law expert the 'northern part of Great Britain' exercised much greater forbearance with the Irish than did the south, 'inasmuch as only one Irishmen is removed out of three liable to removal'.[124] But even this modest ratio seems inflated, for of the numerous entries in the Newcastle minute books for 'Removal to Ireland', far less than half of these correlate with the signed and sealed Removal Warrants. Between 20 February and 9 October 1849, for instance, the pages of the Poor Law books are filled with removal entries,[125] yet only 39 individuals and/or families were actually removed from Newcastle,[126] In many cases the threat of removal was sufficient to ward off the intended victim, for there are abundant entries that read simply, for example, 'Martha Cunan and family ordered into the House to be sent to Ireland – Did not go into House – Disposed of'.[127] No doubt the 'scare technique', also practised in London to cut costs, was equally effective. But it is also obvious from the Poor Law books that many Irish were receiving relief despite their failure to comply with the residency requirements. Even before the great famine influx, the Guardians of the Poor Law were not observing instructions from the bureaucrats in London. When in June 1845 the House of Commons ordered information on whether the regulations of the non-resident relief order had been adopted, the Newcastle Guardians replied that 'the Regulations have not been adopted in this Union'.[128] In fact they stated that 368 non-residents, adults and children, had received relief in their Union between the 21 of December 1844 and the 25 of March 1845.[129]

When the full implications of the famine conditions in Ireland registered, the idea of returning the Irish to their homeland was regarded as absurd. Beginning in March 1847, 70 Irish persons are listed in the Poor Law books of Newcastle as receiving relief varying from one shilling per week plus food, to six shillings per week for two months.[130] This leniency to Irish paupers was observed by an investigator of Sandgate in 1850 who wrote:

> I am informed that fully one third of the persons receiving parochial relief in this Union are Irish and Scotch, and that in All Saints' parish one half are Irish. This corresponds with a statement which reached me from another quarter, and by which it appears that

fourteen years since there was but one Irish family receiving relief under the Poor Law in All Saints' parish, whereas there are now at least 1,200 natives of Ireland weekly relieved in the same district.

The system of deportation ... does not seem to have been vigorously adopted by the Newcastle Board of Guardians, and the few experiments made afforded very little encouragement for its repetition on a larger scale.[131]

There can be no doubt that the relief given to the Irish was in part attributable to the sheer bother of removal procedure, financial considerations, and the distance of local officials from the London Poor Law administrators. But these factors only supply a partial explanation, for at root the Newcastle officials were not ill-disposed to the Irish, at least as compared to elsewhere when judged from the evidence provided by other Poor Law spokesmen before the Select Committees on Poor Removals. That the removal laws were not strictly enforced and that non-resident relief was provided in Newcastle until July 1853 seems governed by genuine sympathy for the plight of the Irish.[132]

The Irish, although not treated in a spirit of camaraderie or in any way exalted in the normal course of affairs, did not elicit in the host population a great deal of hostility. They did not become an omnipresent evil for the expiation of social shortcomings or appeasement for social psychosis – a role they sometimes assumed for other Anglo-Saxon and Scots populations. Within the context of other immigrant groups at least, the Irish were treated with unparalleled equanimity. If a murderer were Irish it was always drawn to the attention of the public, but equal attention was given to murderers such as 'Scotch Charlie' and his comrade 'Scotch Jock'.[133] Or when 'an outrage was perpetrated by pitmen', the press did not fail to mention that the scene of the crime, Hedley Hill, had lost some of its former respectability by 'an influx of Irish *and* Cornish miners'.[134] Indeed, the single most important factor to emerge from the examination of the conditions and social life of the Irish in the North-east, and which contributes to an understanding of their unique position relative to other areas, was the solvent nature of the society into which they entered. The sheer amount of immigration and the mobility of the population made it difficult to target the Irish as the cause of disorder. In other areas, where the industrial expansion was antecedent to the famine influx, the Irish, as the largest immigrant group, could more easily become scapegoats for social ills and unrest.

And yet the fluidity of North-eastern society in the period under study and the relative place of the sizeable Irish community within it only provides a part of the explanation for the toleration shown them. Recourse must also be had to the religious, economic and political fabric of the region, and to the Irish influence within and upon that.

Chapter 3

The Catholic Church

> The Catholics in the place are wretchedly poor, and nothing but zeal of a high order could have induced the purchase of even so humble a structure.
> 'Thornley', *The Tablet*, 11 [20 July 1850], p.461.
>
> He looked upon the North of England as the hope of the Catholic Church in England. In the North they had the vigour and the courage, and the unbroken tradition, and ... a compact solidity to give the Church of this diocese a weight, a momentum, of fruitfulness which they did not possess in the South.
> Cardinal Manning in Newcastle. *Durham Chronicle*, 20 Oct. 1882, p.7.

The Burden of Numbers

Although armchair theologians were slow to acknowledge it, the influx of Irish into Britain turned the 'second spring' of Roman Catholicism into more than a mere seasonal phenomenon. While the leaders of the Oxford Movement awoke advocates and opponents of the faith, it was the Irish poor, not the socially privileged converts to Catholicism, who bloated the congregations. In the North-east, where the impact of the conversion movement was only slightly felt, converts accounted for less than five percent of the estimated Catholic population.[1] Moreover, the converted did not always long remain so. As one priest noted in his enumeration return for the *Status Animarum* of the diocese: 'I am sorry to have to remark that the greater number of Converts whose baptisms are registered and who are still resident in the parish, are not worthy of the name of

Catholics, as they cannot now be induced to enter the Church. I can only point to one convert as a most exemplary member of the congregation'.[2]

The growth of the Catholic population of Durham and Newcastle, in the neighbourhood of 350 percent between 1847 and 1882, was almost wholly attributable to the Irish. Though no complete statistics survive to indicate the size of the Catholic population prior to the influx of Irish, piecemeal evidence suggests that it was probably less than 10,000. The returns made to the House of Lords in 1767 put their numbers in Durham at 2,733.[3] It seems unlikely that there was much increase until at least the turn of the century. If Darlington is at all typical of inland towns, there was a decrease in population, for where eighty-four Catholics had been counted in 1767, only twenty remained in 1800.[4] Within the three large port parishes of Bishopwearmouth, Sunderland and Monkwearmouth, there were 136 Catholics in 1767. By 1808 their numbers had risen to around 300.[5]

Nonetheless, from the turn of the century to the late 1830s there was a sufficient rise in the Catholic population to instill a new sense of mission in the Catholic Church. The growth was mainly confined to the urban centres of Newcastle, Sunderland, Durham, and Darlington.[6] While some of these Catholics would have been Irish, the majority were a residuum from the decay of seignorial estates. Others were the result of the movement into towns of the sons of Catholic yeomanry. As John Bossy has shown through a study of some rural Catholic estates in Northumberland, the growth of the independent town congregations between 1750 and 1850 was partially the result of the migration of the labourers from the estates of the Catholic gentry.[7] Durham and Northumberland along with Cumberland retained the highest proportion of recusant Catholics and these were primarily attached to the land, either on the estates of the Catholic gentry or (especially in Durham) independent small farmers. Thus the migration off the land played a more important role in changing the social balance of urban congregations in the North-east than elsewhere in England. In view of this, it would be wrong to imply that because the figures for the Irish-born in 1841 nearly matched those of the estimated Catholic population of 1821, most Catholics in England in 1821 were therefore Irish.[8] Among other things this fails to allow for any immigration between 1821 and 1841. In fact, without detailed records, it is difficult to state with any certainty what proportion of the 180,000 Catholics claimed to be in the Northern District in 1839 were Irish.[9] And of the 1,500 Catholics found in the parish of All Saints, Newcastle, in 1838,[10] who can say what proportion were Irish when the pecuniary situation of the English Catholic labourer was often such as to make him the neighbour of his co-religionist from Ireland?

For the decade prior to the famine influx, there is little evidence to support the assumption that the Irish played any major part in the progress of north-eastern Catholicism.[11] The Irish-born figures bear little relation to Catholic figures, and in the building of some of the churches between 1835 and 1845 the Irish played only an incidental role. Only in the founding of St. Patrick's, Felling, can we see the direct result of a mainly Irish congregation, amounting 'to nearly four hundred persons' by 1841.[12] The opening of St. Mary's, Sunderland, in 1835 was not the result of any pressing need from a swarming Irish population; Father P. Kearney was thought to be acting presumptuously in opening a church for which there were insufficient Catholics.[13] The building of the cathedral of St. Mary's in Newcastle in 1844 is another case in point, for such pretentious structures were seldom built to serve the Irish hordes, nor were the Irish particularly attracted to such posh places of worship.

The immediate pre-famine church building in Durham and Newcastle is more a reflection of the Church's increased confidence than Irish immigration. In the mid-1840s toleration towards Catholics in the North-east reached new levels. Catholics were gradually emerging from their garrets in back alleys and sequestered chapels. Quite independent of trends elsewhere in England a new life-blood was injected into northern Catholicism which soon overcame earlier persecution and stigma. Counting the heads of Irish Catholics may have accounted for some of this increased confidence but the level of toleration that allowed, for example, Thomas Dunn to become the first Catholic Lord Mayor of Newcastle in 1842 has little to do with it. Though assailed by the Tory press 'for presuming publicly to attend his own church in preference to accompanying the judges to the Protestant Church of St. Nicholas',[14] Dunn, when his term of office was finished in 1845, was elected an alderman by a majority of twenty-seven to two.[15] And in the same year that St. Mary's Cathedral was opened, the first 'Month of Mary' in Newcastle was greeted so successfully that the Catholic *Tablet* remarked 'perhaps in no place has this devotion been introduced under such favourable circumstances, or responded to with so much spirit'.[16]

In Durham the renewed confidence of the Catholic Church was evident in the establishment of new missions and in the rebuilding of old churches. The mission at Birtley was obscure and dwindling in the hands of the Benedictines: the flock was 'a mere handful, widely scattered', the church 'a small, damp, dark, and dilapidated building in an unfrequented corner of the village'.[17] When J.J. Sheridan took over the mission in 1842 he asserted all the Church's new-felt confidence. In two years he transformed the flock 'into a large and respectable congregation, producing ten times the original number of communicants'. At the same time he replaced the obscure church with 'a very handsome Gothic building of stone'.[18] The new church was soon overrun with Irish workers from the Birtley iron works, but in 1842 they were not in the planning. Nor was Rev. J.A. McEvoy of Houghton-le-Spring referring to the Irish when in 1835 he described the 'great number of nominal Catholics in this part of the country' as 'exceedingly fastidious in their notions of accommodation'.[19] Like Rev. Kearney's 'massive and imposing fabric designed by Bonomi'[20] in Sunderland, McEvoy's vision of 'a new chapel erected on the noble Site' was the product of a more self-assured priesthood.

But if the earlier period leaves some doubt as to the actual extent of the Irish influence on the Catholic Church, from the late 1840s no such doubt exists. From then on 'Catholic' and 'Irish' became virtually interchangeable in the North-east. In the first extant and comprehensive census listing the missions in Durham and Newcastle, that of 1847-49, the Catholic population was in excess of 23,000. This figure would have already contained numerous Irish Catholics, but from the extant census to 1882, it is clear that after 1850 the pattern of growth marries with the growth of the Irish population. Consistently, however, the Catholic figures exceed those of the estimated Irish population (see Table 1.5) – a reflection of the indigenous Catholic population and its natural increase.[21]

Table 3.1: **Estimated Catholic Population of Durham and Newcastle**

Year	Population	Year	Population
1847-49	23,250	1874	86,397
1852	38,636	1875	92,013
1855	45,684	1882	106,564
1861	56,688		

Source: Appendix II-VIII.

The extent of growth in real terms is easily measured in the expansion of missions, churches and schools.[22] During the twenty-six year incumbency of Rev. J. Bamber in Sunderland (1852-78), for example, 'Catholics multiplied, and from hundreds became thousands'.[23] From the mother church of St. Mary, missions were established at Monkwearmouth, Seaham Harbour and New Tunstall as well as the building of St. Patrick's and St. Joseph's in the city itself. Seating accommodation rose from 800 in 1851 to 2,700 places in 1872;[24] where two priests sufficed in 1850, nine were required in 1885. A comparable growth occurred in rural iron and coal towns. Representative of many, Brooms grew from a struggling mission with one priest ministering to a congregation said to number about 100 farmers in 1832[25] to become the parent of churches at Blackhill, Byermoor, Consett and Stanley with a population over 7,000 Catholics (the densest area in Durham) requiring five priests in 1882.

By 1876 Durham and Newcastle had a total of fifty-six Catholic churches, chapels and missions. Thirty-one churches, or seventy percent, were built after 1846, along with the founding of ten more missions which would receive churches later in the century. That the greater part of this development was the result of Irish immigration is clear from comparing the location of the churches built before 1846 with those built after (Maps 3.1 and 3.2).[26]

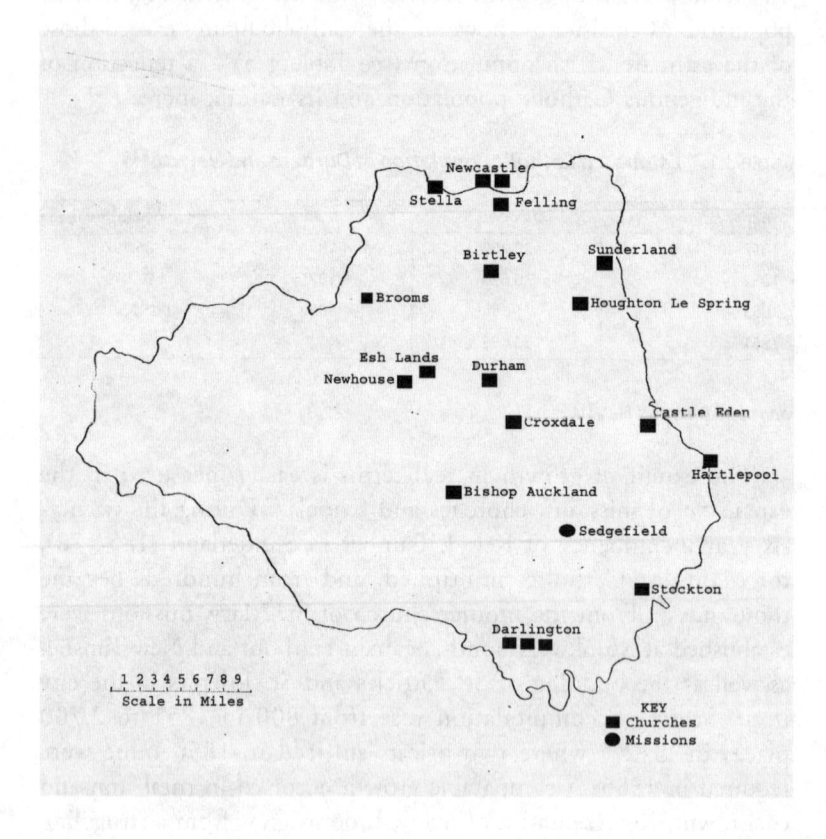

Map 3.1   *Catholic Churches and Missions of Co Durham and Newcastle, 1846*

```
                        Newcastle
              Stella      Felling

                     Birtley    Sunderland

         ■Brooms              ■Houghton Le Spring

              Esh Lands   Durham
            Newhouse■      ■
                              ■Croxdale      Castle Eden

                                                 ■Hartlepool
                     ■Bishop Auckland
                            ●Sedgefield

                                    ■Stockton
                            Darlington
                              ■■■

   1 2 3 4 5 6 7 8 9
     Scale in Miles
                                          KEY
                                          ■ Churches
                                          ● Missions
```

Chapter 3 The Catholic Church   51

Map 3.2   **Catholic Churches and Missions of Co Durham and Newcastle, 1876**

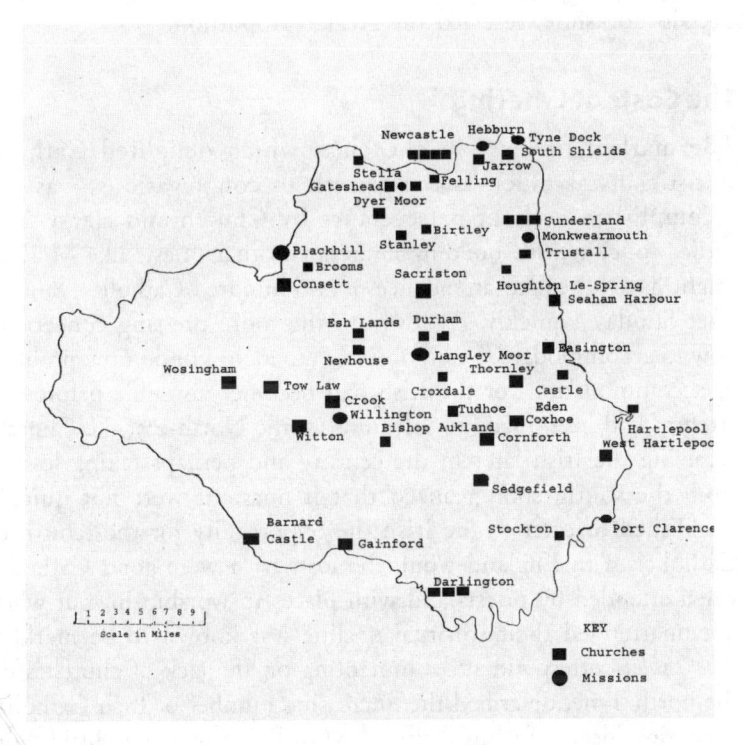

KEY
■ Churches
● Missions

Of those in existence in 1846 only the missions at Felling, Hartlepool and Bishop Auckland were mainly attributable to the Irish. The others were ancient chapels attached to Catholic estates, old regular missions (some redeveloped) and churches built since 1820 to serve 'respectable' urban Catholics. Map 3.2 indicates not only the Irish increase in the urban centres, especially along the coast and Tyneside towns, but also three circles of rural-industrial development: the iron-coal area served from Birtley, Byermoor, Blackhill and Sacriston; the iron-coal area to the south-west of Durham City centred on the River Wear and bounded by the missions at Langley Moor, Bishop Auckland, Wolsingham and Newhouse; and the chiefly coal district between the chapels at Thornley, Tudhoe and Sedgefield. Although the extreme south of County Durham received a good many Irish in the 1860s with the development of the Teesside iron works, Middlesbrough, across the Tees in Yorkshire, received the greater proportion.

The Costs of Catering

The marked increase in churches, which delighted Catholic statisticians as much as the growth in congregations, was not accomplished without perseverance by Church and clergy. The earlier concern with building churches so that priests like McEvoy might have a 'regular attendance of two hundred Catholics, Sunday after Sunday', quickly gave way to the more pressing concern of how to accommodate the numbers.[27] Where in London the problem of accommodation for the Irish had become 'insoluble before any attempt had been made to solve it',[28] in the North-east the Church, receiving the Irish later in the century and perhaps taking lessons from the south, soon realized that if missions were not quickly established to cater to the Irish the opportunity for the rebirth of Catholicism in England would be lost. Irish were good Catholics when attended by priests and with places to worship in, but when left unattended their spiritual decline was known to be marked. *The Tablet* correspondent, commenting on the lack of churches on the north Tyne, described the 'increasing number of Irish Catholics becoming located in this district ... [as] living in a state little short of barbarism'.[29] Outside urban centres the situation was scarcely better. As in isolated coalfields in Wales, where the Irish were said to retain 'very little of what they brought from their own country, save a love of whiskey, and a notoriety for being foremost in a row', across the coalfields of Durham the Irish were perceived as becoming indifferent to their faith.[30] 'What multitudes of Catholics', the Vicar Apostolic exclaimed in 1848:

> in various parts of our District, are deprived of the abundant means of Salvation which our Divine Redeemer has so plentifully imparted to his Church ... multitudes too distant from a Church or Chapel where Mass is celebrated, and where they could enjoy the happiness of approaching the Holy Sacraments ... they are chained irrevocably to the spot which denies them every spiritual consolation ... alas! these instances of spiritual destitution are too numerous and too widely spread over our District ...[31]

But while all agreed with *The Tablet's* solution, to 'take religion to their own doors',[32] the problems of providing accommodation for Irish flocks were staggering. As was said of Provost Platt, the Catholic incumbent of St. Cuthbert's, Durham, in 1850, 'if he saw with great joy that vast number of sturdy Catholics coming to his parish, it must have been too with some sense of terror when he understood the duty of caring for the spiritual needs of an every-day increasing population ... dispersed over a vast area'.[33] Platt concentrated on building another church in Durham City, but it would hardly suffice for those rurally situated from Stanley to Easington. After purchasing the Wheatsheaf Inn and converting its large dining hall into a temporary chapel, he was soon forced to make further extensions into the garden.[34] In the Hartlepools, Canon Knight and Father Harivel faced an equally demanding situation. In 1856 Harivel was holding Sunday afternoon and evening services for 'adults only' in a rented room over a warehouse in West Hartlepool. Ten years later, still unable to house the congregation, he was forced to take a lease on the Central Hall.[35] While the mission of St. Patrick's, Sunderland, was being established above the Magpie public house,[36] in Crook 150-to-200 Catholics were temporarily receiving the sacrament in two houses between which the partition had been removed.[37] In locations fortunate enough to have a church or chapel, three masses on Sunday were common; elsewhere additions were made to the churches wherever possible. Gateshead, in particular, was severely pressed; in 1853 a gallery was added to St. Patrick's, Felling, which doubled the seating capacity, but it was still necessary to hold concurrent masses in a large corn warehouse and in St. John's school.[38] The rest of Gateshead's Catholics went across the river to places of worship in Newcastle, but with three masses being held in each church there was scant extra room.

In the numerous accounts of the tribulations of the pioneer missions to the Irish there lingers the intimation that forces hostile to Catholicism necessitated the use of such inauspicious and overcrowded places of worship. But however much anti-Catholicism deterred the progress of the Church, it was not bigotry but the lack of money that was the chief constraint. Even in the earlier period of building and redevelopment, finances were the restraining factor.

Dr. Briggs, Vicar Apostolic of the Northern District, appealed in 1836 for the 'attention and sympathy' of the wealthy in his flock to alleviate the wants that were 'daily presenting them-selves'.[39] And Rev. McEvoy virtually wrote the epithet for the impoverished mission of the period when he prayed, 'Oh that some benevolent mortal would just give us one thousand pounds what an oasis would spring up in this moral wilderness!'[40] Indeed, the 'charitable friends who sent out appeals on behalf of Father McEvoy' were until the late 1840s, the only source of income for the Catholic Church.[41] In the absence of a Catholic middle class, these appeals were directed at 'those whom the Almighty has placed in easier circumstances'.[42] Of these Durham and Northumberland had more than their fair share. The Salvins of Tudhoe, the Riddells of Felton, the Dunns, Hansons and Bewicks of Newcastle, the Silvertops of Minsteracres, the Erringtons of Highwardens, the Taylor-Smith family of Tow Law and the Charltons of Heleyside were all 'irrepressible Papists' of high social standing and income. But although their names were always to be found beside the £5 and £10 donations at the top of every list of subscribers to the myriad appeals, they were not conspicuously philanthropic with respect to the Irish. Despite the fact that the Bishops implored 'those whom Divine Providence had blessed with abundance of earthly riches, to share a portion of them with their fellow-Christians who are in need', most of the wealthy (excepting the converts) were not generous in aiding those missions burdened with Irish immigrants.[43] Perhaps realising the danger of setting precedents in alms giving to the poor, the gentry tightened their purse strings well before the major influx. When it was revealed in 1844 that the Northern District Fund had amounted in the past year to only £205 16s 4d a writer to *The Tablet* declared:

> Really, one feels not so much indignant as humbled; not so much provoked to passion as sorely grieved at heart upon witnessing what at least would seem such a palpable proof and exhibition of our niggardly disposition, our apathy in religion, and our servitude to Mammon .... Where, then lies the blame? I say it with all respect and a feeling of profound regret, it lies with the Catholic gentry. ... It may probably be that the Croxdale and Minsteracres subscriptions have been swelled by the donation of a few pounds from the respective lords of the manner, but that is all ...[44]

When a 'Constant Reader' attempted to exonerate the North-Eastern gentry by stating that there were thirteen gentlemen in Durham and Northumberland supporting at their own expense Catholic Chapels and priests, the self-styled 'Ecclesiophilist' retorted that the Catholic gentry take no 'lively or active interest in Catholic affairs' and stated, 'If they cannot equal the generosity of the seven Catholic merchants of Liverpool, who have lately presented £50 each to their Diocesan Funds, let them at least bestow their £10, or their £20, towards the same object here'.[45] But the established Catholic families did not hold the Irish in too high a regard – at best the Irish were to be pitied. As the 'Northumbrian Lady', Barbara Charlton, once expostulated after dinner:

> she was 'an English Catholic, not an Irish one, which is all the difference in the world. English Catholics are responsible beings who are taught right from wrong, whereas Irish Catholics, belonging to a yet savage nation, know no better and are perhaps excusable on that account'.[46]

When under the direction of Cardinal Manning the Catholic Church in England reoriented itself towards Irish Catholics landed families, who felt that they alone had preserved the faith, were resentful and even less inclined to help the usurpers of their prerogatives. Thus, while willing to help liquidate debts on cathedrals like St. Mary's[47] or occasionally pay for a stained window in their honour at a new chapel,[48] they seldom made more than a token gesture towards alleviating the destitution and overcrowding at predominantly Irish places of worship.[49]

When the District Fund dropped to £169. 14s 8d in 1846, Mostyn and Riddell were aghast and sought a scapegoat in 'some of the Clergy who do not sufficiently exert themselves to promote it the Fund in their respective Missions'.[50] It was an unfair attack, for many of the priests could barely support themselves; yet it was a clear indication that appeals to the wealthy would no longer suffice and the needs of the poor must in the future be met by the poor themselves. The situation, though extreme in the North-east, was not unique. As *The Rambler* pointed out in 1849 (in part to goad the wealthy):

> The rich and noble can no longer be nursing fathers to the Church. With all that is done by some few among them, they are powerless to extricate us from our troubles; their day of distinction is past; they must take their place as units in the vast crowds of the entire Catholic people, and claim no more consideration from men than they receive from the hands of Almighty God himself. The poor are the only resource that remains to us untried.[51]

Indeed, as Bishop Hogarth was gratified to notice in 1849, the sum collected from the much larger but much poorer congregation showed an increase over the previous years. But still, the amount was 'small compared with our numerous and increasing demands'.[52] In an attempt to rectify this situation, Hogarth struck upon the idea that '*One Halfpenny* bestowed *Each Week* in the year by every Adult Catholic in this District, would abundantly suffice for all the growing wants of the District.[53] Since the 'Catholic Rent' system introduced into Ireland by the 'Liberator', Daniel O'Connell, operated on the same principle of collection from the Irish peasantry, Hogarth's idea, while not novel, had the most fitting of precedents. For those who doubted the scheme, the Bishop could point to the 'unexampled sacrifices of the poor Catholics of South Shields and Thornley' who had provided for themselves 'every facility for the practice of their religion'.[54] Thus was established the general rule that '*One Halfpenny per week shall be collected from every Individual who has attained the age of fourteen*'.[55] Two months later *The Tablet* was commenting on the success of the scheme,[56] and twelve months later was further praising it.[57] After only a year of operation the Fund had risen to 'three times the average of former years'.[58]

However, the Bishop had no desire to shift the whole of the financial burdens of the Church onto the shoulders of the poor; the rich, along with humbler English Catholics, continued to be implored to fulfill their obligations. In his pastoral of January 1852 Hogarth drew the attention of the affluent 'to the pressing need for churches in Gateshead, Wolsingham and Crook'.[59] One month later, perhaps moved by closer observation of his flock, he delivered one of his most pleading pastorals: 'there never was in the entire history of the Church greater necessity of enlarging your Charity than at this period', he began.

> In every part of the empire the poorest and most destitute from the Sister Kingdom, are gathered round our dwellings, bringing distress and poverty, such as men never before witnessed amongst us … demanding from us Church accommodation, such as we have no means, unaided by our more wealthy laity, of procuring … … when we cast our eyes over our extensive Diocese and witness the squalid poverty of the multitudes which are daily added to our flock; when we behold the wretchedness and destitution which accompanies them, where-ever they take up their abode; but above all, when we are made acquainted with the full extent of spiritual misery, to which they have been reduced by poverty, famine and disease; our heart sickens at the contemplation of such scenes. We can no longer silently mourn over the wide spread dislocation of our flock, we feel impelled to raise our voices … we call upon all who have been blessed by his bounty with earthly wealth, to listen to our pleadings for the relief of the poor.[60]

But it had little effect on those it was designed to motivate. *The Tablet*, commenting on the worth of the halfpenny scheme after its second year, stated 'there is no doubt that this principle is not only practicable, but that *to it alone* is owing the great improvement that has taken place'.[61] Hogarth realised this as well and in the following years strove to make the collecting system comprehensive. Pastorals now lavished hosannas on the labouring poor. 'To them', he stated in 1857, the nation 'owes that temporal prosperity … they are our Brethren'.[62] By the late 1850s little thought was given to extracting monies from the wealth, as the halfpennies of the poor became almost the sole source of income for the diocese. Proud of his success, the Bishop declared the scheme to be 'one of the wisest and most beneficial means ever devised or attempted to be carried out for the reformation and re-establishment in society of those who, either from misfortune or neglect, would otherwise become abandoned and entirely lost to society'.[63]

Besides the Bishop's efforts for the central allocation of funds and the countywide collection at every church on behalf of the Catholic Poor-school Committee[64] (also dependent on the Irish pence), there were numerous more local appeals. Partial to his own system, the Bishop scorned these 'painful exhibitions of Clergy wasting their precious time, and often, while exercising this humiliating office, exposing themselves to the grossest insults, when a Church or a School is to erected for the benefit of the poor'.[65] But localism was not without success. That the Bishop of Liverpool was forced to warn against 'the unauthorized begging by strangers ... under the pretence of erecting Chapels, as a sure way of obtaining money for their support', is indicative both of the effectiveness and prevalence of such soliciting.[66] Again, it was the Irish who subscribed their hard-earned pennies. At Jarrow, for example, through 6d donations they raised £900 over five years to provide a Catholic school for more than 800 children.[67] Not that such charity was entirely spontaneous; as Rev. Belaney told the congregation at Bishop Auckland in his visiting sermon for funds:

> No priest ever found the Irish slow to give, where religion is concerned, or where charity is concerned. As this congregation consists chiefly of Irishmen, I know that it will not be found that there is any slowness of giving here. Your only regret will be that you cannot give all you have, instead of the little, as you will deem it, which your humble circumstances limit you to give.[68]

Certainly the former reliance on the wealthy or on the yeomanry for the maintenance of North-Eastern Catholicism had been completely reversed when Belaney declared of the Irish:

> that, without state endowments or any kind, or the assistance of men in power or high places, you build churches and schools as if the wealth of the world ... were yours. In this way, this miraculous way, it is, that ... the Catholic Church ... is now ... through Irish settlers, revisiting her ancient seats, restoring her desolate places, and rebuilding her broken-down altars. This would seem to be *your* mission, and what a glorious one it is![69]

Leakage

Given its dependence on the pennies of the poor, the Church's local building record over only a few decades is impressive by any standard. In view of the increased Catholic population throughout the period, however, it is clear that the pace of building was consistently behind the needs of congregations. Church-to-population ratios indicate that for every Catholic church in 1849 there were approximately

1,300 parishioners. By 1861 this ratio had become 1:2,025, though the average weekly number of communicants per church was less than this, since not all Catholics regularly attended.

A fairly reliable measure of the number of practicing Catholics can be drawn from the list of Easter communicants. For a Catholic to be counted among the faithful, he or she must practice the faith at least once a year during one of the Sundays between Ash Wednesday and the Sunday following Easter Sunday.[70] This duty, the dereliction of which by an able-bodied Catholic is a serious sin, is part of the 'Easter Duties', and a record of those performing them is kept by the presiding priest. Table 3.2 shows the Easter Communicants from the 1840s to the 1880s and their percentage of the total adult Catholic population (as abstracted from only those churches that supplied returns for Easter Communicants). As the ratio of churches to Catholics remained fairly constant, the small percentages in the first three returns suggests that 'leakage' from the Church was considerable.[71] Some of those who had lapsed from the faith before 1855 might have returned to the fold later. But a number of factors, not the least of which was the paucity of places of worship, operated against the Church's total retention of its flock.

Table 3.2 *Easter Communicants in Durham and Newcastle*

	Easter Communicants	% of Estimated Adult Catholic Population	% of Estimated Total Catholic Population
1847-49	4,463	34.1	22.2
1852	10,409	36.1	27.7
1855	19,824	60.0	43.3
1861	22,630	74.4	46.3
1875	28,031	n.g.	35.9
1882	38,203	n.g.	39.1

Source: Appendix II-VIII.

For those Catholics situated in rural areas, the distance to be traveled to attend church was a fundamental hindrance. Although there are numerous accounts of Irishmen astounding the non-Catholic residents by tramping ten miles or more every Sunday to attend mass, the majority of Irish lacked the inclination unless prodded by a priest.[72] In 1865 the church at Stella took in a flock of over 2,000 dispersed over an area of roughly 100 square miles. At Dunston before 1882 Catholics had to walk over two miles to St. Joseph's in Gateshead if they wished to hear mass,[73] while the mission established at Easington in 1866 took in a vast area of eastern Durham containing a good proportion of those Irish Catholics who later in the century would be accommodated by four churches. As missions could not be established for every dozen or so Catholics tied to some obscure colliery, only the most diligent priest could counter the leakage that the country miles encouraged.

Prevailing economic conditions also affected attendance: industrial cutbacks were typically felt first by Irish labourers who were often forced to pack up their households and move to where new employment could be found. In this event a priest who had finally gathered his flock might see it disappear virtually overnight. Protestant clergymen in the region similarly complained that 'a congregation may be collected this winter but before the next members are in great measure dispersed'.[74] The closure of the Rosedale and Ferry Hill Iron Works in the 1880s, for example, forced the newly independent Catholic mission of Trimdon to re-unite with the parent mission at Cornforth.[75] More often than not Irish employment was in an area removed from both priest and mission. The Church was neither able to prevent it nor anticipate it. St. William's, Darlington, was built in 1870 to accommodate an expected influx of Irish labourers at the proposed new iron works, but 'unfortunately the development did not mature owing to the drop in the iron trade'.[76]

One could also point to the workhouse,[77] mixed marriages,[78] working on Sundays, and Protestant proselytizing as factors contributing to the loss of faith of Irish Catholics. Drunkenness, particularly in crowded urban slums, was regarded as a major source of religious neglect; lack of Catholic schools was another. As long as the latter shortage existed, the second generation of Irish Catholics in England would be vulnerable to 'pagan habits', some argued. But most worrisome in the immediate post-famine period was the scarcity of priests, particularly those with sympathy for the Irish.

When in 1851 the Catholic population of Durham and Newcastle approximated 25,000, they were served by twenty-four priests. Newcastle, with a Catholic population between 10,000 and 15,000 in 1851 had but four resident priests. It is perhaps not surprising, therefore, that only 3,389 persons in Newcastle attended morning mass on 'Census Sunday' in 1851,[79] nor that many of the Irish Catholics dwelling in the parish of All Saints, Newcastle, fell into the so-called abyss of irreligion to be numbered with the 'thousands in England with Irish blood in their veins, and indeed baptized by Catholic priests, who are now profoundly indifferent to all religion and absolutely ignorant of the Catholic faith'.[80] In their own country the Irish lived under the eye, if not the thumb, of the Irish priests: 'If they were not at Mass', commented Rev. Morris, 'they were sure to hear of it'.[81] But in the heart of an English slum or the isolation of a pit town, the Irish could become anonymous — unknown by priests, who in any case were far too busy to meet individual needs let alone to seek out culprits falling by the wayside. Since the Irish often harboured a dislike of English priests in general, they were not automatically forthcoming in the practice of the faith.

Moreover, not all English Catholic priests were well disposed to the Irish, especially when their communicants hitherto had been mainly English. While not discouraging Irish attendance, the incumbents at the ancient chapels or at the 'respectable' urban churches (many of which maintained pew rents) did not exert themselves to the extent they might have to prevent the Irish from lapsing. Prior to the Irish inundation, the lives of many English priests had been comfortable; if they lacked the stipends and status of Anglican clergymen, they still enjoyed many of the same comforts, and commanded respect within Catholic circles. The prejudices of English priests were not greatly different from those of their most respected communicants: insular and conscious of class and ethnicity. Though they could hardly express it in public, one suspects that many of the English Catholic clergy held opinions that were not too different from those of the 'Northumbrian Lady'. It was difficult for a priest, used to eating from a well-laid table and provided with his own church, to conceive his mission in terms of Christly suffering, humility and deprivation. Nor was it expected. Where there was a large flock of very poor Irish, such as those in Gateshead in 1843, it was not supposed that a priest should 'attend solely to [them] ... when he could not calculate upon raising above £25 a year from the members of this congregation'.[82] In the 1844 pastoral of Bishops Mostyn and Riddell in which they appealed on behalf of the poorer Catholics of Gateshead, Felling, Bishop Auckland and Easington, the funds were, quite properly, for 'the erection of places of worship suitable to their circumstances'.[83] As late as 1853 it was implied by the *Northern Catholic Calendar* that there was no possibility of a priest 'residing on the spot' of the new St. Patrick's, Wall Knoll, because the 'Chapel was situated in the poorest part of Newcastle, amidst a dense population of poor Irish'.[84] It would, of course, be wrong to imply that English priests did not carry out their ministrations with great devotion, or that they failed to set high examples of Christian charity. Not all lived in easy circumstances. There are many examples of priests early in the century riding on horseback with portable altars and distributing alms at the door of an impoverished mission. But instances of complete sacrifice or emulation of Christ are virtually non-existent. Charity and kindness had their place, but, as *The Tablet* noted, while 'the event of a few stray sheep being brought into the good fold' was the subject of much rejoicing by the English clergy on Tyneside, the truth was that the Irish were regarded as poor remuneration and poor cousins:

> Thousands – mainly of poor Irish – who were baptized in the Church, and who probably at home in their own 'Island of Saints' led edifying lives, now never visit a chapel; and on the Sunday may be seen in groups together, lounging away those sacred hours in idleness and sin which on the Sundays of their youth they spent in the temple of God.[85]

Not only, then, was there a scarcity of priests, but the values and priorities of some of them contributed to the loss of Irish Catholic faithful. Needed to offset this and provide for the spiritual needs of the Irish was, essentially, the re-education of the English clergy. With the Irish rapidly making Catholicism a religion of the very poor, it soon became impossible for English priests to think in terms of significant incomes from their flocks for their own private use and benefit',[86] or to think of 'lavishing large sums of money on some favoured structure'.[87] But it was not the Irish who forced the re-education of the clergy – at least not them alone. Coinciding with their influx into Britain was the equally significant importation of Ultramontane ideas from France, which romanticized selfless service to the poor. What had emerged on the Continent was the 'demand for the re-catholicization of Catholic social methods in a better personal witness to that ideal of "poverty of the spirit" which was reborn in the flowering of monastic and neo-feudal and pseudo-medieval romance'.[88] In Britain these notions of 'holy poverty' were principally extolled by the Brotherhood of St. Vincent de Paul, which was introduced into every major Irish ghetto in England from the early 1840s.

Newcastle formed a 'conference' of St. Vincent de Paul in February 1846 to 'manifest an example of the Catholic virtue ... amidst the decay of piety, and the prevalence of wickedness'.[89] In the first report of the Newcastle Brotherhood in 1848, the city was described as having been divided into 'Visiting Districts' where not only poor Catholics were attended, 'but also sought out were whole families and individuals who, for years had neglected their spiritual duties'.[90] The report also spoke of the great number of famine and fever victims to whom the Brethren had distributed furniture, clothing and bedding. But with only twenty active members each devoting only a small portion of their time to this work, the Brotherhood made no huge dent. However much it proclaimed the Catholic Church to be 'peculiarly the Church of the Poor',[91] and despite the increasing stream of Catholic journalism extolling the 'three things which pre-eminently mark the Christian life and advance it in the scale of holy perfection ..., POVERTY, HUMILITY and PATIENCE', neither the endorsement of its philosophy, nor its practice was immediately widespread.[92] As the Brotherhood noted in its financial report, 'the influx of poor from Ireland since the first commencement of the famine in that country has been very great, so as to render it impossible for the Catholic charities in this Town adequately to attend even to a tithe of their necessities ... but there has been no corresponding increase in the resources of the Brotherhood'.[93] Their income for the two-year period amounted to less than £100 with only £2 being listed as the amount 'Collected For Irish'.[94]

The fact that the Brotherhood was confined to a narrow urban area of mainly Irish poor may help explain the lack of penetration of the concept of holy poverty among the bulk of the clergy. Especially for those without any sizeable Irish flock, the new St. Francis-like priestliness must initially have seemed theologically abstract and out of place. Though it is difficult to set a date on the individual adoption of the concept, the wider adherence to the idea that the poor were the embodiment of Christ seems to have emerged locally in the early 1850s. The 'martyrdom' of Bishop Riddell and the priests who lost their lives in administering to the fever victims in 1847 drew public and clerical attention to this 'Christ-like sacrifice', and such behaviour was dramatically repeated in the cholera outbreak of 1853.[95] While these events set noble examples for other English priests, the daily operation of the concept throughout the North-east could be evidenced in the devoted ministrations of the Irish priests. Though the 'Irish church could not openly approve the doctrine, which was tainted by Italian anti-clericalism,[96] ministering to the sick and poor without expectation of fame and fortune was second nature to many priests in Ireland. Provost Consitt, on a visit to Donegal in the 1850s was greatly influenced by Irish poverty and piety. Upon his return to Durham 'he spoke most feelingly of the heavy trials of the poor people, and seemed to be quite won over by the noble qualities he had observed in the devoted parish-priests and their flocks'.[97] When it was realized in England that the wealth of the Catholic Church was dependent on the Irish poor, the priests were heartily encouraged to let the Irish 'feel and see that the Church is preeminently the Church of the poor. Let them see in us no signs of a spirit of worldliness and dependence on secular maxims'.[98] The predominance of this rhetoric when set next to its personification in the Irish priests or in the Brotherhood of St. Vincent de Paul was successful in shifting the clergy, if not to the 'opposite extreme' of complete humility, as *The*

Rambler claimed, then at least closer to the romantic vision of sacred poverty.[99]

By such means the Irish came to be regarded not only as the numerical salvation of the faith in England, but as embodied vehicles for true Christian piety. While holy poverty was not the death knell of the aristocratic tradition for many of the laity in the North-east, after 1850 it is more difficult to point to instances of a prejudiced clergy. It is far easier to identify sacrifices on behalf of the poor. Non-Catholics, as well, noticed this change and often praised 'the fidelity and devotion of the Roman Catholic Church, which never shrinks from ministering to the poor, the sinful, and miserable'.[100] The Irish thus came to find their place in the re-invented bosom of the English Catholic Church. And in the juxtaposition of their plebian chapels (barren of all liturgical adornments save a statue of St. Patrick) with the older pretentious edifices, one could readily perceive the new orientation of Church and clergy.

The Irish responded to the increased warmth of the English clergy. It could be seen, for example, in the building of St. Dominic's, Newcastle, where 'Irish labourers ... manifested their zeal and interest in the movement, by gratuitously giving their work in the digging of the foundations, which [was] done in the hours they had to spare after the conclusion of their ordinary vocations'.[101] It was apparent as well in the increasing stream of pennies for the Church. More significant still was the rise in Easter Communicants. That they accounted for approximately seventy-five percent of the flock after 1861 indicates that the disruption and displacement occasioned by the Irish was, by that date, overcome. As the diocesan calendar stated in 1876 after praising the many new churches: 'there has been a corresponding increase of Religion, of Catholic feeling and devotion. The services of the Church have been improved and multiplied .... Confessions and Communion are now much more frequent ... Bishops and priests are better known and more influential'.[102]

Irish Priests

While priests from Ireland played an important part in changing the orientation of Catholicism in Durham and Newcastle between 1840 and 1880 they never composed more than twenty-three percent of the total clergy. In other words, there were never more than seven Irish priests present at any one time. In view of the shortage of priests and the heavy proportion of Irish Catholics after 1847 this low percentage is surprising. Cardinal Manning remarked in 1887 that he had spent his life 'working for the Irish occupation in England ...; that occupation is the Catholic Church in all the amplitude of faith, grace and authority'.[103] Yet at mid-century the priesthood was still seeking to remain as English as possible. What was true for England was also the case in the North-east where the Anglo-Catholic establishment was proud of its long heritage. Cardinal Wiseman, though his mother was Irish, had been raised in Durham and educated at Ushaw and Rome. That the major influx of Irish took place while he headed the church in England is seldom remarked upon in his writings. For Wiseman the English Catholic Church was responsible to Rome; as with many eminent Victorians, Ireland and her emigrants held no prominent place in his conscience. It was the spirit of Wiseman rather than that of Manning that dominated in the North-east.

As 'local and particular duties and works ... could be discharged by no central body whatsoever', the selection and procurement of priests rested with the local diocesan authorities.[104] In the North-east the Church preferred to be supplied by her own priests from Ushaw College, rather than by those from Ireland. Few priests, therefore, were brought over to meet the local demand. Some of those who did arrive, like Rev. M. Bourke, had emigrated with their families themselves to escape the starvation.[105] Dr. Chadwick, the second bishop of the diocese, was born in Drogheda, but like many other graduates of Ushaw he was only nominally Irish.[106] Since his youth he had lived in England. The only obvious case of actual importation of a priest from Ireland was that of Rev. Robert Foran, who was brought in to serve the Irish in Newcastle. That

Foran's brother James later came to work among the area's Irish suggests that personal rather than official connections may have been more important.

Despite preference for their own priests, however, the English Catholic hierarchy was not unappreciative of the labours of those from Ireland. At an important *Conventu Ecclesiastico* in 1852, for instance, five of the sixteen select clergy invited to attend were Irish.[107] Indeed, the Irish priests exerted a disproportionate influence on both clergy and congregations. It was certainly no secret that the Irish 'exhibited a preference for the priests of [their] own country over those of any other'.[108] The Irish priest was held to understand his countrymen's 'habits of thought, and modes of expression in a way in which no foreigner could understand them'.[109] To the Irish faithful it was the difference between merely the 'praste' and the 'Fayther', the latter being both confessor and friend. It was he who 'stopped the street fight when the police were afraid to intervene';[110] he who was the caretaker of morals, disciplinarian, adviser, helper and leader.

If the priest knew the Gaelic he was even better off, for there were many Irish in the diocese unfamiliar with English. As Father R. Foran 'preached in Irish to crowds of his admiring countrymen',[111] his brother James, who also 'had the Gaelic', is reputed to have had his confessional 'thronged from all along Tyneside'.[112] The value of Gaelic could be seen during Rev. Platt's incumbency at Stella (1847-57) where the influx of Gaelic-speakers was so great that Platt undertook to learn the language that he might 'be able to hear confessions and have freer intercourse with that portion of his flock'.[113] It was this sort of effort on the part of the English clergy, encouraged by the example of Irish priests and the rhetoric of holy poverty, that gained the respect of the Irish and allowed the term 'Father' to enter common usage for English as well as Irish priests. Hence Rev. Consitt, 'English to the backbone', could be affectionately referred to by an Irishman in Gateshead in 1858 as *'the great Father Consitt'*.[114] Fortunately, his parish was not in Consett.

Irish priests were generally assigned new missions where the Irish had hitherto been unattended and where the presence of a 'foreign' priest was likely to command little respect. As the non-Irish Father Torregiani discovered upon his arrival in Pontypool, in Wales, 'there arrived a deputation of Irishmen ... not for the purpose of welcoming ..., but to say that, as they did not wish for a foreign priest, they should refuse to contribute anything to his support'.[115] The role of Irish priests, therefore, was to assemble otherwise difficult flocks; to live with them as much as possible; and to encourage them to the regular practice of their faith. But with so few Irish priests available the job was arduous, involving both short incumbencies and a great deal of traveling between often isolated flocks. Father Patrick Matthews, for instance, not only established St. Godric's, Durham, but between 1866 and 1879 set up missions at Easington, Callaly Castle, Sacriston, Stanley, Byermoor, Dunston and Chester-le-Street, all of whose congregations were Irish.[116] Once the spade work was done, it was easier to introduce an English priest. But the Irish often intimated by their attendance that they would prefer an Irish pastor. This was particularly so in rural settings where greater motivation was necessary to induce flocks to regularly journey the considerable distances to places of worship. Thus the Gaelic-speaking Father Gilligan took over the mission at Sacriston,[117] while another Irish priest, Jeremiah Foran, carried out brief incumbencies at Blackhill, Darlington, Stella, Thornley, and Hebburn in order to revitalise those Irish missions.[118] Only after an Irish priest had served in such a manner was he granted a more permanent position, invariably in a predominantly Irish parish.

This exclusive use of Irish priests for Irish congregations was a deliberate appeal to the ethnocentricity of the Irish. As Rev. Belaney spoke of the Catholic faith to the Irish at St. Wilfrid's, Bishop Auckland:

> It is that which sheds the light of heaven upon your trials and sufferings of life. It is that which turns your earthly sorrows into spiritual joys; which makes you feel at home where you are treated as aliens; which enables you to compassionate the ignorance, the prejudice, or the unbelief which treats you with scorn because you are Irishmen, or because you are Catholics.[119]

Such sermonizing on the indivisibility of Irish faith and nationality ('hallowed by persecution ... in the harsh realities of his exile')[120] emphasized that if nationality was lost, so too was faith. This lesson was reinforced and perpetuated by Irish instructors in the Catholic schools. The Christian Brothers were imported into Sunderland in the early 1840s, and among the Sisters of Mercy could be found many Irish émigrés, the most notable of whom was Rev. Mother Zavier (formerly Ellen O'Connell), a close relative of the 'Liberator' himself.[121] But whether through Irish Catholic instruction in schools, or by means of itinerant Irish priests, the Irish brought within the fold and who listened to the panegyrics on the homeland were, by all accounts, much stronger Catholics. Thus was the Church insured against Irish leakage. As well, the Church's exploitation of Irish ethnocentricity solidified separate Irish communities, while the mobility of the priests gave a degree of cohesion to all the area's Irish.

Faith Renewed

This chapter has outlined the difficulties the Catholic Church faced in the North-east in accommodating, controlling and providing for the influx of Irish. We have also observed the internal adjustments the Church and clergy made in order to retain the souls of the Irish immigrants. The swollen numbers of the faithful, the new churches and schools, and the altered conceptual framework of the priesthood all served to enhance the confidence and enterprise of Catholicism in the North-east. It is erroneous to presume, however, that the less submissive Church was merely a continuation of that spirit of confidence that had been manifested in the mid-1840s. Far from hastening the gradual emergence from the traditional roots of Catholicism in the area, the response to the Irish was initially a diminution of the earlier hopes for the progress (or for some, the status quo) of the Church. There undoubtedly was, as Manning declared of North-Eastern Catholicism, 'an unbroken tradition', but as he himself was only too aware, English Catholicism had been radically recast since mid-century. Indeed, between 1845 and 1855 the Church in Durham and Newcastle underwent a metamorphosis from which it emerged more powerful and more confident. It was a transformation for which the Irish alone were accountable. It could hardly have been otherwise, for at the lowest unit of the Catholic hierarchy, that of priest and flock, Catholicism was forced to become open and outward looking. As one writer reflected, 'whatever may be said to the contrary, the presence of the more boisterous Celt had a very salutary effect in correcting the air and habit of timid reserve so long noticeable in the bulk of native English Catholics'.[122]

The new confidence, apparent in the church building of the 1850s, was unmistakably present by the 1860s. There is a glimpse of this in the opening of St. Mary's, Sunderland, in 1851, at which Wiseman presided and for which 'special trains ran from several towns, and ... great numbers availed themselves of the facilities offered'.[123] Yet by the 'solemn dedication' and perhaps by the fact that the Church 'was filled, but not crowded', moderation can still be seen to be the order of the day. Nine years later, however, in the same town, the foundation stone for St. Patrick's was laid without the slightest sign of restraint. With that distinctly Irish blending of the sacred and the profane, a large procession laden with shamrocks ('especially provided from Ireland') flowed through the streets with their bishop until, arriving at a Protestant church, they entered the opposite field and began the holy ceremony.[124] In Newcastle in 1872, it seemed to the *Newcastle Courant* that Roman Catholicism had reached its apogee when 'the health of the Pope was proposed before that of the Queen' during the ceremony to mark the completion of the spire on St. Mary's Cathedral.[125]

Symbolically, the resurgence of confidence was nowhere more evident than in Durham City. Tremendous efforts were made by Catholics throughout the district to raise enough money in order that the architectural designs by A.W. Pugin Jnr, might materialise and hence attract glances away from that omnipresent citadel of 'Anglican usurpery', Durham Cathedral. The large but ragged collection of Irish hardly merited such a 'grand design' of Gothic revival, but the Catholics were not to be outdone by the other denominations. In 1861 a site with a 'commanding view' was purchased near the centre of the Irish community.[126] On Whit Monday 1863 brass bands paraded with banners through the streets followed by the bishop and a flock of clergy. After erecting the cross on the site of the future high altar, the Very Rev. Cannon Consitt 'spoke in moving terms of Durham's great Catholic past, emphasizing that his hearers were brothers in the faith and rightful heirs of those who had worshipped God in the Mass in the cathedral and all the ancient Catholic churches of Durham'.[127] In November the following year St. Godric's was opened by Dr. Manning (Wiseman was ill) who rose to the occasion and spoke of their beloved Cardinal, who as a youth had been stoned by anti-Catholic mobs in the city.[128] With the Protestant Mayor as a guest of honour and an audience 'not only [of] communicants to this branch of the Christian faith, but many citizens of Durham and the neighbourhood who profess the reformed religion',[129] Manning and the bishop of the diocese eulogized the wonderful local achievements of Catholicism. Durham City indeed continued to be something of a showplace for Catholic ostentation: in 1866 the first Catholic cemetery in the city since the Reformation received the extraordinary double interment of a priest and a nun, the date marking the twenty-eighth anniversary of the funeral of two local priests who were forced to be buried in the Protestant churchyard.[130]

Such ritual displays of power and position often appeared to have little to do with the Irish. To the casual observer it was the same drama of the 'liberated Church' that had been acted out in the building of the cathedrals in Newcastle and Sunderland twenty and thirty years before. Except where the communicants were almost totally Irish, the Celts seemed to provide only a statistical backdrop: the *raison d'être* of the noticeable proliferation of churches and schools. Behind the scenes, however, in the bureaucracy of the Catholic Church in Durham and Newcastle the Irish influence was understood. The earlier quiet confidence of the Church had been shattered by them; the former status quo undermined. Through the rebuilding – the burdensome sowing and cultivating for a real 'second spring' – it was apparent to the Catholic hierarchy that the focus of the faith had significantly and irrevocably changed. In forcing the Church to become extrovert to an unprecedented degree, the Irish had laid the basis for a much stronger and more demonstrative faith. The days of the 'mysterious faith' dominated by an exclusive elite were ended; the flowering of a viable social religion for the masses had begun.

Chapter 4

Anti-Catholicism

> He was an Irishman and a Catholic. On my expressing my hope, that, amidst his hardships in this world, he was supported in his spirit by the consolations of his religion, and prepared for a better lot hereafter, he seemed surprised to hear a few charitable and kindly words drop from the lips of one, whom he seemed instinctively to regard as a Protestant, and with much emotion, said 'Indeed, sir, you are the first of your sort of people that ever spoke to me in that way in my life.
> *Inquiry into Newcastle Poor*, 1850, pp.18-19

> How much 'No Popery' continued to matter after the so-called 'Catholic Emancipation' in 1829, and in what parts of the country, on what occasions, at what periods in particular, are questions to which I can propose no firm answers ..., too little attention has so far been given to this wide and weighty phenomenon'.
> G.F.A. Best, 'Popular Protestantism in Victorian Britain', in Robert Robson (ed.), *Ideas and Institutions of Victorian Britain* (London, 1967), p.116

Few rich seams in Victorian history are so under-explored as that of the crusade against the Pope and Catholicism at mid-century. Like the progress of Catholicism, the history of its confrontation by militant Protestants has concentrated on several well-defined issues: Catholic emancipation, the Oxford converts, the Maynooth issue, the establishment of the Catholic hierarchy, the Pope and Italian liberalism, and the Vatican decree controversy. All have received their due from those concerned with the period's major political and ecclesiastical issues. In terms of the larger society, however, particularly at the provincial level, little has been written. This is not surprising; to attempt to understand the social ramifications of No-Popery is to enter a labyrinth of confused, uneven and inconsistent prejudices. After 1850, with the noticeable shifting of the social base of Catholicism toward the Irish, the maze becomes even more complex, for it is increasingly difficult to differentiate between 'anti-sacredotalism' and anti-Irish feeling.

Certainly the Bishop of Durham's publication of Lord John Russell's letter in 1850[1] is made famous least of all by any implication of anti-Irish sentiment. As with most attacks and counter attacks in ecclesiastical battle, the blows were directed well above the heads of the lowly Irish.[2] The Bishop specifically stated 'I hope ... my censure has been seen to direct itself against the *system,* not against individuals'.[3] But at the same time, Bishop Maltby felt the need to make a distinction 'between English Roman Catholics and others of that persuasion'. What is more, when the high-powered charges filtered to the street – via politicians, evangelical Protestants and ranting preachers – the theological arguments were lost in waves of pedestrian bigotry that was commonly directed at vulnerable Irish Catholic populations. Confrontations between the Established Church and the temporal sovereignty of the Pope had a popular chauvinistic appeal and the Irish were doubly vulnerable for being unpardonably 'foreign' *and* 'papist'. Just as the cry in the 1830s against 'O'Connell and his Popish and infidel coadjutors' had brought the Protestant-Tory response of 'I Will Die First' rather than submit to 'Popish superstition and tyranny',[4] so in the 1850s the 'horrors' of the Romish Church unleashed a national fervour that was not diminished by the invasion into purist England of the 'Catholic Priesthood and their Infatuated Dupes the Irish Peasantry'.[5] Between the Oxford Movement and the political tail of Maynooth (the years of the heaviest Irish immigration) No-Popery in England attained proportions which had not been witnessed since the Gordon riots after the passage of the Catholic Relief Act of 1778. As one contemporary regretted to note, the Irish in England as Catholics, 'live in the midst of controversy'.[6]

The North-east, as a stronghold of Catholicism and as a centre for Irish immigration, was not immune to waves of anti-Catholicism. During the turbulent days of No-Popery in the early 1850s, even the liberal press was wont to call a convert to Catholicism a 'pervert'. The *Newcastle Chronicle* agreed 'with much that is said of the insidious and aggressive character of the Papal system, and we of course think it would be infinitely better if the whole population of the United Kingdom were Protestant'.[7] Meantime, petitions against papal aggression were received in Parliament from Wesleyan and New Connection Methodists in Newcastle, South Shields, Sunderland, Houghton-le-Spring and a host of smaller towns throughout Durham.[8] The Tory *Newcastle Journal* made no pretence of diminishing animosities; it made as much political hay from anti-Catholicism as it could. Whilst supporting the brief Derby administration in 1852, it provoked *The Tablet* to castigate the supporters of the 'Scorpion' government, whose agents:

> could not have vomited forth more blasphemy against the most sacred objects if Beelzebub himself had been behind the editor's desk. Catholics may endure personal abuse, but when the Mother of God becomes defiled by the irreverence of men, and the Saints of God are held up to profane ridicule, it is difficult to suppress feelings of indignation ....[9]

During the preliminaries to the election of 1852, in which the Maynooth issue figured so prominently, feeling was strong against candidates with any leanings towards an endowed Maynooth. A Liberal candidate for Newcastle who expressed sympathy in the Commons with the Catholic cause thus found it expedient to admit that 'He was never a "thick and thin" supporter of Popery ...; was not brought forward by the one hundred Romanist voters for Newcastle, [and] ... his religious opinions were as much opposed to it as any man's in the empire of Queen Victoria'.[10] Notwithstanding this confession, his public endorsement by local Catholics led to his electoral defeat.

Sustained by the general tenor of the times, 'ranters' invaded Irish-Catholic ghettoes provoking the kind of hostile reactions that would further deprecate Catholic claims. 'Since the Premier's attacks on the Faith and practices of the Catholic Church', commented *The Tablet*, 'there is not to be found a ranter preacher in the north who has not become more zealous than ever to make perverts among poor Catholics, and for several Sundays back it has been usual for one or more of these fanatics to attend in the vicinity of Sandgate'.[11] Like the infamous incendiary, William Murphy,[12] these 'itinerant bigots' with their 'infuriated harangues'[13] were masters at incitement and the exploitation of sexual fantasies. While the press gave glowing accounts of the celebrated 'Miss Talbot's Case', with titles such as 'Getting Young Females into Nunneries to Obtain Their Property',[14] the ranters proclaimed nunneries to be exclusive brothels for priests. 'Evidence' was easily obtained from the mannered speeches of the 'honourable' Earl of Shaftesbury, Sir William Harcourt, or a 'distinguished' MP such as H. Drummond who had 'asserted that nunneries were either prisons or brothels'.[15] One ranter, at a meeting of the Protestant Alliance in Newcastle in 1852, 'created a great sensation amongst his audience by pledging his word that at present the Pope had 30,000 prisoners confined in his awful dungeons in Rome'.[16] As *The Tablet* commented, 'there seems at present a rivalry amongst the 'prim Parsons' as to who can coin the greatest lie'.[17] Ever eager to help widen the rift, the *Newcastle Journal* pointed out that 'such splendid Romanish Ecclesiastical structures arising around us, as if by magic' were 'cemented with the hearts' blood of defrauded families'[18] – defrauded, it meant, by extortionist priests plying their wares at death-beds. Ranters thus had an abundance of 'authentic and indisputable evidence' on the 'mummeries of the priestcraft' and the 'national Catholic conspiracy' with which to entice and provoke their audiences.

The Irish, unlike the more martyr-conscious church, were not inclined to let pass these slights on their faith. As an investigator of Sandgate noticed of even the quieter missionaries, they 'can provoke no discussion among ... the native inhabitants; but they may among the Irish, who are considerably more susceptible of religious feeling'.[19] Unless restrained, they tended to spontaneous physical demonstration of their faith. This was dramatically displayed on a Sunday evening in May, 1851 when 'Ranter Dick preeched frey a chair, /'While singin' oot wi' cuddy blair, /'An' gi'en the Pope a canny share /'O'hell-fire confort, aw declare', sparked 'The Horrid War i' Sandgeyt'.[20] The Irish, according to *The Tablet*,

> unable to restrain their feeling, commenced an attack on the preacher, who had speedily to fly to save himself from a severe chastisement; some of the people present took part with the preacher; the Irish rallied on their side, and a general row commenced; for an hour or two, in spite of the police, the Irish were in possession of that part of town. ... upwards of sixty Irishmen were taken into custody ....[21]

In cooler terms, another correspondent wrote:

> A row took place amongst the Connaughtmen [sic] and the Northumbrians in Sandgate (Newcastle), last week, in consequence of a No-Popery sermon preached by a dilettante, who may be specified by the adage: '*Respice finem, respice funem*'. The rope-maker took to his heels ....[22]

In the *Newcastle Chronicle's* coverage, it was denied that a street preacher had been the provocateur and the incident was cast in terms of the 'national character' of Irish-English antipathy. 'As often happens in such cases, poor Pat came off second-best' for there 'came the turn for English vengeance' and 'Lynch law was invoked'.[23] While not exactly xenophobic, these sentiments paralleled the *Chronicle's* anti-Catholicism. In a surprisingly moderate tone, the *Newcastle Journal* did not vouch for the presence of the ranter, but realized 'that for some time past they the Irish have been cultivating feelings of hostility towards the English portion of their neighbours, in consequence of the recent agitation on the Papal question'.[24] Both papers were anxious to show that the Irish Catholics were the perpetrators of the riot, and both quoted the rather dubious statement reputed to have been heard in the course of the battle: 'Och, by Jasus, we'll take Sandgate to-night, and be revenged on every English ------ in it'.

While in Durham there was no incident comparable to the 'Sandgate riot', similar prejudices existed against Irish Catholics. In Gateshead it was noted in 1851 that 'the Catholic religion is daily insulted by the most insane cries', but except for 'two cases of partial rows, confined to public houses', no serious disturbances took place.[25] In and around Durham City, there was apparently 'a strong feeling of contempt' surrounding the Irish, 'which manifested itself in every way; their religion was attacked, vilified; they had for safety-sake when going to church at Durham to wait at the top of Findon Hill until they form[ed] a group; they dared not go into a public-house where they might meet a company of men who were not of their own nation; they were considered as belonging to a race altogether inferior'.[26] And from Anglican pulpits throughout the area, the exposure of the 'error and superstitions of the Romish Church' did little to improve the public's estimation of the Irish Catholics.[27]

However, on the basis of the hostilities of the early 1850s, it would be mistaken to pass judgment on the general state of prejudices in the North-east. Extreme situations can bring to the surface deep-seated biases hitherto dormant, but they can also generate panic conditions, regionally ill-grounded and historically ephemeral. It is noteworthy that even at the height of mid-Victorian No-Popery (during the debates on the Ecclesiastical Titles Bill) the petition from Newcastle with the most signatures was from 1,067 residents who were not concerned with the aggrandizements of the Catholic Church, but with a 'modification of the tax upon carriages' in the proposed income tax bill'.[28] And while Maynooth was a 'household word' during the election of 1852, an anti-Maynooth meeting sponsored by the Protestant Alliance in Newcastle drew an attendance 'so meagre that the proceedings were adjourned *sine die*'.[29] According to the *Gateshead Observer*, 'this result was mainly attributable ... to the little interest which the public generally take in the narrow Maynooth question'. Disinterest was also manifest in the poor attendance at the Alliance's anti-Maynooth meeting in Durham City.[30] Even *The Tablet*, whose claims against the bigots tended to be overstated, viewed the 'paltry efforts that were made by placards to mar ... the object and success' of a fund-raising bazaar for St. Patrick's, Wall Knoll, in October 1852, as part of the generally 'inoffensive movement of sectarians who *supposed* that a new church would be most objectionable to Protestant feelings'.[31] Again, during the St. Patrick's Day celebrations of the same year, the Irish paraded through the streets of Newcastle unhindered by attacks. The press could find little at fault with the procession, and opinion was basically in agreement with *The Tablet's* comment that 'there is no doubt but during the last few years in the north of England Irishmen as a body have considerably improved their condition in society, and it is self-evident they are every day becoming a more influential portion of English society'.[32] It is noteworthy too, not only that the 'Horrid War' in Sandgate had no sequel, but also, that it was soon rendered into comic verse.

In the period from Catholic emancipation in 1829 to 1850 there were few local instances of overt hostility to Catholics. As indicated by the election of Thomas Dunn to the mayoralty of Newcastle in 1842, local residents held the Catholic gentry in high regard. This was clear when W.T. Salvin contemplated running as a county candidate in 1837. Henry Morton, chief agent to Lord Durham, wrote to his employer that 'informed estimates suggested that his Catholicism would cost the liberal party only two hundred out of over two thousand votes'.[33] Attitudes toward the Catholic gentry were not of course necessarily synonymous with those expressed towards Irish Catholics. But from the religious point of view at least, the keen interest of the Irish in their churches and pastors more often excited curiosity than hostility from the majority of the population, many of whom had never seen the spectacle of the 'mysterious faith'. The Rev. John Lenders has cited a rather incredible case of the residents of Bishop Auckland peeping into the Catholic mission 'to see if the Irish people had really claws!!' and insists that 'This is a fact'.[34] Though hardly, if true, a widespread occurrence, it underscores the extent to which fanciful notions of Irish and Papists entered common consciousness – evidence of which could be seen in the attendance of non-Catholics at Catholic ceremonies, or the fascination in the 'confessions' of an ex-priest. Lack of enmity to the Catholic poor was demonstrated in Bishop Auckland in 1842 when, through 'the kindness and liberality of a Protestant gentleman', a large room was donated as a temporary chapel.[35] Indeed, the spirit of toleration shown by Protestant landowners and municipal corporations was more the rule than the exception in the North-east. Even 'in the teeth of seeming difficulties', in 1850, Rev. Betham of Gateshead managed to obtain 'half an acre of Freehold ground in the very centre of town'.[36] The land for St. Mary and St. Andrew's was virtually given by the Newcastle corporation,[37] while in Hartlepool, when an Anglican incumbent protested against the clamorous pealing from the belfry of the new Catholic Church, 'the authorities ... gave no countenance to the application'.[38] The death of Bishop Riddell in 1847 brought profound lamentations from most quarters: crowds 'thronged the public thoroughfares ... anxiously waiting to witness the mournful procession ...; every available spot from which a view could be obtained was crowded'.[39] The *Newcastle Journal* could not refrain from commenting that 'the chapel was crowded with spectators during the performance of mass, many of whom appeared impressed with superstitious awe, but, by far the greater portion were anxious only to gratify their curiosity, by seeing High Mass performed by Romanish Priests'.[40] It admitted, however, that the deceased 'was descended from an ancient and honourable family in the county of Northumberland'.[41]

After mid-century popular anti-Catholicism rapidly declined in the North-east. Once seen that the establishment of the hierarchy had not enslaved Protestant England – indeed had not made the slightest difference to anyone except a handful of Catholic administrators – the flourish of anti-papist fervour faded fast. What had been propounded, pornographically and otherwise, as the great Romish horror, lost potency when set next to the reality. In the North-east awareness of the fallacy of papal domination seems to have been realized fairly early. An Anglican in Darlington 'ashamed of the violence and hypocrisy of those pure members of the diocese of Durham' wrote to the local press in January 1853: 'It is a good job the two Hierarchies are fairly before the country; it is of little consequence what our Clergy may advance as to the doings of the Pope at Rome so long as his servants here behave themselves'.[42] While not wishing to countenance the spread of Catholicism, the writer continued,

A Hogarth, whether a Bishop or anything else, will be appreciated and respected, independent of his creed, and people will judge of a tree by its fruits ... The Romanists will gain influence in proportion to their usefulness in society; busy meddling, vainglorious, and consequential Protestants only advance the cause they profess to battle with.

The Tablet concurred, remarking that 'John Bull is once more returning to his senses'.

Through the efforts of individual priests, in particular, Catholicism became innocuous. Evidence of priests controlling the wildness of the Irish where the police failed; priests confronting 'dangerous' secret societies and advocating temperance reform or, later, acting responsibly as members of school boards and guardians of the poor law, all served to promote an image of the Catholic Church as a valuable social force. The result was praise, rather than harassment or chastisement. There was even envy by other denominations who saw the Irish poor responding to their priests and attending their chapels while their own poor remained 'lost' in the slums. The depiction of an English Catholic priest in 1856 as a favourite object of attack on whom 'every eye is directed ... with an unfriendly glance ... and every tongue is filled with his reproach',[43] simply did not hold true in Durham and Newcastle. The death of the Rev. Gillow ten stirring years after the death of Bishop Riddel drew from the Protestant press praiseworthy comments about 'a gentleman of great suavity and sweetness of manners, and of a generous, open disposition'.[44] At least, as the *Northern Catholic Calendar* remarked of Rev. Bamber in Sunderland, 'if his foes did not love him, at least they respected him'.[45] Obviously this held true for Bishop Hogarth as well, for upon his death in Darlington in 1866, Francis Mewburn (Hogarth's Wesleyan neighbour) wrote in his diary: 'The shops in the town were shut, excepting that of a baker, whose obstinacy, I regret to say, gives me a dislike to the man. The concourse of people in the streets was beyond all comprehension'.[46]

The Church and her ministers were not unaware of the more tolerant conditions obtaining in the North-east, and the good fellowship of their neighbours was continually toasted. No better example of this exists than the release from Durham Gaol in 1860 of Rev. John Kelly of Felling after forty hours of incarceration for not revealing the secrets of the confessional. Rather than soliciting a blazing invective against Protestant bigotry, or a poignant martyrdom rhetoric, Kelly wished only to take the

> opportunity of expressing my deep sense of gratitude to the Press, as also to the honourable gentleman who had the great kindness to introduce my name and defend my character in the House of Commons; and to all others, particularly those of the Protestant communion, who have done me the favour of expressing both publicly and privately, their kind sympathy toward me. Of these the 'Protestant juryman' (the gentleman, the Christian, and the scholar,) claims the first place.[47]

It is difficult, therefore, to refer to any locally significant No-Popery movement. What agitation there was seems mainly to have been confined to a small group that relied for sustenance on the passions raised by outside agitators on national tours. The election in Newcastle in 1857, for instance, would have been void of religious hostilities had not an outsider, the anti-Maynooth Liberal, Mr. Carstairs, decided to sit for Newcastle. When at a meeting of Protestant dissenters a Dr. Bruce stated 'he had made up his mind never to give his vote in favour of a candidate who would allow the tax-gatherer to take money out of their pockets for the support of "idolatry"',[48] the rest of the dissenters were coerced into endorsing Carstairs. Religious frictions were thus revived by an outsider's appeal to, as the *Newcastle Chronicle* put it, 'the section of the electors which thinks ecclesiastical of more importance than political questions'.[49] Proposing the question 'Who, then are Mr. Carstairs' friends?' the *Chronicle* answered, 'A small knot of religious bigots, who pride themselves on their attachment to extreme Protestant principles, in whose eyes Roman Catholicism is an invention of the evil one, the Pope Antichrist, and the college of Maynooth an utter abomination'. The paper had shifted from its former anti-Catholicism. It must also have carried a good proportion of its readership (the majority of whom were dissenters) for Carstairs was the only Liberal in Newcastle to be defeated in the election. By the late 1850s therefore, despite the trumpeting of a minority, the anti-Catholic vote lacked the sufficiency that contributed to the defeat of the Liberal candidate for Newcastle in 1852 mentioned above.

Although the sensation of an ex-priest or a farcical ranter could still draw a crowd, by the 1860s the public was less inclined to take them seriously. When, in 1862,

> a gentleman in black, white neck-clothed, spectacled, and got up in the true orthodox style, and calling himself John Tadini, LLD, of the University of Pavia, an Italian exile, and formerly a Romish priest, was announced to deliver a lecture in the East Street United Presbyterian Church, South Shields, on 'Auricular Confession, Jesuits and Nuns, Popery as it was and as it is ....[50]

he was bound to get the church at least half full. However, when the mistress of a commercial hotel in Newcastle arrived 'greatly excited' and 'accused Tadini, who had been staying at her house for about seven weeks, of having decoyed away her daughter, a young woman of about 22 years of age, and left without paying his bill,' the congregation showed no hesitation in stoning 'Dr. Tadini' out of town.

Such incidents contributed to a growing impression of the exponents of No-Popery as charlatans and, alternatively, of Catholicism as less fearful than purported. It is against this background of an ephemeral anti-Catholicism that we can explain the lack of success of evangelical missions to the Irish Catholics in the North-east.

******

'It seems to us abundantly plain', wrote the *British Protestant* on the first page of its first number in January 1845:

> that the impending and paramount controversy of the age will be between *Romanism* and *Protestantism*. The supremacy of Tradition – the Priest – and the Church is the essence of the one, and the

supremacy of Scripture, as the only rule of faith, lies at the root of the other. These two points are the poles of the increasing movement, and towards the one or the other every party and church and ceremony seems rushing to its place.[51]

So the great mid-century battle for the souls of the nation began, and as nowhere else in Victorian society was there such abundance of the boisterous and the bizarre. Though satirized and dismissed as hypocritical by almost every significant contemporary,[52] the evangelical zealots with their trenchant morals, their well-worn bibles and their stock of puissant tracts, were an unrelenting force. Their progress could be traced in the anti-papal *Record*, which served as a clearing house for all and sundry Protestant missionary societies. Every spring the *Record* gave a full review of the annual or inaugural meetings of organizations ranging from the Church of England Scriptural Reader's Association, and the Colonial Church and School Society, to the Moravian Missions, Prayer-Book and Homily Society, and the Operative Jewish Converts' Society.[53] There were close to 100 such societies by 1861. Chairing their assemblies were the leading Protestant evangelicals: the Earl of Shaftesbury, the Bishops of Durham and Ripon, the Archbishops of Canterbury and York, along with members of parliament and outspoken members of the clergy. United in zealous faith, they laboured at home and abroad to make the world secure in the true faith. Jew, Moslem, Hindu, Buddhist or Catholic, none was overlooked and none would have cared to dispute at least the strength of commitment of these missionaries.

The faith of the Irish Catholics in England was tampered with by missionaries on several fronts, including the Bible Society and the Religious Tract Society. However, at least four agencies were more exclusively concerned with converting them: the Home Missionary and Irish Evangelical Society (which sought to correct the 'ignorance, ungodliness, and crime' of society, and found that converting Irish Catholics was a means to this end);[54] the Church Pastoral-Aid Society (which similarly worked against 'those sinks of infamy and pollution' in the major centres of England);[55] the British Society for Promoting the Principles of the Reformation (which aimed at reversing the 'alarming progress of the Romish leprosy over the body of the visible Protestant Church' in England, and worked in a manner analogous to that of the Irish Church Missions in Ireland);[56] and, last but not least, the English Church Mission ('a Church of England Society, established for the conversion of Roman Catholics in England' that claimed 'prescriptive rights to Irish converting').[57] In addition, there was the North of England Protestant Alliance, which was less concerned with converting Catholics than with combining

> all classes of Protestants, whose object is not merely to oppose the recent aggression of the Pope as a violation of national independence; but to maintain and defend, against all the encroachments of Popery, the Scriptural doctrines of the Reformation, and the principles of religious liberty, as the best security under God for the temporal and spiritual welfare and prosperity of this Kingdom.[58]

All of these societies had their heyday between the 1840s and the 1860s, after which funds and fervour declined. During their assent, however, they were obsessed with the conviction that the Catholic Church was 'concentrating her efforts upon England, knowing that if she could accomplish the conquest of this land, Europe would lie prostrate at her feet'.[59] Against this spectre they set up missions throughout the country. The North-east was early noted as 'inviting material'; a committee of the British Reformation Society [BRS] had spied Northumberland as one area where the Roman Catholic 'increase [was] particularly observable'.[60] Efforts were made in 1831 to rectify this 'lamentable ignorance upon the subject of religion' by establishing auxiliaries in Durham City and Newcastle. But they went largely unsupported and, in contrast to the other auxiliaries, no funds were remitted to London.[61] The BRS Committee reported in 1831 that the two meetings held at Newcastle were 'very interesting' and promised a further deputation to the city in the following year.[62] This second delegation met with some success and remained in Newcastle for three weeks holding seven meetings and six sermons and allowing the 'Society's Agents ... to distribute tracts to a very considerable amount'.[63] There were also meetings and sermons at Durham and Sunderland. But little zeal was shown by the locals: while the contributions from other auxiliaries steadily rose after 1834,[64] Durham and Newcastle raised only £6 in 1832 and nothing the following year. To remedy this situation, the BRS sent another delegation to the North-east in 1834 but it was received, in their own words, 'amid great coldness'.[65] As the Society was only too aware, 'In all these localities around Newcastle the success of Romanists is so palpable'.[66] It was not until 1839 that the Society, having carried out visits to the area's major cities, announced their first success: 'Two careless Protestants who were married to Romanists and had been nearly brought over to Popery by them'.[67]

When a petition appeared in the *Gateshead Observer* in 1840 signed by twenty Protestants requesting that the Catholic priest of Hartlepool continue his annual winter lectures on the doctrines and principles of the Catholic religion (because the Protestants were frequently 'disgusted by the evidently exaggerated statements, which they heard'), the BRS lost no time in dispatching the Reverend Brabazon Ellis to deliver a fiery harangue on 'No Peace With Rome'.[68] To one Protestant minister in Hartlepool the Society must have instilled something more than xenophobia; he suddenly became loudly convinced that the Pope was the devil, that nuns were nymphomaniacs, that priests were lechers and that 'Socialism was a branch of Popery ... got up to divert our attention ... it is a senseless, brainless, dirty swine, rolling itself in a puddle-hole'.[69] Direct mention of the Irish was also made at this Hartlepool meeting by a Protestant incumbent from Stockton who, believing that 'some of the Irish Roman Catholic peasantry' were present, stated:

> I believe you were sent to this country, not to convert us to Popery, but for us to convert you to Protestantism ... you are brought here under the providence of God, that we may convert you to the knowledge of Christ, for when I meet a Roman Catholic peasant I have these feelings to try and do him good.[70]

Although the Hartlepool meeting fired enough enthusiasm to launch a BRS auxiliary in the town, interest soon lagged in spite of the noticeable growth of Catholicism in the North-east in the mid-1840s.

To an agent unfamiliar with the history of the BRS in the North-east, the region appeared propitious for evangelical inroads in the 1840s. With neophyte zeal, a missionary wrote to London in 1843: 'Newcastle might be one of the Society's best stations, if an Annual Meeting be held. The Romanists are very numerous here, and are now building a new church on a most extensive and magnificent scale'.[71] So yet another deputation was sent to Newcastle in 1844, headed by no less a figure than Rev. John Cummings, one of the nation's leading exponents of No-Popery. *The Tablet* was on hand to record 'the altered state of the Reformation Society', but that it was a 'downward progress in public estimation, amongst even Protestant communities, was strongly indicated by the absence of every man in Newcastle of standing or importance from their meeting at the Music Hall'.[72] Despite that the meeting also imported Rev. Dr Townsend, Canon of Durham, to show that not everyone in the North-east was apathetic to their cause, it was obviously difficult to provoke anti-Catholicism where even the mayor of the town was Catholic. Even Townsend (who was to make his mark in 1850 by attempting to convert Pope Pius IX) had no large following: he alone seems to have made up the Durham auxiliary of the BRS with his annual submission of £5 to the central fund.[73]

It was perhaps the general failure of the evangelical missions to secure any foothold in the North-east that prompted the North of England Protestant Alliance – the 'rump of the Reformation Society'[74] – to set up operations in Newcastle in 1852 in order to muster local No-Popery forces. But as witnessed in their endeavour to make Maynooth an issue of local significance, they met with as little support as the BRS. The Alliance seems only to have created mild disturbances in the towns they visited, merely ruffling feathers for instance when they arrived at the seat of Bishop Hogarth in Darlington. As for the English Church Missions,[75] the Pastoral-Aid Society and the Home Missionary Society, their efforts in the North-east barely merited even Catholic attention.

Between 1860-63, however, the efforts of the Durham City missionary for the Protestant Reformation Society (the renamed

BRS) began to receive an inordinate amount of attention in the quarterly reports of the Society. In October 1859 the *British Protestant* wrote of

> a most urgent application for a missionary ... made by some sound Protestant Christians of this city [Durham]. There are few places where such instrumentality is more needed. We are truly thankful that we have been enabled to establish a Mission in that important stronghold of Popery.[76]

The Protestant Reformation Society was even more fortunate than it had at first imagined, for the missionary who went to Durham was fired with evangelical fervour, and was well suited to converting Irish Catholics: from Dublin, he had a smooth and quiet manner, was ardently pious and firmly believed in the integrity of his work. His many letters to the Society's offices were thus profusely quoted in their reports in an effort to model this ideal evangelical. A part of his résumé of accomplishments for January 1860, for example, illustrates the prototypical grass roots missionary:

> The first example is that of a young woman (Mrs. M.) whom I visited after I came here, but who at first refused to receive me. However, on asking her what part of Ireland she was from, and learning it was from Dublin, and then telling her I also had come from that city, she invited me to come in and sit down. We conversed for some little time about Dublin, etc. I then took the Douay Bible, and read to her what the Scriptures say about our state by nature, the necessity of being born again, etc., and how the change is to be wrought, and then read for her some texts, which speak of the efficacy of the blood of Christ to cleanse from all sins, and contrasted them with the teaching of the Romish Church. She said she liked very well what I had read for her, and also received a tract, and said she would be glad to see me often, and made me promise to call frequently.... This I continued to do up to a fortnight ago when she told me her mind was much shaken in the belief of several Romish dogmas, and at the same time said she would follow my advice, and take her children from the Romish school and send them to the Protestant school; which she did on the following Monday, where they continue to go regularly.[77]

Such a slow and laborious method of converting left much space for Catholic resistance and opposition, however. For this reason the Durham missionary, although he continued to visit as many 208 families in one month,[78] opened 'a controversial inquiry class' which (he reported) Catholics attended 'in great numbers'.[79] But that he made many converts among the Irish seems doubtful. His zeal succeeded only in having the auxiliary in Durham run by a local committee, which was an advance over the single representation of Rev. Townsend ten years before. He continued to list the two or three converts he had made in each quarter of the year, describing how they arrived at enlightened conclusions such as 'I now see clearly that the Catholic Church teaches false doctrines, and is an apostate church, and I shall never join it'.[80] But his two greatest accomplishments were, first, in warding off potential converts to Catholicism by exposing 'the legends and 'lying wonders' of Father Furniss [sic], through means of handbills, public meetings, and newspapers ... [which] had the effect of opening the eyes of great numbers of Protestants of all ranks'.[81] Second, he kept a vigilant eye on the Catholic school and prevented any Protestant children from attending. '*I am not aware*', he reported in July 1861, '*of a single Protestant child being in attendance at a Romish school*'.[82]

Beyond this and the rescuing of some children of mixed marriages from the clutches of the Sisters of Mercy, the missionary's success was curbed by the Church. Priests in Durham warned their congregations against attending the discussion classes on pain of excommunication and, according to the missionary, the Catholics were instructed 'to keep a strict watch' upon their neighbours and report anyone who attended the meetings.[83] As a result the Catholic attendance came to a halt and the missionary was given a sound beating by 'a violent Roman Catholic'.[84] In having Protestants occupy the seats in the discussion class vacated by Catholics, the missionary had, by the standards of the Protestant Reformation Society, achieved as noble a victory as chalking up any number of converts.[85] The opening of St. Godric's Church in 1864, however, points not only the ineffectiveness of Protestant efforts, but the paradox of No-Popery in stopping some of the sources of leakage from the Catholic faith.

Indeed, one of the major effects of the evangelical outcry in the North-east was to make it impossible for Catholics to be indifferent about their religion. As the editor of the *Newcastle Chronicle* commented in July 1851: 'Ever since the first appearance of the famous Bill for dividing England into Roman Catholic sees, we have had a strong impression that one of the main objects of the measure was to provoke in a certain degree the Protestant feeling of the country and thereby to attract attention to the claims of Romanism'.[86] Or, as a local priest confirmed at a social gathering of Catholics in Newcastle a year later,

> there was no denying the fact that the government's penal measure had given the Catholics a position of attention which they had for some years been desirous to obtain. .... Thanks to the bigots, thousands were now discussing the subject of religion in this country who hitherto never had permanently turned their minds to such a subject.[87]

For the Church's concern with leakage, the exposure wrought by anti-Catholicism was a blessing in disguise. *The Tablet* correspondent noticed on Easter Sunday 1852 that attendance at the principal Catholic Churches in the diocese was 'very considerably increased – immeasurably increased'.[88]

Naturally the Church did everything it its power to obstruct the path of evangelicals or, when such was impossible, to minimize their influence. While Viscount Seaham presented local petitions against papal aggression, the Liberal, M. Headlam, was selected to put forward petitions from the Roman Catholic laymen of Durham and Minsteracres.[89] When the Bishop of Durham made his position clear in his 'Letter to the Archdeacon of Lindisfarne', a local priest quickly retaliated with a pamphlet on *Protestant Aggression* that charged the Bishop 'as allied with this band of religious incendiaries: nay more, I point to you as a leader – bearer of the torch of persecution'.[90] The priest went on to warn:

> Beware, how you make approach to this volcanic question, for the indications of convulsion around you, are awful to contemplate. The Catholic millions of Ireland *may* sit down and weep in silence

over their *political* thralldom, but depend upon it, they will arise to a man, should the usurper advance to set foot within the precincts of the sanctuary.'[91]

And when a local dispute in Gateshead caused the unofficial precedent of allowing Catholic children to be escorted from the workhouse to mass to be removed, an incensed priest raised the cry: 'And now Irishmen, these children are all Irish! Englishmen, are we to permit this state of things in our own country? Members of the Defence Association, are we to go to sleep? Irish Brigade, up, guards! and at 'em in the next session of parliament'.[92] Nor was this priest unsupported by the rest of the clergy when, in 1853, he dispatched a petition with 804 signatures (raised within forty-eight hours) to the House of Lords to oppose the proposed Nunneries Inspection Bill.[93]

Although in the field of proselytising, organisations like the Protestant Alliance had greater financial reserves for a single cause, Catholics were not without counter-organisations such as the local Defence Associations and the Association for the Propagation of the Faith.[94] If the tracts dispensed by these associations or those distributed by the Brotherhood of St. Vincent de Paul[95] 'made no wide or deep impression on the mass of English unbelievers as a body',[96] they were no less effective (or ineffective) than those distributed by the Protestants. Catholic lecture tours such as those by the eloquent Jesuit, Charles Larkin, on the 'Spiritual Jurisdiction of the Pope', were also used to attract attention and to disseminate information to non-Catholics.[97] But, like the tracts, the lecture tours served to bolster the faith of co-religionists against militant Protestantism. While priests such as Father Kelly in South Shields were delivering lecture courses in defence of the doctrines and practices of the Catholic Church' on Sunday evenings,[98] other priests were using the same propaganda on local tours as a convenient means to raising funds. Rev. Betham of Gateshead, for example, commenced his crusade for St. Joseph's Church in 1851 'which he said he would make subserve a double purpose – that of setting the new church afloat, and of vindicating the Church and the Holy See against the calumnies by which they had been assailed'.[99] And while the British Reformation Society missionary in Durham City struggled for one or two souls, 7,000 Catholics gathered at Ushaw in 1860 to hear 'very inflammatory speeches made by the priests who were present' on behalf of the collection for St. Godric's.[100]

The *Dublin Review* was right that anti-Catholicism at mid-century tended to arrest the 'tide of conversions', but in the Northeast there was little truth to their further claim 'that the growth of all the works of the Church had been indefinitely retarded'.[101] No-Popery in general, and the local evangelicals in particular, alerted the Catholic Church to its weak spots. By 1852 the Bishop's Pastorals were deeply concerned with the efforts of *'those who persecute and calumniate us'* and who offer relief to the Irish poor *'on condition that they will abandon the faith of their Fathers and allow their Children to be trained up in schools, where the doctrines of the Reformation are taught!*[102] The clergy were exhorted

> to represent to their respective flocks the dreadful consequences, which must result from the system which is now so universally adopted by the enemies of our Faith, and that they would urge *in season and out of season* the necessity of using every means in their power to procure funds to enable the Catholic School Committee fully to carry out their projects for the religious education of the poor, as the most effectual barrier against the evil which threatens the Children of their flocks.[103]

The response was immediate and thorough and it was not long before comments lauding Catholic education began to appear. The *Newcastle Chronicle*, commenting on Consett, remarked: 'the particular faith to which they the Irish, belong claims especially the superintendence of their children's education. It is not the least pleasant and remarkable feature of the Roman Catholics of the present day, that they are most careful in training up their children'.[104] And while souls of children were being more zealously protected priests 'exerted a greater vigilance in slum areas to protect the Irish from lurking and luring infidels.' There came to be some truth in the earlier cry that the Romish Church was being aggressive,[105] but what the No-Popery evangelicals could never acknowledge was that it was their own efforts that were behind it, accelerating the Church's ameliorative exercises.

Beyond giving encouragement to the very force they intended to defeat, the evangelical missions to the Irish Catholics failed for a number of other reasons.[106] Among these was the narrowness of the evangelical pursuit in contrast to the breadth of the Church, its lack of financial and moral support when national fervour declined,[107] the amateurness of its zealots and/or mountebanks attempting to encroach upon better trained and equipped clergy,[108] the inability of the various missions to unite into one central more effective agency,[109] the delay in establishing missions to the Irish Catholics until at least four years after the major tide of immigration, the inability to justify the cause through numbers of converts,[110] and finally, the evangelicals' general inability to fathom the meaning of Catholicism to the Irish,[111] hence generating antipathy toward those whom they endeavoured to convert.[112] The contest was thus one of unfair advantage for the Catholic Church. In the North-east the evangelicals were at an even greater disadvantage for they were far removed from the thumping energies of Exeter Hall, at the same time as their London-based headquarters were largely out of touch with local affairs. Moreover, because Catholicism in the area was more firmly entrenched and respected than elsewhere in England, it was easier for the Church to protect her flock when necessary. Being urban-oriented, the evangelicals neglected the extensive Irish Catholic population in the rural areas of Durham for which they also had insufficient manpower. Finally, there was the lack of local enthusiasm for the cause of the evangelicals, a problem which also faced the Protestant zealots elsewhere in Britain but which in the North-east was more prevalent.

The ephemeral nature of No-Popery and the inefficacy of the evangelical attempts at proselytising the Irish were also dependent in part upon the general religious composition of the area. To fully appreciate the position of Roman Catholics it is necessary to view them relative to other denominations. Table 4.1, extracted from the *Religious Census* of 1851, outlines the area's major denominations and their seating capacity.

Table 4.1: **Places of Worship and Seating Accommodation in Durham and Newcastle**

	Number of Places		Seating Accommodation	
	Durham	Newcastle	Durham	Newcastle
Church of England	189	12	70,648	10,488
Wesleyan Methodist	204	6	45,633	3,652
Other Methodists*	169	11	35,142	3,838
Presbyterian	14	5	6,550	2,770
Independents	27	2	9,575	1,036
Roman Catholic	24	2	5,250	1,744
Baptists	22	7	4,678	2,148
Others	26	9	4,927	3,738
	675	54	182,403	29,414

*Includes Primitives, New Connexion, Wesleyan Reformers and Wesleyan Methodist Association
Source: *Census of Great Britain: Religious Worship* (1852-53), pp.418-21.

After a century of debate it is now conceded that the barrister responsible for the *Religious Census*, Horace Mann, was close to the truth when he stated that 'the general facts and totals of the census are substantially correct'.[113] But for Durham and Newcastle, this concession to Mann must be seriously questioned, for as we observed in Chapter 1, there was an unprecedented population increase in the area at mid-century. Consequently, there was an unparalleled shortage of churches – indeed Durham and Northumberland had the second lowest percentage of seating-accommodation-to-population for all England and Wales.[114]

The Roman Catholics, for whom as a body we have more detailed statistics, were not untypical in having accommodation for only 5,000 communicants in Durham while their estimated population in 1851 was around 25,000. Even if each pew was occupied three times on 'Census Sunday', the figures do not tally. Because this discrepancy with the Catholic figures also applies to other areas of Irish-Catholic immigration, Maps 4.1 and 4.2 can only give a positional bearing on the places of established Catholicism in England,[115] not on the strength of the faithful. This is made clear in

Map 4.3 where the heavily shaded portions reflect the traditional roots of Catholicism, while areas like South Shields and Sunderland, which had extensive Irish populations by 1851, are shown to have an index of attendance of less than two. As indicated by the comparative maps on the Catholic Chapels and Churches in the area (Maps 3.1 and 3.2) most of the church building took place after 1846, the bulk after 1851. At least for Durham and Newcastle, then, some credence must be given to the *Rambler's* interrogatory: 'What argument as to population can be drawn from the number of church-sittings, when the supply of these must depend on the wealth as well as on the wants of different sects?'[116]

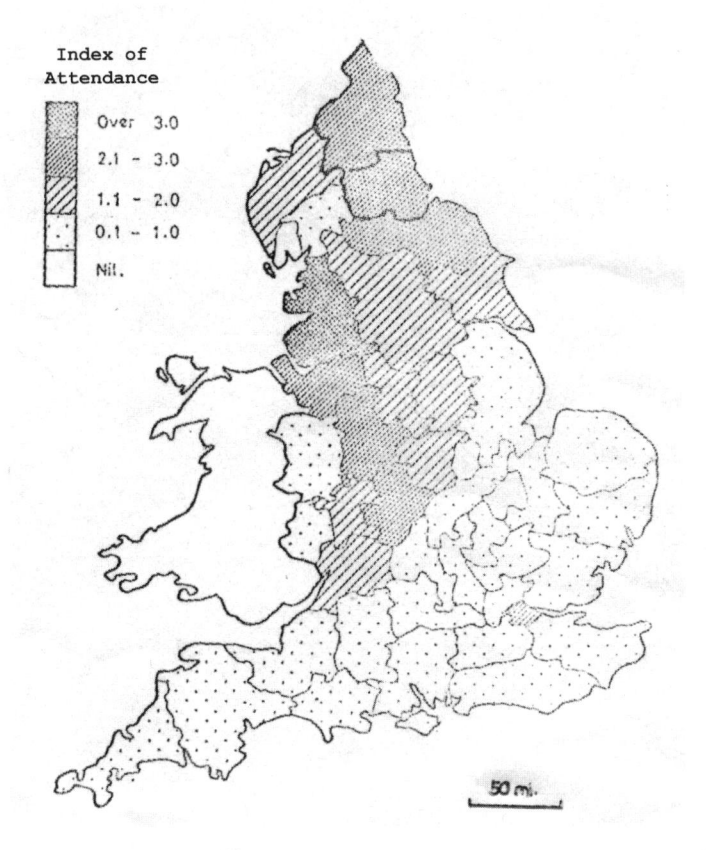

Map 4.1:   *Distribution of Roman Catholics in England, 1851, by Census*

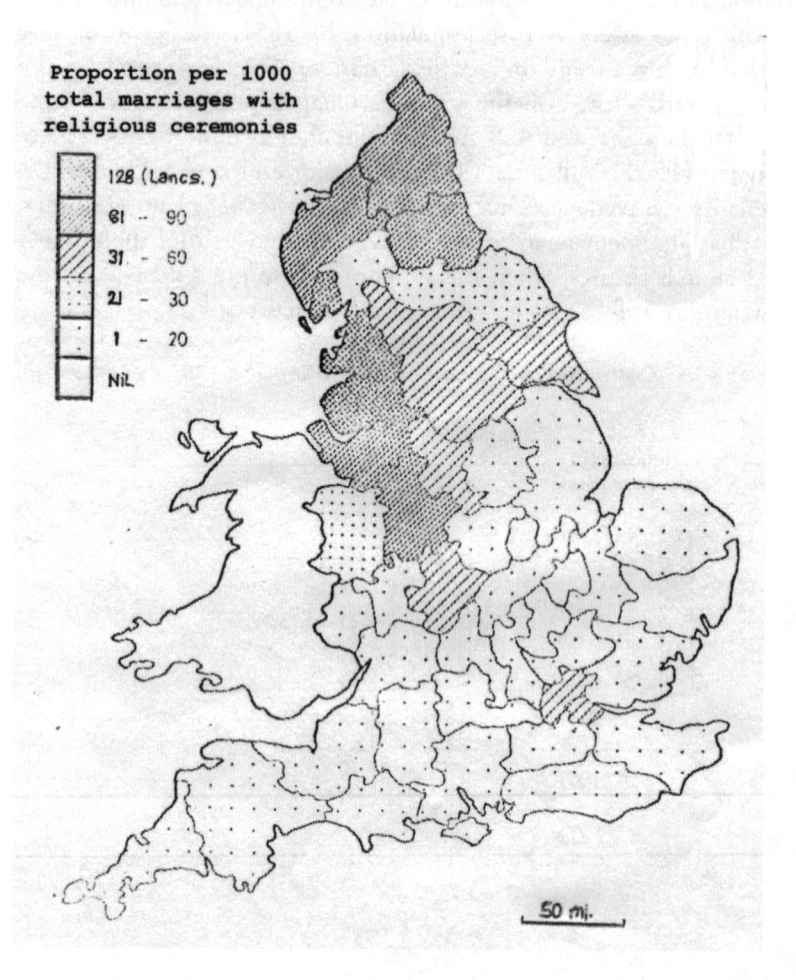

Map 4.2: *Distribution of Roman Catholics in England, 1851, by Marriages in Roman Catholic Churches*

Proportion per 1000
total marriages with
religious ceremonies

128 (Lancs.)
61 - 90
31 - 60
21 - 30
1 - 20
Nil

50 mi.

Map 4.3: ***Distribution of Roman Catholics in Co. Durham and Newcastle, 1851, by Census***

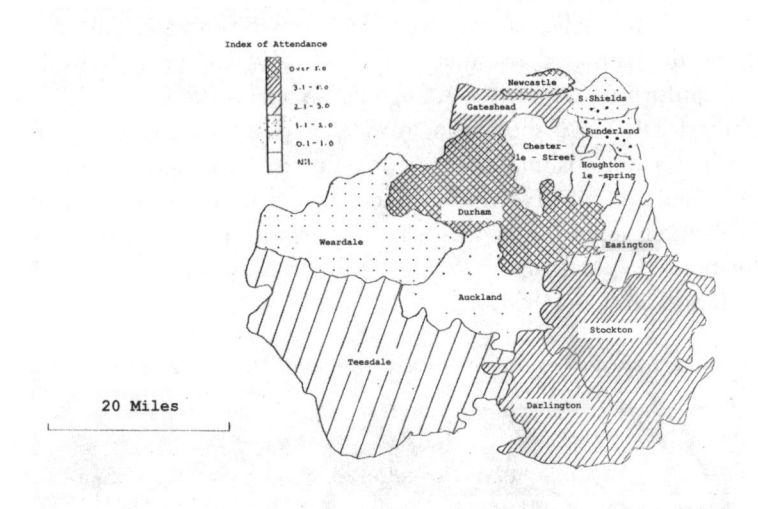

What is equally germane here is the similar predicament of other denominations in Durham and Newcastle in *their* struggle to provide accommodation for the vast influx of labourers and to meet the local needs stemming from the consistently high (and nationally exceptional) birth-rate among the working classes. The Anglican incumbent of Gateshead observed in 1843 that in 'all these places – Gateshead, Newcastle, North and South Shields, and Sunderland, with its contiguous parishes, numbering a population of nearly two hundred thousand, contained within the area of a circle of five or six miles radius, have scarcely, on an average, a church for every 7,000, and less than one clergyman for every 5,000 people'.[117] Eight years later, though great efforts had been made, the situation was no better. Among the thirty-six towns in Britain that had an index of attendance of less than the average for large towns (49.7) were Gateshead (32.9), Newcastle (40.0), South Shields (46.3) and Sunderland (48.5).[118] While abstinence from religious worship 'was most common where the largest number of working class people lived',[119] the implication that the working classes were relatively indifferent to religion cannot be assumed in the North-east due to the shortage of places of worship.

Although Anglicans, too, were aware of the shortage, the onus of the demand and responsibility lay not with them, but with Nonconformists (Baptists, Congregationalists, Presbyterians and Methodists). Since the advent of Wesley, the Church of England had had a diminishing place among Protestant congregations. By 1851 Durham and Northumberland were the two counties where the Established Church was least important. Table 4.2 indicates the relative position of the Church of England to the other denominations in 1851.

Table 4.2: **Relative Position of Church of England, National and Local, 1851**

	% of Seating to Total Population		% of Available Seating	
	C of E	Other	C of E	Other
England and Wales	29.6	27.4	51.9	48.1
Durham Co.	17.6	28.9	37.8	62.2
Northumberland	18.1	30.7	37.1	62.9
Newcastle	11.7	22.8	33.9	66.1
Gateshead	15.2	20.2	42.9	57.1
Sunderland	13.7	35.2	28.0	72.0

Source: *Census of Great Britain: Religious Worship* (1851), p.cclxxiv, p.ccxcii.

Even without taking into account the scarcity of Nonconformist places of worship, it is clear that the position of the Church of England was extremely weak. This situation was in marked contrast to London, for example, where in every borough except Tower Hamlets Church of England attendance was much higher than that of Nonconformists.[120] While in Lancashire the proportional seating of the Church was also very low (19.1 percent), the difference between that county (and all other areas of Irish immigration) and the North-east, was the position of the Methodists. While the ratio of Anglican-to-Methodist percentage accommodation in Lancashire was 1:0.46, in West Yorkshire 1:0.96, and for all England and Wales 1:0.41, in Durham this ratio was 1:1.24.[121]

In the decades after 1851 this gulf between Anglicans and Nonconformists was widened. Although the Church made a determined effort to enhance its position, its appeal to the new working classes met with little success.[122] In 1872 the *Newcastle Daily Chronicle* pointed out that

> the upholders of State Churchism have worthily betaken themselves to gigantic efforts in multiplying their seats and their adherents ... by revival prayer meetings to floral fetes; from whitewashed cottage Bethels to gorgeous and gorgeously-appointed temples; from popular Penny Readings to ornate musical ritual; by polite adaptation of article and rubric to all sorts of conditions of men; by saintly enthusiasm and monkish rigours; by unctuous Evangelism; by natural-tinted Broad Churchism; by daring avowals of rationalism; and by sailing as near the wind as possible without splitting on the rock of St. Peter ... the Episcopal Church have endeavoured to make for their sect an ascendancy in the councils of Authority and their practical monopoly of such disbursements from the public funds as the law places at the disposal of Government.[123]

But, as the article went on, in being so absorbed, the Church had failed to notice the even greater progress of dissenters. Quoting the findings of a religious census carried out by *The Nonconformist*, it stated that 'Newcastle shows seventy-six per cent of Dissenting increase alongside of forty-six Church increase' in the number of churches built since 1851. While the places of the Church increased from eleven to nineteen, the seating capacity of the Catholic Churches more than doubled in Newcastle and Congregationalist places increased threefold.[124] The Newcastle MP, Joseph Cowen, in opposing the Bishopric Bill in 1878, pointed out that in the two counties of Durham and Northumberland,

> the Dissenters and the Catholics have, during the last quarter of a century, not only expended as large a sum in building chapels and schools as the Church has done, but that they have absolutely expended one half-as-much again. The consequence is that the position of the different bodies to-day is not altered for the better, so far as the Church is concerned. On the contrary, Dissent and Catholicism have increased, not only as fast and as much as the Church, but they have progressed fully one-half more.[125]

For Irish Catholics, the state of religion in the North-east meant greater levels of religious, if not racial, toleration. In the first place, the building efforts of all the denominations reduced the amount of attention drawn to the increase in Catholic churches and communicants. Furthermore, in articles like 'Hartlepool – Chapel Building Extraordinary' Catholics received as much praise as other denominations for playing their part in bringing religion to the people.[126] The sheer numbers of communicants to be accommodated also made local proselytising attempts for one or two Irish Catholics seem fatuous. Local missionaries such as the Scottish evangelical Dr. Rutherford paid little heed to Irish Catholics who were the best provided group in the slums, and concentrated instead on instilling religious feelings in those slum dwellers who had no faith at all.[127]

Finally, in light of the limited place of the Church of England among the indigenous population, the social and religious life of the area and the attitudes of the inhabitants were primarily influenced by Nonconformist leadership. Despite the presumption of the commissioners appointed by the Anglican Bishop of Newcastle in 1883, who 'thought it right to take the entire population as the basis of our calculations' for the spiritual wants of the district;[128] 'that body [as Cowen claimed in 1878] never had, and has not now, any strong hold on the affections and convictions of the people of the North'.[129] This is evident in the social affairs, political meetings and entertainments of the population. At the opening of a Wesleyan Chapel near Newcastle in 1869, for example, shipping magnate Charles Palmer used the occasion to advance the argument that 'the Church of England is not keeping pace with the intelligence and increase of the population of the district, and he regards the Methodists as doing the work which the Church has left undone, and which it was her duty to have accomplished'.[130] Palmer, doubtless expressing the sympathies of his audience, went so far as to call some of the Anglican clergy 'drunkards, bankrupts and men of impure life'. While the Wesleyans were not over-warm either to Catholics or Irish, the problems facing that denomination at mid-century tended to distract them from anti-Catholicism. The 'spiritual earthquake' in the twilight of Jabez Bunting's very Tory 'Premiership of Methodism' (1808-48) forced the Wesleyans to become more closely allied with the popular liberalism of the Northeast.[131] In Newcastle, Gateshead and Sunderland, Wesleyan membership was cut almost in half by the disaffection of less conservative members.[132] For the Methodist body as a whole, the internal difficulties at mid-century mollified much of the earlier rigidity and stiffness. Among Primitive Methodists, who were strongest in the mining districts and costal seafaring villages, religious views largely determined a political outlook that leaned towards the 'radicalism' of labour spokesmen like Thomas Burt, John Wilson, William Crawford and Joseph Cowen. Exactly *how* far this liberalism reduced antipathy to Catholics or to Irish in daily life it is difficult to say. The point is that Nonconformists generally went out of their way to underscore their disapproval of the unfairly endowed State-supported Church, and in so doing were unwilling to follow its anti-Catholic lead.[133] Since the politics of Irish Catholics in the region also tended to Liberalism, and since their religion was Establishment-dissenting, it was difficult for Irish Catholics to serve as a focus for hostility from the religious majority.

Two other factors operated to reduce antagonism to Irish Catholics. The first is the lack of Orange lodges in the area. This meant that little moral or practical support was given to the particular union of Tory politics and State Churchism that rendered Irish Catholics favoured victims. While there is evidence of registered Orange lodges in Newcastle in 1814 and 1830, there appear to have been few later in the century.[134] Excepting one murder which took place in 1858 outside The Ellison Arms, commonly called 'The Hole' it being an Orange Club in which the victim was 'a Roman Catholic, but not a Ribbonman or a member of the proscribed Hibernian Society', there are few references to Orangemen in Newcastle.[135] There are no local reports of Battle of Boyne Day celebrations, nor any references to Orangemen raising havoc on St. Patrick's Day. For Durham, too, the evidence is scant. One of the few reports of disturbances on 12 July came from the strong Irish Catholic centre of Consett in 1882. Here an Orange lodge had been established in 1868,[136] but its strength might be measured by the fact that the melee of 1882 required the import of Orangemen from other places, for 'upon the arrival of the last train from Durham at Benfieldside, a batch of Orangemen were met at the station by a number of police who escorted them to Consett'.[137] Crook also had an Orangemen's association in 1881, but its membership was less than eighty.[138]

The other factor working in favour of the region's Irish Catholics was the liberalism of several of the most influential Anglican families. The Ravensworths, the Greys and the Lambeths, for instance, generously gave land and building materials in order that their Catholic workmen could be spiritually provided.[139] Other Protestant landowners such as Sir Hedworth Williamson were renowned for their 'generosity of heart and liberality of sentiment'[140] and were willing benefactors to every Catholic fund for a church and school.

Hence, with (i) a sizeable Catholic gentry quite highly regarded and easing the reaction to the Irish Catholics; (ii) a strong dissenting population of break-away Methodists who could not easily join with the Establishment in the cry against the Pope and who were also preoccupied with their own internal schism and church building; (iii) few Orangemen; and (iv) a traditional liberalism among many of the leading Anglican families, anti-Catholicism was confined to a very small minority of devoted upholders of the Establishment. But though these were few in number, they were neither insignificant nor without power. Indeed, among them were the high and mighty. 'Some there are', wrote the *Newcastle Daily Chronicle*

> who will never, if they can help it, tolerate any opinion contrary to their own. The present Bishop of Durham appears to be one of these. His lordship failed to put in an appearance at the opening ceremony connected with a most excellent charity ... because the Roman Catholic Bishop of Hexham and Newcastle had been invited. He would not stand on the same platform with Bishop Chadwick.[141]

The five bishops of Durham from Maltby to Lightfoot were all men of 'strongly Protestant inclination' with no tendencies to High

Churchism.[142] For them, Protestant England was dependent upon the stalwart principles of those political factions violently opposing the papacy – that 'gigantic lie which attempts to stand between the soul and Christ'.[143] Dissenters were naturally frowned upon, but even an orthodox Presbyterian might sometimes serve as a welcome ally. Thus Bishop Maltby in 1851 acted with impunity in presenting 'a liberal contribution towards the erection of a Presbyterian Chapel in his diocese',[144] but Bishop Lightfoot, thirty years later, led a charge on the Salvation Army so riddled with 'discriminative criticism' that it shocked even the Episcopal Bench.[145] Local support for the bishops, came from those who had vested interests in the Established Church, and for whom the 'Church in danger' acted as a powerful charm. Among this group could be found the almost stereotypic judges and magistrates who brought anti-Catholicism to the courts and hence into the immediate vicinity of arrested Irishmen. Rev. Major, the parish incumbent of Thornley as well as the magistrate, appears to have been a representative of this class: much to the chagrin of the Irish, he levied fines on them that were twice those handed to the non-Irish.[146]

An order of bastardy brought against a Catholic priest in Stockton by the daughter of an Anglican incumbent further exposes these sentiments of the bench. The combination of Catholicism and sexuality naturally drew those who delighted in erotic fantasies about the priesthood. The magistrates were obviously opinionated as well, for the railway attorney, Francis Mewburn, having 'read the evidence carefully' came 'to the conclusion that the priest is perfectly innocent and he is the victim of a clever and abandoned woman'.[147] Nevertheless, the magistrates found the priest guilty, though they could not convict him for lack of corroborative proof. 'I fear', said Mewburn, 'the magistrates allowed their prejudices to get the better of their judgment'. This was made all the clearer when it became the priest's turn to charge the woman involved with felony and extortion. 'The magistrates, however, did not commit her for reasons they did not express' and the case was dismissed.[148]

But the best example of anti-Catholicism and anti-Irishness, inextricably linked to Tory-Establishment views, is that presented by the Dowager Marchioness of Londonderry in her treatment of the Irish Catholics at Seaham Harbour. In light of the high degree of toleration shown to Irish Catholics in the North-east, the incident is unique in the history of the Irish in the region and for that reason all the more historically revealing.

******

Towards the end of the summer of 1860 the Dowager Marchioness of Londonderry received a letter requesting a small grant of land on which the Catholics of Seaham Harbour could build a chapel, a school, and priest's house. The author was Rev. Robert Belaney, a Catholic convert from a background of learning and social standing.[149] His mettle, like that of many clerical converts, was being tested in the grim reality of a struggling, impoverished provincial mission. Belaney's position was all the less enviable in that he and his flock were in the fiefdom of one of the most formidable and entrenched Anglican-Tory families in the North-east. The Londonderrys behaved in a manner that, if erratic in other ways was consistently autocratic. The Dowager, Frances Anne Vane Londonderry, was as strong a personality as the late 'Fighting Marquis', and attracted only little less odium, if thinly disguised under a reputation for a 'noble and noble-hearted lady' of benevolence.[150] Not without a hint of irony, the historian Sir Archibald Alison wrote of her in 1861 as 'a tall and elegant figure and uncommon personal beauty, [who] was endowed at that same time with a fascination of manner few could withstand'.[151] Robert Blake in his biography of Disraeli notes that she was 'odious and overbearing' and 'famed for her opulence and her arrogance', while Disraeli himself, after years of flattering her, recalled her as 'a tyrant'.[152] It was in character therefore for her dismiss out of hand Rev. Belaney's request. Her Seaham agent, J.H. Ravenshaw communicated her coldness on the subject, leaving Belaney to administer the sacraments in a garret above a hayloft, and pray that the misguided lady might a change of heart. When providence failed to intervene, however, a second letter was dispatched. Though couched in priestly humility and over-adorned with terms of respect, Belaney minced no words:

> I can hardly imagine your Ladyship to be aware of the misery and inconvenience which these persons – a large proportion of whom have been your Ladyship's faithful though poor workmen for many years – are at this time enduring from want of a proper place for Divine Worship and a school for their children. Their present spiritual destitution is only transforming men who might be a benefit to the community in which they live by their virtues, into a curse by their vices. There is an amount of vice, especially of drunkenness, in this town which I should hope has nothing to equal it in any other town in England; by day one cannot move without seeing it, and throughout the night its horrid sounds are heard in every street .... My business here, and my aim here, is to rescue that portion of the people of the town who profess the Catholic religion from the danger and guilt of contributing to the stream of depravity which is flooding the very floor of peoples' houses. But without a Church, and without a School, my aim, be it ever so good, can avail nothing.[153]

Not content with this, Belaney went on at length espousing the cause of 'the poor Irish brought over and settled ... by your Ladyship', emphasizing that the Lady's own knowledge of the Irish should make it perfectly clear to her that they would not be 'better workmen if they became worse Catholics'.

Lady Londonderry did not reply. Instead, she addressed a letter to the Rev. G. Howard Wilkinson, the Anglican incumbent of Seaham Harbour, enclosing Belaney's epistle, and trusting that he would 'be able to contradict a statement respecting the town ..., which I should be very sorry to think was true'.[154] Like the Marquis of Bute's pride in spending £400,000 developing the dock and shipping facilities on his property in Cardiff,[155] the Londonderrys were proud of their investments in Seaham which gave them their own port for coal export. These 'civic efforts' were the reason for the town's sizeable population increase between 1841 and 1851.[156] Not only had the church and house of the Anglican incumbent been furnished by the Londonderrys in 1841,[157] but the Third Marquis had corresponded with the Archbishop of Canterbury to secure a perpetual curacy in his name.[158] Conscious of all this, as well no doubt of the proven temper of Frances Anne, Wilkinson had little difficulty in replying that 'by whatever standard its morality be measured, Seaham Harbour will not stand unfavourably, when compared with other towns'[159] While he admitted that some drunkenness existed and that he had even gone so far as to urge 'upon all classes the duty of uniting to arrest its progress', he thought it 'most unjust that a whole population should be branded with infamy on account of the degradation of a comparatively small portion of its members'. Having heard what she wanted, Lady Londonderry proceeded to publish her correspondence in the *Seaham Weekly News*, prefaced by her reply to Rev. Belaney. She announced her happiness in receiving the incumbent's contradiction and, though no further proof was needed, had received from her son, Lord Adolphous Vane, an assurance, 'that from his little experience, as a magistrate, he thinks there is far less crime in Seaham than in many places of similar size'.[160] She concluded her letter to Belaney 'Having thus disposed of your sweeping abuse of the place and inhabitants, I have only further to add, that when the Roman Catholic population shall have reached such a figure as will render it necessary, I shall be ready to grant a site for a Church for 99 years on the same terms I grant leases to other denominations'. *The Record* was delighted to see a 'Romish Priest' put in his place, and scorned his insolence in the face of such Protestant magnanimity.[161] Belaney, outraged at reading in the local press the reply he had never received, lashed out:

> the visits of a lady (whose visits to a town are paid in a carriage and four) are not likely to give her much knowledge of the moral condition of the poor. Their state is not to be discerned, like objects at a distance, by the telescope. You only see it from the windows of a palace or of a stately carriage ... If I were myself to go by such evidence as Mr. Wilkinson puts forth ..., I should conclude that the couple of hundred people who are grouped and huddled together before me in a hayloft on Sundays ... were all saints. Their readiness would also do honour to people who had twice their means.[162]

Effectively this sealed the fate of his Irish congregation, and for more than a year nothing further was heard of them. Belaney was dispatched to Ireland and was later kept occupied with local collections for St. Godric's in Durham City.[163] However with the unveiling in that city of the equestrian statue of the Third Marquis by Disraeli on 2 December 1861 the issue was reopened. The *Hull Advertiser* asked if Disraeli, while the guest of the Marchioness at Seaham, was aware that his hostess 'who makes such beautiful maternal speeches at the annual public dinners which she gives to portions of her tenantry – has for years refused to give, sell, lease, or allow to be occupied upon her property at Seaham, a spot of ground upon which to erect a chapel and a school for the use of some hundreds of poor Catholics'.[164] In the execration that religious issues alone could provoke, the *Advertiser* went on:

> the lady's No-Popery zeal is equal to her ability as a lecturer upon agricultural, social, and domestic economy; and failing to persuade her Catholic colliers to show their respect for their employer by adopting that employer's religion in preference to their own, she dooms them, as far as in her power, to a life of irreligion, and their children to be reared in worse than heathen ignorance.

Supposedly quoting an informed source in Seaham Harbour, the article exclaimed:

> But, thank God, she is mortal, like the rest of us, and in a few years she will possess less land than we want for a chapel and school. Her earthly possessions will be limited to the space occupied by her coffin, and the poorest of us will obtain as much without even doing her the courtesy of consulting her about it. When she is gone there will be changes in the management of the property.

Surprisingly, the Marchioness' response was calm, reasoned even: she instantly commission her chief agent, Robert Anderson and, independently, Rev. W.A. Scott,[165] to carry out a census of the Irish Catholics in the Seaham area. Anderson found no Catholics at Seaham Colliery, forty-four Catholics at Seaton Colliery and 475 in the town of Seaham Harbour.[166] Scott gave no account of Seaham Harbour and also found no Catholics at Seaham Colliery, but listed the names (all Irish) of fifty-eight Catholics in Seaton Colliery.[167]

Curiously, however, given the figures, the Marchioness felt able to exonerate herself. Adolphous was thus instructed to write the libellous journal to reclaim his mother's good character. 'Acting on the principle she has ever laid down for guidance ... on her estates in Ireland, of giving full liberty of conscience in religious questions', he wrote, Lady Londonderry, upon receiving the application for a site, investigated 'as to satisfy herself with the numbers of the R[oman] C[atholic]s at Seaham Harbour'.[168] He concluded that her Ladyship did not think that 500 or so Catholics was a sufficient number to warrant the building of a church when they already had a place of worship – failing to add its exact nature.

But if the Marchioness was certain of her ground, the Catholics were no less determined for theirs. In March 1862 a local landowner, R.L. Pemberton, was approached by the priest for the purchase of a plot of land ostensibly for Catholic burials. Pemberton was not adverse to such a sale, but, like the rest of the inhabitants of Seaham, he had no appetite for crossing swords with the all-powerful matriarch. Instead, he informed her that the priest had stated that 'there are 1,000 souls of that [Catholic] persuasion in the place who have to take their dead great distances or pay double fees which seems a hardship'.[169] Anderson was again solicited to investigate, and dutifully reported that there were '*no double Fees*' on Catholic burials, adding that 'If the priest obtains a piece of ground for a burial ground from Mr. Pemberton, he will build a Chapel on it, close adjoining your Ladyship's Estate – and say he was obliged to go there, because you refused to grant him a site on lease'.[170] Once again the Dowager was caught between her erstwhile reputation and her 'principles'. Adolphous warned her:

> The application from the RCs to Pemberton is very awkward for either he would come forward and do what you have refused or you would have to ask him to refuse and you would have to do it yourself on compulsion. This latter would be only apparent for I know had you been left at peace instead of this endeavour to thrust you into this concession you could have done it of your own accord.[171]

Adolphous went on to state that he had 'always expected' that his mother would be branded a religious bigot through the affair and this was the last thing he desired. He urged her to get out of the situation that she might not appear as always having her actions influenced by 'unpopular' sentiments. But the Marchioness did not budge; she procrastinated and the Catholics got neither Pemberton's land nor a leasehold.

The final approach to the Dowager was made in December 1862 by the Catholic convert, Priscilla Beckwith, wife of General Beckwith,[172] who was sometimes resident in Seaham. Beckwith appealed to her Ladyship's connections with Ireland, 'by Parentage, by Alliance, and by Property', and declared her certainty that her Ladyship 'must feel a deep sympathy with these poor people. They are ignorant and probably uncivilized, but all the more reason is there that they should be instructed and brought under the influence of Religion'.[173] She emphasized the social advantages of a church and resident priest, and hinted that the Bishop would take special care in the appointment. And she spoke of new financial arrangements made possible by the Church Fund, enclosed the Bishop' s address that her Ladyship might not have to deal with lessers and, finally, attempted a variation on the burial ground idea. But it was all in vain; the feminine touch was no more effective than the appeals that had gone before. The Dowager was sceptical of an 'unsupported application' made by a woman who did not want 'the General' to know of her appeal.[174] Perhaps, in view of the distress caused by the defection to Rome in 1855 of her daughter-in-law, who was to become Marchioness of Londonderry,[175] the Dowager also resented being approached by a convert. At any rate, the reply to Beckwith contained but vague references to Earl Vane, the future Fifth Marquis, and to other advisors and previous letters. And there the matter rested for two years until the death of the Dowager in January 1865.

The statement in the *Hull Advertiser* thus became prophetic, for with the passing of the estate to the Fifth Marquis, the land was at last granted to the Catholics 'on ordinary terms of ground rent under a lease of seventy-five years'.[176] Fifteen years after Bishop Hogarth had made his appeal for the 300 to 500 totally unprovided for Catholics at Seaham Harbour,[177] his successor, Bishop Chadwick, laid the foundation stone for the plain little structure that would be dedicated to St. Mary Magdalen, patron saint of those rescued from the devil.

In more ways than one, the story of Lady Londonderry and the Irish Catholics of Seaham Harbour is a tempest in a teapot. But that is the point; compared to the riotous proceedings against the Irish in places like Stockport or Glasgow, the triviality of what went on in Seaham is an exemplification of Anglo-Irish relations in the North-east. The Nonconformist faith of the majority allied with their political liberalism made behaviour like the Marchioness's as exceptional as her wealth and hauteur. No-Popery directed against the Irish Catholics in Durham and Newcastle was not only momentary in its passage but, while passing, countenanced by only a very small portion of the population. Bishop Bewick, surveying the past three decades in 1882, concluded that 'We are at perfect peace with all the population of the district. We have received many substantial proofs of their good-will in the past, and we shall not fail to see them in the future'.[178] There was no other Catholic Bishop in England with as large a flock of Irish who had any desire to record his 'deep sense of gratitude to the press', let alone be able to state without hyperbole that

> the great employers of labour ... co-operate with us in promoting the social, moral, and religious improvement of our labouring classes, and the education of our poor children in our own schools. Exceptions there may be, but they are rare .... They look to us and our clergy to do our utmost, and to exercise all the influence we possess.[179]

Such was peculiarity of the North-east, and why, historically, incidents like the Sandgate riot or Seaham Harbour, so far as they stand out at all, do so for being hugely exceptional.

Chapter 5

Occupational Place and Labour Relations

> Little did they bring with them but sturdy limbs for toil.
> *6th Annual Report of the Catholic Poor-School Committee*, 1853, p.29
>
> They undergo a very rough and laborious kind of work, do they not? – They are excellent labourers. Do you think from your knowledge of that locality and of the North of England generally, that they could do well without those Irish labourers? – I think we could not do without them.
> Assistant Overseer of the Newcastle Poor Law to the *Select Committee on Poor Removals*, 1855, q.599-600. p.40

Where the occupational place of the Irish in nineteenth-century England has been studied at all, the source has been mainly the wealth of evidence contained in the reports of the select committees of inquiry, in particular 'Appendix G' of the 1836 parliamentary *Report of the Poor Inquiry (Ireland) Commission on the Irish Poor in Great Britain*. Such commissions substantiated what had been observed from the turn of the century: that the Irish formed a significant substratum of the labouring population of England and that their labour was among the most fatiguing, degrading and lowest paid. Abundant testimony pointed to the primary place of the Irish within the large manufacturing centres: in the woollen and linen industries, building trades, chemical and soap works, and a host of related sundry trades. These were mainly unskilled jobs for which the demand was high and the attraction to the English low.

The government inquiries also indicated that the Irish had assumed a definite place in employment outside urban centres, as migratory agricultural labourers and on railway cuttings. By 1850 the seasonal migration of Irish agricultural labourers was no longer a significant phenomenon, but from the 1830s the Irish increasingly moved into railway and dock excavation.

The government Blue Books provide little information on Irish labour in the North-east. However, it is clear from local sources that here, too, they occupied the bottom of the labour hierarchy. Many of their jobs were similar, but the industrial emphasis of the region was significantly different from other Irish centres in England. 'From a combination of causes', noted the Newcastle correspondent to the *Nation* in 1872, 'there are classes and varieties of labour to be obtained which are met with in few other places .... In this respect [the Irish] fairly contrast with their kindred in most other towns'.[1] The weaving industry, with which the Irish were so closely identified in Lancashire and the Midlands, did not exist in the North-east. The textile industry was small and specialised and few Irish gained entry. While agriculture and the chemical and glass-making industries were significant sources of Irish employment, the major industries in Durham and Newcastle – coal, iron, engineering and shipbuilding – were not, at least initially.[2]

With regard to coal mining in particular, the lack of Irish experience delayed any significant entry before the 1860s. The point is worth making, for those who *have* acknowledged an Irish presence in the North-east have invariably looked to this industry and drawn all-too-easy conclusions. Besides lacking the requisite skills, the Irish were thwarted by the pride and jealousy of the indigenous labour force whose skills were their only property and gift to their sons. As important was the disastrous colliers' strike of 1844 which left in its wake a surplus of skilled workers in cut-throat competition.[3] A decade later the surfeit of skilled miners was still a subject of concern.[4] It was not until the late 1850s that the trade began to revive, ultimately to flourish with the development of iron production. By 1866 the general manager for one of the chief coal entrepreneurs, Lord Londonderry, was reporting that he had 'inserted advertisements in all the local newspapers, and hoped to be able to secure some workers in this way'.[5] While some Irish entered the pits at that time, the bulk of the new recruits were brought in from South Wales, Derbyshire, Staffordshire and the local lead mines. Lord Londonderry secured Cornishmen, widely regarded as the *crème de la crème* of miners, not only because of their skill but, morally, for 'neither howl[ing] like a frantic Irishman, nor curs[ing] with the bitter oaths of the drunken collier of the black country'.[6] Where the Irish were employed in the coal trade – primarily in new pits around Durham, Easington, Thornley and Sedgefield – their labour was confined to the low-paid surface jobs, at the coke ovens, or in 'patching' or unloading – jobs peripheral to hewing. With the further expansion of the industry during the Franco-Prussian War more Irish made their debut in it. And when wages fell during the depression that followed that war, forcing many local colliers to emigrate, the Irish took up the slack. But until the mid-1870s coal was the local industry that was least penetrated by them.

If before 1850 the regional 'forces of capitalism...consisted in one word, ... coal',[7] after 1850 other industries became nearly as important. For Irish employment, these other industries far surpassed that of coal. As in Wales, it was especially to the iron works that they were recruited.[8] Its rapid expansion in north Durham during the 1840s provided countless jobs for anyone who had strong arms and a willingness to work. The Irish met the need, their foreignness proving no obstacle to the stoking of blast-furnaces or the labour-intensive demands of the rolling mills. Unlike the coal industry, the iron works were too recent to have any strong patriotic claims on the locals. The iron works at Consett, Birtley, Witton Park, Tow Law, Weardale, Gateshead and Sunderland were, almost from their inception, heavily dependent on cheap and accessible Irish labour. And as their labour there was increasing appreciated, their employment opportunities expanded along with the industry itself (on Teesside from three blast-furnaces in 1851 to fifty in 1861 and 122 in 1871).[9] By 1886 some 14,000 men were employed in the north of England iron works, 'not more than half of this number [being] employed twenty years ago'.[10] The concentration of Roman Catholics in areas like Consett (2,000 according to a report of 1854)[11] only suggests what the Census Enumerators' manuscripts confirm, that the industry was the chief employer of Irish in County Durham by mid-century.

Shipbuilding, like the coal trade, took on relatively few Irish before the 1860s. Until then the industry was a small-scale employer.[12] In 1851 only 5,000 persons were employed in it the North-east, and 'only eight firms employed more than 100 men and none more than 250'.[13] On the Wear, the trade was typified by small family firms with a mean size of thirty-three workers each.[14] But between 1850 and 1880 the growth of the industry was as dramatic as the iron and steel production upon which it depended. The growth on the Tyne and the Wear was as much as five-fold by the end of the century, by which time each shipyard was employing a thousand men or more.[15] Charles Palmer, himself employing 3,500 men, estimated that there were about 8,000 persons employed in iron shipbuilding in the area in 1862.[16] Half of these, he judged, were on the Tyne, 2,500 on the Wear, and 1,500 on the Tees. Later in the century the general manager of Palmer's works at Jarrow reported that 'the principal part of our labour is performed by the Irish'.[17]

As in the steel mills, so in shipbuilding, the Irish needed few skills. Although some entered the ranks of the 'unskilled' and worked as helpers to platers and riveters, the majority were delegated to hard labour, such as the lifting of the hundredweight sheets of iron onto the decks. Many were continuously employed in dock excavation and on the expanding dry-dock facilities. Although only a few of the first generation had much hope of advancing beyond the rank of general labourer, some of the second generation entered the skilled trades. John Denvir, the contemporary chronicler of the Irish in England, remarked of Irish progeny in Sunderland that they 'are generally put to trades, chiefly, as along Tyneside, in connection with iron shipbuilding, so that you now find a considerable number of Irishmen and boys in the fitting and engine shops, besides those employed as platers and riviters [sic]'.[18]

As elsewhere, the building of the churches marked the labour inroads of the Irish. St. Joseph, the 'patron of the artisan and the horny-handed labourer' gained a church in Sunderland in 1873 in 'a new and thriving part of town, where the ship-wrights, riveters, and others engaged in the shipbuilding yards of Deptford, Millfield, and Pallion, mostly reside'.[19] The mission at Tyne Dock, as well as the churches at Jarrow and Hebburn, were almost exclusively for the shipyard Irish. By 1880, perhaps as many as one-quarter of the Irish in Durham and Newcastle were involved in the industry.

But while the major industries took on an increasing number of Irish, there was, throughout the period under study, a vast number of Irish (40 percent would not be an unreasonable estimate) in occupations that rarely received contemporary comment. The glass works of Messrs. Hartley in Sunderland and John Candlish near Seaham, for instance, both made extensive use of Irish labour. The chemical works at Gateshead, Jarrow, Sunderland, and Port Clarence also depended on them, as did Darlington to become one of the country's leading centres of railway engineering. As historian John Treble has noted, the Irish also played a fundamental part 'in speeding up the pace of environmental change' in the north of England through their involvement in the building and construction trades.[20] The vast suburban expansion of Newcastle in the period[21] accounts for many Irish listed in the Census Enumerators' Manuscripts as bricklayers or masons' helpers. The building trades, in turn, created a demand for Irish labour in the brick factories, and in the region's many limestone quarries. Southwick-on-Wear is an example of a town whose population was doubled by the Irish who came to work in the expanding quarries and limekilns.[22]

Another Irish occupation seldom remarked upon in history books was the use of young men for the coastal shipping. According to an article in *The Tablet* in 1852:

> boys under the age of eighteen years, who come over here almost daily from Ireland in search of work, and are induced by lodging-house keepers (who are allowed a commission by the ship-owners) to ship as sea apprentices in the Tyne. ... it is a fact that nearly one-fourth of the boys who now apprentice to sea in this district are, or were, poor destitute Irish boys – tramps seeking employment.[23]

As with most other employments, the initial hesitancy in hiring Irish soon gave way to more eager acceptance. 'Formerly', it was claimed, 'there was on the part of ship-owners and captains much unwillingness to receive Irish boys, but that feeling has considerably abated – they are found on board ships as useful, as obedient, and as skilful as Scotch or English youths; hence ship-owners now, generally speaking, have no reluctance to Irish boys as such'.[24]

Of course, in the urban slums of the North-east, as we have noted, a great many Irish were living off their wits, self-employed. Particularly in the 1851 Census, Mayhew-like depictions of such 'employment' are commonplace. Identified in one part of South Shields, for instance, were shoemakers, rag pickers, tinkers, weavers, hatters, musicians, tailors, barbers, knitters, cartmen, pipemakers and dressmakers.[25] Additionally, there were Irish fish and produce vendors, as well as publicans and lodging housekeepers. But while many Irish were consigned to these vocations upon arriving in the area, the commentary on their improved circumstances by the early 1850s (cited in the last chapter) suggests that by then a significant number of them had been assimilated into the main industrial workforce.

Railway construction not only employed many Irish but deposited colonies of them throughout the region. More than fifteen separate branch lines were opened in Durham County between 1840 and 1868.[26] Many of these, such as that from Seaham to Sunderland or that from Hartlepool to Ferry Hill, were scarcely twenty miles long but their terminals were often fruitful sources of employment. Witton-le-Wear, for example, found itself with a sizeable Irish population attributable, said the Census, 'to the influx of labourers and their families employed on railway works, and to the establishment of iron works'.[27] At Durham City the Irish population was much increased by the labourers who assisted in the massive railway cutting and viaduct at Redhills in 1857. It was these Irish who forced the decision to build the church of St. Godric.[28]

The question as to the number of Irish employed on railway construction is one that is no more answerable today than it was during the great railway age. The *Select Committee on Emigration* of 1841 and the Census report for the same year, as well as the evidence before the *Select Committee on Railway Labourers* of 1846 gave the proportion of Irish to other workers at between 10 and 50 percent.[29] Terry Coleman, in his study of railway navvies, is probably not far off the mark with his estimate that about one-third were Irish.[30] If true, then for Durham and Northumberland approximately 700 Irish would have been employed in railway construction in 1851, 1,100 in 1861, and slightly less than this in 1871 and 1881.[31]

But however many Irish were employed on certain lines at specific dates, it seems certain that within the railway gangs, the Irish retained a position at the bottom of the labour ladder. Few Irish attained the prestigious rank of 'navvy', receiving the highest pay for the performance of the most skilled jobs such as tunneling. The Irish were mostly found among general labourers, although the example of Redhills and that of the construction of the Knaresborough viaduct (where 26 percent of the labourers were Irish)[32] also suggests that many were employed as helpers to the bricklayers and masons who were setting the huge blocks for the viaducts.

Finally, note should be made of the Irish agricultural workers in the North-east. Traditionally the Irish harvesters had migrated to Yorkshire and counties southward. Very few appear to have made the pilgrimage to the North-east. In south Durham their entry can be dated from 1830 when Francis Mewburn wrote in his diary: 'This summer an immense number of Irishmen came into the county and superseded the ordinary harvest labourers, few of the lower classes either in the towns or villages being hired for the harvest'.[33] Paradoxically, when in the 1860s the Irish element was 'nearly extinguished' at harvest in the more southerly counties, Irish reapers continued to come to the North-east.[34] In 1861 the population of Sandgate, Newcastle, was reported as 'doubled ... in the height of summer' as a result of 'the immigratory Irish, who flock here in prodigious numbers in the harvesting time'.[35] Not all came directly from Ireland; many migrated from the south of England specifically for the harvest. Mr. Grainger, who was in Newcastle in the autumn of 1853 to deal with the cholera outbreak, received reports of 100 to 150 'Irish labourers coming from the south for harvest work.' They disembarked 'from a Hull steamer, [and] immediately walked up in a troop to the already densely packed houses in Sandgate'.[36] But whether from Ireland or from the south of England, increasing numbers of them remained behind to swell the ranks of the 'half-mendicants' in the region's labour pool.

As all the above would suggest, there were few employment opportunity for Irish women and children in the region. Without any woollen or linen industry, the North-east had none of the scope for family employment of other areas. Nor were there factories to which school children could be transferred 'for the sake of *gaining* a shilling or eight pence per week' to add to the family income.[37] Schools for 'Catholic – chiefly Irish – children employed in factories' were never proposed for the North-east.[38] Children had been used as 'trappers' in the coal pits, but before the Irish made any significant dent in that trade religious, governmental (Lord Ashley's Act of 1842) and educational pressures had eliminated this employment for boys under thirteen. Thus when Catholic authorities in the area complained of fluctuating attendance at schools, it was seldom because children were at work; more often it was due to the mobility of their parents. This was quite unlike Liverpool, for instance, where contemporaries estimated that only a quarter of the children attended school in 1861 and that 'even these are removed at an early age, to add to the family's earnings'.[39] In the North-east it was rare for the Census enumerators to list children between the ages of six and thirteen as other than 'scholars'.

As for women, it was noted by Newcastle's superintendent of police in 1838 that 'the female population of the town have very few sources of employment, either in trade or manufactures'.[40] This remained largely unaltered to the end of the century.[41] Women rarely undertook even the lighter harvest work. The Assistant Overseer of the Poor Law in Newcastle complained that when the Irish go to harvest, 'their wives and families, in the meantime, become chargeable'.[42] Although some women were 'to be found in the lower and dirtier departments of the factories on the Tyne – in nursery-gardens and in field work – some even in brick yards ... [with] average earnings ... at from 4s. to 12s. per week', employment for Irish women was confined principally to domestic service, from scullery maids to laundresses.[43] In the absence of alternative employment, and in response to the market, many Irish girls turned to prostitution. There are numerous references and allusions to brothels and harlots in the Irish quarter of Newcastle,[44] though it was Sunderland's boast that 'notwithstanding that we are a seaport, we are below Tynemouth, Newcastle, and Hartlepool, or any of those surrounding places, both as to thieves and abandoned women'.[45] The occasional reference in the Census enumerators' manuscripts to Irish 'sisters' occupying single houses in colliery villages also suggests the scope for this profession outside urban centres. In general, however, employment opportunities for women, as for children, were not plentiful, thus compelling Irish family income to rely mainly on the male wage earner. Thus our estimated Irish population for Newcastle and Durham in 1861 of 46,000 (Table 1.5) would have been almost wholly reliant on the income generated by 17,000 Irishmen.[46]

Had this reliance on the male wage earner existed in other areas of Irish settlement, the most destitute conditions would have been greatly worsened. But the attraction of the North-east to the Irish – the relatively higher wages as a result of the demand for labour – meant that an Irishman's wage was often in excess of that of a whole family elsewhere. The area's fortuitous combination of coal, iron, and shipbuilding permitted incomes for common labourers as high as 24s. a week. If one was to believe the Assistant Secretary of the

North of England Iron Trade at Middlesbrough during the iron lockout of 1865, the lowest paid iron workers, the puddlers, had weekly average earnings of £2 11s 6d.[47] According the *Durham Chronicle*, which reported it, this was an income 'not reached by many clergymen of the Established Church'. Or, if one chose to believe Charles Palmer in 1866, while warning his men against striking: 'Labourers on the Clyde are earning from 12s. to 14s. a-week, while here they are paid from 16s. to 18s.; platers on the Clyde earn 30s a week, while here they receive 33s.; riveters there earn 25s., while here they earn 30s.'[48] Although this was far from the average wage of an Irish labourer, the epithet for Durham and Newcastle in the second half of the nineteenth century, as 'a poor man's Eldorado', is not without substance.[49] The Crimean War, the American Civil War, and the Franco-Prussian War all served to bolster the local economy, and a margin of the considerable profits filtered through to workers. To Irish immigrants, whose wages at home were estimated to average 6s. per week in 1861,[50] the North-east was a haven, for it was rare even in other parts of northern England for the average weekly wage to exceed 15s. In the North-east it commonly did.

Yet, while the region's average wage was comparatively high, the financial circumstance of Irish labourers was rarely as happy as this suggests. A great many of them did 'find constant employment at good wages', and enjoyed a 'condition of comparative prosperity', but the majority did not, and many were only seasonally employed.[51] In contrast to the Irish at Jarrow and Consett who liberally donated to Catholic schools,[52] the Irish at Seaham were 'out of work a considerable portion of their time', and (if the priest Belaney is to be believed) found it extremely difficult to raise £20 a year for church ground-rent.[53] The priest at St. Godric's, Durham, told the Poor Law Guardians in 1879 that many in his flock were 'unable month after month to pay to the school fees on account of unemployment'.[54] And the vicar of St. John's, Newcastle, believed that there were thousands in his parish earning less than 12s. in consequence of the layoffs in the shipyards in the early 1880s.[55] So while there were times of unexcelled prosperity, there were also times of considerable hardship and privation.

Although the recession in trade directly or indirectly affected the whole population of the area, the Irish were usually hit first and hit hardest. If work gangs had to be trimmed to meet slack in trade, the Irish were the first to be laid off. Moreover, in the iron trade, where labourers were paid on a 'piece work' basis in accordance with the current market value of the product, those who were not laid off saw reductions in their pay. Unlike skilled craftsmen, the Irish (along with other common labourers) seldom had any savings to fall back on, or any union agreements for a minimum wage. In the coal trade, even after it was unionised, there were great fluctuations in wages in relation to the 'sliding scale' of market prices. In 1873 the highest paid men in the pits, the hewers, were earning 7s. 9d. per day, but a year later only 4s. 6d.[56] In at least one industry, that of the glass and bottle works, foreign competition eliminated hundreds of jobs. Sunderland had thirty-six bottle houses in 1876, but only fourteen ten years later.[57] Newcastle's Board of Commerce noted in 1886 that 'whereas this locality was one of the chief seats of the crown glass and glass bottles, these industries have left the district'.[58] Thus, as one health officer noted of Newcastle earlier in the century, 'As in other seaports and manufacturing towns, there is a constant gravitation of unskilled labour towards this centre of commercial industry ... to make that valuable and important portion of the community feel the first effects of any stagnation of trade, or economic convulsion'.[59]

Strikes among the skilled trades and industrial lockouts were further threats to Irish livelihoods. Few Irishmen listening to Rev. Belaney would have cared to contradict his opinion of 'those ruinous and most suicidal things – called strikes', for, as non-unionised labour, they were most often its unintended victims.[60] Unable to draw union benefits while the strikes lasted, they reaped no rewards if union demands were met. The 1871 engineers' strike on Tyneside was sustained by the strikers obtaining outside employment, but the Irish labourers could do nothing but endure the consequences. The iron lockout of 1865 and the strike of 1866 forced many labourers who 'received no support', to sell their belongings to buy food.[61] Thus in 1877, the Bishop of the Diocese once again 'pleaded ...

the cause of the distressed poor (chiefly labourers in the iron works) of the Darlington district'.[62]

If the generally higher wages in the North-east served to compensate (sometimes generously) for the chiefly male employment, not all the Irish can be seen to have benefited, while their precarious place in the workforce meant that few could ever be economically secure. Since one of the consequences of the population increase was pressure on accommodation, rents remained consistently high – often higher than they were in London.[63] 'Very few rooms could be got in the worst part of Newcastle for less than 3s.', reported the commission of an early 1880s inquiry into the housing of the working class, 'and if they wanted a small back one as well they would have to pay 5s'.[64] In times of cutback, therefore, many Irish were left with little more than the average town labourer in Ireland had under normal conditions.

******

The willingness of the Irish to work for lower wages has often been interpreted as a motor for ethnic antipathy with the English. At the root of this not-unqualified argument lies the premise that the surfeit of Irish in some industries lowered the demand for, and hence the remuneration of, indigenous labour. Native workers, it is claimed, sensed a threat to their standard of living and therefore lashed out at the Irish competitors. As expressed before the Committee on Emigration in 1827, the anticipated effects of Irish immigration would be:

> most fatal to the happiness of the labouring classes in England, because there will be a constant and increasing immigration from Ireland to England, which will tend to lower the wages of labour in England, and to prevent the good effects arising from the superior prudence of the labouring classes in this country.[65]

Although some, such as Sir Robert Peel, did not wish to 'condemn too precipitately the incursion of Irish labourers into England', the opinion of others that the Irish could have only a deleterious effect upon the country was widely heard.[66] It was blatantly obvious during the famine that the crowds of Irish paupers 'seeking Employment in England, and willing to work for the lowest Wages, were thus reducing the Remuneration of Labour, and lowering the standard of Comfort and of Subsistence in this Part of the United Kingdom'.[67] And there can be no doubt that many entrepreneurs ruthlessly exploited the cheap and available Irish labour, and in so doing undercut the cost of English labour. In downturns in trade when the labour market was glutted, such as after the Napoleonic Wars, Irish labour could often be cheaply procured when the English workers refused to take a cut in wages. Or in industries where employment for common labourers was restricted the Irish, if available, were eagerly sought after. The Irish reaper, for example, who 'always bargained for money, milk, and some beer', frustrated co-operative attempts by the English for higher wages and was, therefore, welcomed by farmers.[68] In Morpeth in 1850 local labourers were demanding 3s. per day for the harvest and it was 'much to the disappointment of the masters that the grey-coated Irish are wanting'.[69] Conversely, other employers in the area were pleased with the 'great number of Irish reapers ... fully employed in cutting the corn'.[70] Indigenous workers were naturally indignant. Mewburn noted that the consequence of the Irish reapers coming to south Durham in 1830 was that 'an extraordinary degree of exasperation arose amongst the labourers in the village, and in many places the Irishmen were completely put *hors de combat*'.[71] Lord Durham's agent, Henry Morton, remarked in 1837:

> I dare say you have often observed that the poor Irish have been mobbed and driven away from the public works by the English and Scotch labourers. They drove them away from the Hartlepools, and I know that the Farm Labourers in Northumberland frequently drove them away during harvest in order to get higher wages. The working classes have all a decided dislike to Irishmen whom they consider lower the price of labour in this country.[72]

Morton's use of the word 'consider' bears weight, for it is not clear that the Irish *did* lower English wages wherever they went. Evidence in 1836 permitted the commissioners reporting on the Irish poor in Great Britain to conclude that 'when it is said that the Irish settlers in Great Britain have lowered wages, nothing more is probably meant than they have enabled the actual extent of work to be done at the existing rates'.[73] The commissioners went so far as to state that it was conceivable that wages 'might perhaps have been lower, if the manufacturing districts of England and Scotland had not at their command a large and (as compared with their wants) an unlimited supply of Irish labourers'. Moreover, it was only in specific occupations or in those sections of certain industries where the unskilled labour of the Irish and English were in direct competition that the Irish inadvertently prevented wage increases and, thereby, nurtured animosities.

The economic boom in Durham and Newcastle ameliorated the forces conducive to ethno-religious discord. The demand for labour through the expansion of the economy reversed the earlier competition for jobs. Thus 'the importation of Irish families for the working of the mills and ironworks recently established in [Darlington]',[74] or those imported into Seaham Harbour by the Londonderrys (referred to by Belamey)[75] created no disturbances and raised few eyebrows in the local press.[76] This was in marked contrast to Wales where upon the arrival of hundreds of famine victims in Newport (who had been sent by Irish agents) an era of troubled race relations was initiated.[77] Whenever the Welsh economy slackened violent clashes resulted, such as that which forced the expulsion of the Irish from the Rhondda Valley in 1857.[78]

In the North-east, the demand for labour relaxed even the tightest traditional controls, for the earlier dependence on jobs such as agriculture, mining and railway construction was greatly reduced. With an abundance of employment for both Irish and English, the former's threat to the other's security was nearly abolished. In agriculture, the Irish were opposed decreasingly as a result of migrations of indigenous labour to town industries.[79] Quite literally, the field for Irish employment became more open.

Under these conditions it was both impossible and undesirable to inhibit Irish employment, but discrimination against them *within* trades was widely practiced. Although the 'greater majority of those entering the region during the peak phases of immigration were...without particular skills',[80] it was the non-Irish who gained the greatest economic mobility.[81] The English worker was preferred for the semi-skilled operations and could, without difficulty, advance to the skilled trades; the Irish worker was almost always bound to manual labour. This was not necessarily the effect of prejudice; as the *Newcastle Daily Chronicle* opined,

> If in the workshop the sons of Erin are sometimes subjected to a little chaff, they are seldom the victims of prejudice. This, which we believe to be the general state of sentiment in England towards the Irish race, is in an eminent degree the sentiment of these northern parts. Tyneside is famous for its hospitality.[82]

However, the reality was probably closer to the view expressed by an alderman from Sunderland in the course of the 'Fenian scare' in October 1867: 'ill feeling might be prevented if Irishmen were treated with proper respect and had the chance of appointments for which they were otherwise well qualified'.[83] Yet this occupational discrimination may actually have served to minimise friction between the 'races', for it permitted non-Irish wages consistently to surpass those of the Irish. This, together with the knowledge that the Irish would be the first to be laid off during cut-backs, gave the non-Irish further security, while the lack of Irish occupational mobility meant that they would take over only the lowest-paid jobs. To some extent this eliminated the scope for animosities in the immediate working environment; more importantly, it prevented the Irish from undermining the occupations and wages of the non-Irish.

Closer examination of the frictions that existed between Irish and non-Irish in the North-east indicates that occupational competition was rarely the source. On railway construction, low-paid Irish labour amidst alternative employment for the non-Irish, meant that the Irish were little threat. The few reports of disturbances that reached the press from the isolated railway camps more frequently point to clashes over differences in religious practice. Most common was the outrage of Scotch Presbyterians at the Irish attitude to the Sabbath as a day of recreation rather than God-fearing piety.⁸⁴ In places of labour shortage, like West Hartlepool, clashes with the Irish were frequent, but had more to do with urban growing pains than occupational threats or racial intolerance.⁸⁵ As the *Newcastle Chronicle* noted of the 'mixed nationalities' at Consett, 'together in the harmony of labour … sometimes unhappily their differences break out when they are at 'play'.⁸⁶ Such 'play' could become 'alarming', as in one riot between the Irish and English in Consett which lasted 'for several hours, during which from forty to fifty on each side were more or less disabled by cuts and bruises', and from which three persons subsequently died.⁸⁷ But riots like this were infrequent and, like the more common Saturday night affrays in public houses, were largely extraneous to occupation.⁸⁸ The prosperity of the population as a whole, in tandem with social and religious factors discussed earlier, meant that persecution was minimal. For Durham and Newcastle, therefore, particularly apposite is E.P. Thompson's insight that 'it is not the friction but the relative ease with which the Irish were absorbed into the working-class communities which is remarkable'.⁸⁹

The apparent exception was in the coal industry, where the use of Irish 'blacklegs' or 'knobsticks' is reputed to have played an instrumental role in defeating the aims of striking colliers. Repeated allusions to the use of Irish in the pitmen's strike of 1844 have tended to give rise to an undisputed legend of the widespread use of Irish strikebreakers in the North-east. Because the Irish *were* utilised in that strike, it has tended to be assumed that they were deployed similarly in other of the region's labour disputes.

In fact, Irish strikebreakers were a rarity. There is no evidence that they were employed in the coal strikes prior to 1844, while the experience gained through that strike, as we shall see, did not encourage their further use. As regards the use of Irish in labour disputes in other major industries there is little evidence. In the iron lockout of 1865 and the prolonged strike of 1866, when the workers refused to take a 10 percent cut in wages, the Irish were themselves locked out and in some instances resorted to militant action.⁹⁰ It was only after they had been unemployed for seven months and had suffered the worst consequences that some of the Irish in Middlesbrough and elsewhere began to defect from the ranks. But in the majority of strikes in the North-east the Irish could not act in a subversive manner, for the strikers were most often skilled tradesmen while potential Irish blacklegs were nearly always not. Thus seldom was any thought given to the introduction of Irish labour to replace striking craftsmen. Ironically, the prolongation to twenty-one weeks of a shipwrights' strike at Hylton,[91] near Sunderland, was caused by the disputed use of non-union Irish labour for 'boring', but no attempt was made to employ these Irish during the course of the strike. Again, in the better-known engineering workers' strike on Tyneside in 1871,[92] the labouring Irish did not replace the skilled workers. Some tradesmen were imported from Ireland, but the overwhelming majority of blacklegs were secured by agents sent to Denmark, Germany, Holland, Belgium and other dockyards of England.

The use of Irish in the miners' strike of 1844 has not only engendered popular misconceptions concerning the use of blacklegs in the North-east, but has itself given rise to myth. Typical, is the view of historian Eric Strauss that 'the abuse of Irish labour as blacklegs against British workers was not confined to the industrial west coast nor to the textile trades: the great strike in the Tyneside collieries in July 1844 was defeated, at least in Durham, by the mass importation of Irishmen'.[93] An examination of what actually transpired between April and September 1844 reveals that the number of Irish imported was relatively small and that they were not responsible for the defeat.

It is true that the mass importation of Irishmen, was often publicly *threatened* by the owners in attempts to scare the miners back to work. Only eighteen days after the strike's commencement rumours began to circulate, supposedly from the Coal Trade Office, that 'arrangements are in progress for introducing several hundreds of Irish labourers into the collieries'.[94] A month later the *Tyne Mercury* announced that:

we are informed a positive offer has been made to bring a large number (from 5,000 to 10,000) of Irish workmen to Newcastle, the expense of doing which would be moderate, the steam-boat fare being only 2s 6d per passenger across the Channel, and workmen would be landed within five hours distance of the Coal district.[95]

But another article in the same issue of the *Tyne Mercury* revealed that a deputation of union delegates had already met with:

> an authorised party as the representatives of the Newcastle Hibernian Society, and the result of the interview was that the Hibernian Society had transmitted communications to London, and to the repeal wardens of different towns throughout England and Ireland, advising them to prevent the immigration into Northumberland and Durham of more Irish labourers.[96]

The *Northern Star* spread the alarm; in a 'Warning to Irishmen' it appealed:

> to the warm and generous hearted sons of the Green Isle to remain at home, and as a warning, the whole of their brethren in Newcastle-upon-Tyne have held a public meeting in order to apprise them not to be duped or deluded by any fair promise the employers or their agents may make to them .... At the above meeting the following resolution was unanimously agreed to – 'That the meeting having heard the manly and straightforward statements of the deputation of miners, do hereby agree to use all legal and constitutional means to prevent our countrymen from being deluded and entrapped by being induced to leave their native land to crush the miners of Northumberland and Durham'.[97]

That the owners had only been employing scare tactics was made clear in the 'Address of the Special Committee .... To the Coal Owners' of 29 June, which was subsequently published in the local press.[98] There it was stated that the time had at last come for the owners to have 'recourse to the extreme measure of obtaining a supply of workmen from other parts of the United Kingdom'. But the union, in earlier giving countenance to the rumours of a threatened Irish importation, had in effect, pulled the rug from under. Although the address of 29 June was itself partially for effect, the warning to the Irish was in part responsible for the failure of the Coal Owners' Association to act upon their threat.

With the exception of Lord Londonderry, those owners who managed to procure Irish blacklegs did so from other parts of England and in small groups only. Fifty men, 'principally Irish' were reported to have been conveyed to Cramlington pit in early June,[99] and others were reported to be employed at Seaton Delaval. Most of these Irish were secured by the coal owners' agents who, armed with promises of high wages, beer, tobacco and protection, lured workers from the railway and dock excavation crews. Of course the owners were anxious to show that the Irish workmen were as valuable as the locals, and the anti-union press made space for their eulogies. But few Irish took a liking to the work and most soon left the employment. It was stated at a meeting of pitmen on 15 July that '12 Irishmen at one colliery, and 14 at another. . .had already left: that 36 more had gone from Seaton Delaval and Cramlington'.[100] As stated before the Poor Law Commissioners in 1855, when they asked about the numbers of Irish in the area's pits: 'they are very rare; they do not make good miners'.[101] The owners learned this the hard way during the course of the strike, making the arrival of 204 Welsh miners at Cramlington and Seaton Delaval a typical welcome event.[102] Indeed, references to 'strangers' in the *Miners' Advocate*, as in the reports of the Coal Owners' Association and the local press, are most often to men brought in from other parts of England, Scotland, and Wales.

The Irish retreat from the pits was hastened by the hostile atmosphere surrounding all blacklegs. Though, compared with the 1832 strike, violence was negligible,[103] small affrays and verbal belligerence greeted blacklegs wherever employed. Reports such as the fracture of the shaft rope at Thornley, which killed two blacklegs and brought 'great shouting and marks of rejoicing' from a 'mob, consisting principally of women' served as widespread discouragements.[104] The Irish had no desire to provoke such antagonism for work which neither suited them nor was the goldmine they had been promised.[105] Most therefore, departed the pits well before the strike was over.

The best instance of the use of Irish blacklegs in the strike of 1844 (and the example most commonly relied upon to substantiate the general claim of Irish strikebreakers in the North-east) was Lord Londonderry's importation of workers from his estates in County Down. Londonderry's action has been seen as in character with the ultra-Tory aristocratic individualism that made him as much the despair of the members of the Coal Vend as he had formerly been to his 'colleagues' in the House of Lords.[106] He has been described as a man with 'a slightly crazy consistency, especially in the extremism with which he conducted cavalry charges against any measure or men who threatened to override the basic principle that a man should be allowed to do what he liked with his own'.[107] An uncompromising autocratic entrepreneur, Londonderry was untypical of other local coal owners and was entirely dissimilar to the other two 'grandees' of the local trade, the Earls of Durham and Ravensworth. Neverthless, his place in the pantheon of industrial ogres is deceptive, for Londonderry often displayed surprising sparks of humanity and tolerance, or at least *noblesse oblige*. Towards the Irish and towards Catholics he often sounded the most un-Tory opinions.[108] In the strike of 1844 his behaviour was not without some of these quirks.

For at least the first two months of the strike he had nothing to do with blackleg labour. With stockpiles of coal with which to oversell the Coal Vend prices, the strike was a source of considerable profit. While other owners before the end of April were desperately seeking means to crush the strike and hiring blacklegs at considerable expense, Londonderry and his chief agent Nathaniel Hindhaugh were delighting at their unbounded profits.[109] It was not until early June, when the stockpiles were exhausted, that Londonderry grew concerned. Desirous that his pits should be first in operation to take advantage of the inflated prices, he held a mass meeting of his colliers and implored them to return to work, threatening that he would supplant them with workers from his Comber estate in Ireland.[110] Unlike the Coal Owners' Association, Londonderry was prepared to back up his threat, but it is noteworthy that he proceeded with caution. He wrote to Hindhaugh on 28 June: 'I am curious to see what moral effect the arrival of our 20 Irishmen will create', adding 'the Coal Trade are very wrong in thinking to force a general turn out of the miners from their houses. Each Colliery must be left to its own Discretion ... Keep our efforts quiet'.[111]

In fact, thirty-five Irishmen arrived on 29 June and were immediately dispatched to Rainton Colliery where 'the women got about our men and a Catholic priest was sent to speak to them from Houghton-le-Spring who invited them to chapel to-day, however, they resisted all these things'.[112] Londonderry's overviewer, George Hunter, described them as 'a few as likely men as I ever saw for the purpose', and recommended that the importation be vigorously followed up with 100 more Irishmen, adding the enticement that they 'will work for less wages than our old Colliers'.[113] Under guard, the Irish were put to work in Adventure pit where 'they did extremely well the first day earning 2s 6d or 2s 8d'.[114] They were all, reported Hunter, 'in capital spirits and have written to their families and friends in Ireland to come to them. I have no doubt but these people will answer our purpose, at least as far as we can judge at present'. Hunter implored Londonderry to allow him to 'send for another 100', for 'if we continue to bring over a supply from Ireland I think we will soon put an end to [the strikers] ... proceedings, in fact I see no alternative but to establish our Collieries in full work with these men from Ireland'. But Londonderry was not so keen, leading Hunter to complain on 2 July 'you are wrong in preventing me from getting more people from Ireland'.[115]

Londonderry's private reservations were not those he exposed to the striking miners in the broadsheet he posted on 3 July. In this he pointed out that the pits were operating in spite of the strike and implored the men to 'look upon the ruin you are bringing on your wives, your children, your county, and the country. In twelve weeks more the collieries will be peopled by foreigners, and you will have neither shelter, protection, or work. While there is time – reflect!'[116] Below this the broadsheet warned:

> I have now brought Forty Irishmen to the pits; and I will give you all *one more week's notice*. And if by the 13th of this month a large body of my pitmen do not return to their labour, I will obtain one hundred more men, and proceed to eject that number, who now are illegally and unjustly in possession of my houses; and in the following week another one hundred shall follow.

The ultimatum, which admittedly was cast 'not [in] the language of tyranny, but of pleading' was interpreted as the limit in pomposity.[117] As the *Dublin Monitor* put it, 'Lord Londonderry has taken just such a part in the affair as any one might expect that he would'.[118] With bitter sarcasm, the paper went on:

> There is wisdom, too (if you could understand it), in replacing them strikers with your Irish serfs. It will hide the workings of the property system in this country. An excellent mode it is of draining the over-charged surface of Downshire, to carry off the superfluities a hundred fathom or so beneath the spires of Durham Cathedral. Nevertheless, it seemeth unkind toward these convenient, easy tools or your marquisate's high displeasure, at the very moment when you are using them for so agreeable a purpose, that you should brand them as *foreigners*. 'In twelve weeks more', you say, 'the collieries will be peopled by foreigners'. That is an ugly word, my lord; Irishmen do not like it.

The effect of this publicity was to exonerate the Irish by making them appear as the serfs of the Marquis, while Londonderry's own character was thoroughly blackened. Londonderry of course cared less. Only a day after his broadsheet was tacked up over the county, he wrote: 'I am fully aware [that] the importation of Irish is a great evil. Discord and Disaffection around us, poverty increasing, Poor Rates more burthen ... yet it is of Evils the least, because standing still is Ruin – No Coals – No Money'.[119]

Meanwhile, the agent at Comber proceeded according to his instructions to make ready the sending off of 100 men in 'portion of 50'.[120] Londonderry's other agents were becoming 'anxious ... to do without them, but there is no alternative and if another week does not bring the men to work, we may allay our Accounts and act upon what you state in Hand Bill'.[121] Thus by 13 July neither

Londonderry nor his agents had much appetite to follow through the threat in the broadsheet. Grimly they stuck to the policy that 'our movements in Ireland must be governed by the Conduct of our Men here'.[122]

A gap in the extant letters prevents tracing the introduction of the promised Irishmen or determining exactly how many arrived. And, as Londonderry wanted to keep the Coal Trade Office in the dark about his activities during the strike, the Office's circular of 17 August (one of whose questions asked for the number of outside 'strangers' imported for the strike) was not answered. 'I think you will agree with me', wrote Hunter, 'that these Questionnaires are quite unnecessary'.[123] Two years later, however, Seymour Tremenheere, the Commissioner for the *Report on the State of the Population in the Mining Districts*, was told by one of Londonderry's agents that [only] 180 Irishmen had been imported.[124] This figure is probably correct, for by the end of July 1844 some of the strikers were returning to work and Hunter was of the opinion that 'we ought not to send for any more Irishmen at present, as it is evident we will get old Hands of our own to work'.[125] As less than 200 men could scarcely put one pit into full operation, it is obvious that among Londonderry's fifteen or so collieries, the Irish could have had little effect in breaking the will of the strikers.[126] Although Londonderry was quoted in the *Sheffield Independent* on 3 August 1844 as saying that from personal experience the Irish made the best blacklegs and that 'though at first rather inefficient hands, they are now tolerable workmen',[127] he was on the same day recruiting 'from 200 to 500' miners from Gloucester, and 50 to be sent from Wales.[128] Scare tactics were swept aside; the object became 'only to *Make Hay* and care for Nobody but ourselves'.[129] It now became Hunter's turn to show restraint, but Londonderry had lost all patience and castigated him.[130]

By August the men had been out of work for over four months. They were all in debt and not a little strike-weary. Their leaders told them that 'all the Irish in the world can do us no harm if we only stick firm',[131] but numbers of men were leaving the union and, worse, the weekly output of coal was rapidly increasing through the use of experienced miners from other regions.[132] The miners assumed that they would be given preference over the Irish at the strike's end, but they were less sure that they would supplant the Welsh and Cornish miners whose importations had cost the owners as much as £6 and £7 per family.[133] If importations continued not only would their demands be sabotaged, but they would lose their jobs. The colliers therefore broke their own ranks and offered to return to work because the pits were filling up with competent miners who were starving them and their union out of existence.

In the aftermath of the strike it became apparent that only Londonderry had procured Irish blacklegs in any forthright manner or in any significant proportion.[134] But even Londonderry gained little immediate satisfaction. When the Irish expressed a desire to leave the employment, Hunter had 'no objections ...; it will be well if the Irish will go, as they are a heavy charge upon us – indeed (as no one wanted to admit during the strike) 'they don't average above *half a man*'.[135] By October 1844 another bunch of Irish were 'for being off at the end of the Month', to Hunter's relief since the Irish had not been the mindless serfs he had hoped:

> the change of pay being altered has made a wonderful difference amongst them – those who did only hew 6, 7, 8, & 9 tubs a-day are now hewing 12, 14, 16, & 20 tubs – only look at such knaves – the fact is they have not acted honourably with us at all.[136]

By 25 October seventy-seven Irish remained at Rainton Pit and a dozen at Pensher. But 'from the notices', wrote Hunter, 'we calculate that we will have notice from 39 this week, which will leave us fifty ... I think they will all dwindle off'.[137]

Irish blacklegs cannot, therefore, be seen to have played a significant role in the outcome of the 1844 strike. Their use by Londonderry did little in itself to frighten the men back to work, nor to inspire other coal owners to adopt the same tactic. That the Irish later entered the pits in considerable numbers and did so unopposed, suggests that they did not become the ogres of local folklore they are reputed to have done in Wales.[138] Non-Irish blacklegs were always seen to be more culpable than the Irish for the union defeat,[139] but the blacklegs themselves did not blind the union men to their real enemies, the employers. Thus the legends surrounding figures like Londonderry came to have much greater meaning in the local history of the workers' struggles, while the small part played by the Irish blacklegs was fairly soon forgotten.

******

If the significance of Irish blacklegs in the North-east has been exaggerated and mythologised by historians, so too has the alleged 'natural' reluctance of the Irish to join local trade unions. Admittedly, the evidence for the latter is readily marshalled. Already in 1836 it was being posited that 'the Irish in Great Britain are not in general members of trades, or mechanics, they have not often been placed in circumstances in which it was possible for them to appear as leaders in such associations'.[140] Admitting that 'they appear to have been at least as active as the natives whenever they had an opportunity of combining', well into the 1880s these opportunities were infrequent in the North-east.

A number of factors prevailed. The fact that wages in the better areas of employment seemed high, compared to the poverty the Irish had fled, delayed initiatives to join unions. As well, the nature of the employment, often piece-work on contract, was not conducive to co-operative bargaining efforts. Piece-work put the labourer in competition with his own exertion and, ultimately, in competition with other workers performing the same job employed in the same way. The emphasis was thus on the individual. It is noteworthy that the only category of Tyneside workers containing Irishmen that attempted to form a union in the 1870s were the 'helpers' in the shipyards who were paid on a time-work basis.[141]

The congregating and eventual monopoly of Irish in certain industrial sectors also tended to shelter them from the ideas and institutions of the native workers. The Catholic Church furthered this protection and separation. By waging its implacable war against 'secret societies', the Church divested the Irish of the working-mens' clubs, which had previously served as links with English trade unionists. A salutary role played by the Newcastle Hibernians in the strike of 1844, for instance, was no longer possible after the Church's suppression of such societies. The substitution of Church-controlled and priest-led organisations was no substitution at all. Catholic Friendly Societies or branches of the Catholic Institute were hardly respected by non-Catholic labourers, while the societies themselves gave little encouragement to the solidarity of Irish workers for bargaining purposes. Without effective labour organisations and leadership the Irish were, in effect, industrial eunuchs.

Prior to 1840 the Catholic Church had followed a fairly strong anti-unionist policy based on the suspicion that secret oaths were involved in initiating union members. The case of the Tolpuddle Martyrs in 1834 convinced the Vicars Apostolic that their suspicions had been correct and that trade unions smacked of subversion. But with the wider adherence of working men to trade unions and their less secretive nature, the Church relaxed its stand. The social condition of Irish immigrants, and their obvious exploitation, forced many priests to side with the workers and in some cases to openly criticise employers.[142] Church leaders remained non-committal, however, and it was not until 1865, with the introduction of Cardinal Manning's brand of social Catholicism, that the Catholic clergy got a better steer. Manning generally shifted the clergy more towards sympathy with workers and largely abolished the stigma against Catholic involvement in trade unions, even if he was careful not to commit the Church too far. Papal legitimacy had to wait until Leo XIII's *Rerum Novarum* of 1891.[143]

For the most part, as long as there was neither secrecy nor subversion, Catholic workers had no impediments to entering a union after 1840. But since Irish employment was primarily outside the trade-organised unions and among the lowest-paid, there was little opportunity for such involvement. It was not until the rise of 'New Unionism' in the 1880s and 1890s, with the organisation of unskilled workers, that the bulk of the Irish could become union-affiliated.[144] By 1893 the general manager of Palmer's works could state that 'we are not employing a single man at the present moment who is not in one society or the other – from the highest skilled mechanic down to the commonest labourer'.[145] On Tyneside many of the Irish were incorporated into the Tyneside and National Labour Union, later the National Amalgamated Union of Labourers.[146] The number of Irish names among North-eastern labour spokesmen in the reports of commissions of inquiry into labour in the 1890s also suggests that once unionised they soon assumed roles of leadership in the local unions.

Ironically, before 1880 the place of greatest union penetration by the Irish in the North-east was the miners' union. Almost from the inception of the Durham Miners' Association (DMA) in 1869, the Irish played an important part. Aside from the ostracism that often resulted from not joining, the DMA offered many Irish their first real chance for economic security. By the 1880s the Irish were an integral part of the Association, as may be judged by the executive's minutes where numerous wage and rights appeals on behalf of the Irish in local branches are to be found. A list of candidates who had been elected by the local lodges in 1885 to stand for the election of the executive reveals that at least 10 percent were Irish or of Irish extraction.[147] William Crawford, the first head of the new union, was always sympathetic to the Irish and throughout the 1880s he made numerous speeches disapproving of coercion in Ireland and in support of Irish nationalism.[148] And at the DMA's annual galas there was always at least one Irish politician of national reputation on the rostrum, from J. O'Connor-Power in 1876 to T.D. Sullivan in 1890.[149] Although there continued to be a number of small strikes in an industry that employed blackleg labour, few of the blacklegs were Irish. The fact that the executive repeatedly exposed the hypocrisy of the miners in mingling with non-union men 'at home over your glass of beer, in your chapels, and side by side you pray with them' hardly suggests that they were Irish.[150] Indeed, John Denvir's mention of a coal strike near Seaham in 1890 points to the place of the Irish in the trade by that date:

> A recent strike at New Silksworth showed them Irish that this process of eviction was not entirely unknown on this side of the Channel.

The colliery owner was the Marquis of Londonderry, and on his behalf the work people with whom he had the dispute were evicted from their dwellings. It was singular that, when the first cottage was broken into and the furniture ejected, the first article brought out was a picture of Robert Emmet, and the second a picture of St. Patrick. When added to this the 'man of the house' was named Dunleavy, there cannot be much doubt as to his faith and nationality.[151]

A rather extraordinary strike at Ushaw Moor in 1882[152] further indicates the place of the Irish in the DMA as well as revealing the attitudes of the Catholic Church, non-Irish workers, and the public in general to the striking colliers. Ushaw Moor was a fairly new colliery which, like others of its kind, had attracted an Irish workforce. Not all of the approximately 200 workmen were Irish, but there were enough to warrant the a sizeable Catholic school and compel enlargement of the church at Newhouses.

The dispute began in the last week of 1881 when the president of the local union lodge was dismissed, allegedly for filling the coal tubs in an incorrect manner. A hasty meeting was convened and the men walked out. When the secretary of the DMA arrived he was careful to point out that 'the strike was for union principles, and exhorted ... [the men] not to remove away from the village on being evicted from their houses, as by so doing they would be abandoning the strike'.[153] Little did he realise the lengths to which the men would stand by the principle. Next on the scene was the local priest, Rev. Philip Fortin, 'respected by all classes of dwellers in the Dearness Valley', according to the *Durham Chronicle*.[154] Fortin 'expressed his warmest sympathy with the men and their families ... and proffered the use of the large schoolroom at Ushaw Moor for the women and children to shelter in'. Meanwhile the lodge president obtained the permission of Rev. C. Gillow of Ushaw College to erect a tent on one of the adjoining fields.

From its commencement the strike captured public sympathy. The evictions came at the worst time of year for weather; the remark by the pit's manager (Thomas Robinson) in the presence of William Crawford that the men were a 'set of lazy b———s;'[155] the kindness of Father Fortin and Ushaw College; the revelation that Fortin's generosity would cost the school the loss of the government capitation grant of £140;[156] and the exposure that the houses the men were driven from were the worst imaginable – all contributed to open the public's hearts and purses to the miners and their families. Even after nineteenth months of its 'somewhat monotonous history',[157] public support was not diminished. Provocation sustained it, not least that by the manager Robinson who sought to incite the Irish to violence by planting intimidators about the pithead, by smashing the Irishmen's pig crees before they had sold their pigs, and by harassing the women and children in the schoolroom.[158] Before finally resigning, he was prosecuted four times for crimes ranging from cutting down a private footbridge which lead to the pit, to shooting a young boy.[159] Fortin himself in the course of conducting his pastoral duties became the victim of Robinson's outrage. 'Much has been said about tyranny and despotism at Ushaw Moor', he wrote to the press:

> but now the manager seems determined to rule over the souls as well as the bodies of the unfortunate creatures in his power. This however, is not the first time he has outraged Catholic feeling ... Without any warning or notice he turned the Catholic teacher out of her house, throwing the furniture on the high road, where it still remains, and he has publicly expressed his desire to have 20 pounds of dynamite to blow up the school.[160]

'There is a limit', added the *Durham Chronicle*,

> beyond which no one in authority ought of go; and when it comes to pass that one placed in the capacity of an employer takes upon himself to say that those whom he employs shall not receive the ministrations of the clergy of their own faith, the public will be inclined to declare that the bounds of prudence have been overstepped ... No one can properly find fault with what Mr. Fortin has hitherto done.[161]

The public indeed felt that the limits had been overstepped and support for the striking miners was unbounded. Funds flowed in from all of the lodges as well as from Irish centres such as at the Consett Iron works;[162] several co-operative stores donated supplies, and cart loads of bread arrived weekly. Moreover, the Durham and Northumberland miners' hearty endorsement of the strike – shown also through their pilgrimages to the site for mass demonstrations – resulted in raising the strike pay from the usual 10s. per week to 16s.[163] When some isolated voices were raised in opposition to the strike, they were either condemned or ignored. One member of the Durham Board of Guardians in February 1882 attempted to use his position to attack the authorities of Ushaw College for their unparalleled behaviour. The result was a vote of condemnation against the member from the rest of the Board.[164] Noteworthy as well was the letter from a dissenting clergyman who wrote to the press to 'remind Father Fortin that the Roman Catholics, who possess the land of Ushaw Moor, will not allow the Dissenters to have a piece of land, for either love or money'.[165] But the anti-Catholic approach, even from a dissenting clergyman, could not alter the feelings of the mining population. Father Fortin, who earned himself the lasting title of the 'Pitmen's Priest',[166] was too highly respected.[167] And when Anglican Tories condemned the strikers from the bench and the pulpit,[168] or called Robinson' s management 'long, successful, and generous',[169] it only served the righteousness of the cause in the eyes of the majority. As the *Durham Chronicle* wrote at the fortieth week of the strike, 'Great interest is still displayed in the dispute, and the support given to the men on strike by their fellow workmen throughout the country is nearly as good as it was at the commencement of the conflict'.[170]

In his efforts to secure blacklegs, Robinson inspired further condemnation, but while his initial endeavours were frustrated, he eventually met with some success. Although Crawford stated in December 1882 that ' a full year has now passed away, and ... [full employment at the pit] has not yet been accomplished',[171] the pit was by then in partial operation. The strikers never defected. Nevertheless, by the strike's anniversary it was clear that the union had nothing but its existence to bargain with, while the owners had 'not the least intention of making an arrangement with them [strikers]'.[172] The men celebrated the anniversary with speeches from union delegates and Father Fortin, followed by a rendition of the

'True-Hearted ... ', 'sung in a very credible style'.[173] But there was a hollowness to both; the union was stumped and it knew it.

Ashamed to admit defeat, the strike continued. The men took their daily stroll to the pit-head to badger the workers and then went to Newhouses to show their gratitude to Father Fortin by volunteering their labour towards the rebuilding of the church. When the church reopened on St. Patrick's Day, 1883, the men were still on strike although in February the villain of the piece – Thomas Robinson – had resigned. When in August the Lords of the Privy Council 'expressed a desire that the school should be restored to its original use',[174] and the women and children were removed to the neighbouring villages the noose was tightened. For another four months the strike endured; the men were as united as ever but defeated in purpose. In November Crawford resolved to terminate the ordeal but the union, 'in its continued support of the men', rejected the proposal. Finally, in December, Crawford put the matter before the county, reciting the history of the strike, describing the plight of the evicted miners and, in a face-saving appeal to martyrdom for the 'sacrificed men', called for a vote from the miners to bring the strike to its sad conclusion.[175] An affirmative vote was counted.

The cost of the strike, £5,707 3s 6½d, has been described as purchasing 'nothing but ridiculous defeat'.[176] Yet for the Irish Catholics in the coal industry of Durham, the strike was a *succes d'estime*. No one could dispute that they had nobly served the union's cause for a principle basic to the rights and integrity of working people everywhere. The hanging of Father Fortin's portrait between the other 'worthies' at DMA headquarters was to be a lasting tribute to the privileged place of Catholicism among the miners as well as a proud symbol of the position of the Irish in one of the area's major unions.[177] If nothing else the case gives substance to the reflection of T.P. O'Connor in 1917 that 'the Irish miners very soon were able to form the friendliest relations with the English miners of Tyneside. They took part eagerly in the various movements of the Trade Unions to improve the conditions of their class'.[178]

The conclusions to be drawn from this material are not those which have persistently surrounded the history of the Irish in England. While the industrial composition of the North-east resulted in a relatively different spectrum of Irish occupations, the pace of the expansion heightened the need for, and the remuneration of, Irish labour as well as diminishing the potential for hostility surrounding it. As strikebreakers, their role has clearly been exaggerated and distorted by historians, while their role as strikers has been largely overlooked. Although their entry into unions was delayed by their position in the workforce and by combined socio-religious factors, when the opportunity for unionisation emerged it was seized. In short, on the shop floor too, Paddy met Geordie on terms not untoward.

Chapter 6

Political Awakenings

> Dungeons might enclose their bodies, sin might cover their souls inches deep, the drink of English public-houses might damn them ten thousand times, but they would never lose the love of their country.... Let Irishmen, then, rise in their thousands and do the best they could for themselves in a peaceful and constitutional sort of way. They must band themselves together firmly, must enter upon their great political campaign with ardour, and must never cease their agitation.
> Dr. Mallen at the 'Great Amnesty Demonstration on Newcastle Town Moor', *Newcastle Daily Chronicle*, 28 October 1872, p.3

> ...the worst thing about the Irish is that they become corruptible as soon as they stop being peasants and become bourgeois.
> Engels to Marx, 1869

> Nowhere had he found the exiles from Ireland more warm-hearted or more determined to do the best that in them lay for the welfare of their native land. .... He had also to thank the people of Newcastle for the care that they took of the interests of Ireland during the last general election. In dealing with Irish subjects, they got the greatest assistance from the two members from Newcastle-upon-Tyne.
> Parnell at the 'Great Meeting in the Town Hall', *Newcastle Daily Chronicle*, 10 Aug 1880, p.2

For the majority of Irish who came to Britain in the nineteenth century political action or direct involvement with English politics was not initially an option. Though often fervently patriotic for Ireland, the mass exploitation of that attachment for specific political ends had to wait until more basic struggles for existence had been dealt with. For many, in poverty, it was hardly possible to have more than a sentimental attachment to the politics of their more comfortably situated brethren. Some never got beyond the politics of the Catholic Church, while others found more interest in local politics than those particular to the homeland. Over the last third of the century, however, there was a general political awakening which developed into a national movement. This chapter traces that emergence, the politicisation of the Irish, and the local reactions to it.

******

Despite the evident desire of some historians to show a connection or at least a degree of empathy between the Irish immigrants and the early political movements of the working classes, few such bonds existed, while those that did were extremely tenuous.[1] Illustrative is Feargus O'Connor's failure to carry any large body of Irish immigrants over to Chartism and away from the politics of Daniel O'Connell.[2] O'Connor might have been 'an Irishman in the strictest sense of the word' but his nationality became incidental to his appeals for the People's Charter and did not serve as a basis for Irish support.[3] His relative lack of impact is palpable when compared to the popularity of the Lancashire-born, working-class Irishman Michael Davitt a quarter of a century later. Nor did Ribbon lodges in England make any significant contribution to Chartism. Not only were they constrained by the Church's opposition, but their agrarian concerns with tithes and rents in Ireland had little in common with the aims of English labourers.[4] Where the Irish did become involved with Chartism, it was most often to the detriment of the movement. By standing on the side of their employers, as in Wales,[5] or in deliberately disturbing Chartist meetings, as in Manchester,[6] they contributed only to its defeat.

In the North-east, where Chartism was weak, the Irish response to most labour movements was similarly adverse.[7] The interruption of Robert Owen's 'perpetration of blasphemy'[8] in Newcastle in 1843, for example, by a gang of Irishmen who 'forced an entrance, and soon compelled the audience to retreat through the doors and windows',[9] suggests that Catholicism was by far a stronger force. As noted by the Commissioners to the 1836 report on the Irish poor in Britain, 'the Irish appear to have little sympathy with the political or religious feelings of the natives, either in England or Scotland, and have taken little part in elections'.[10] As late as 1856, even though some urban Irish were enfranchised by the Small Tenements Act of 1850,[11] it was still possible to maintain that the Irish were 'upon the whole a peaceable body of men, who trouble themselves but little with the politics of the country'.[12]

The Irish were more interested – if interested at all – in the political affairs of the homeland. But although some early attempts were made to organise the Irish in England behind various Irish causes, their success was limited. Bernard McAnulty,[13] Newcastle's leading Irish spokesman from mid-century, is reputed to have established the Irish 'Precursor Society' as early as 1842, but it appears to have elicited little support.[14] Repeal Associations, backed by the moral force of Daniel O'Connell, fared better but, break-away factions, the death of O'Connell, and the failure of the Young Ireland uprising of July 1848 was to render Repeal an increasingly sterile issue over the next thirty years. As John O'Leary recollected of the Young Ireland movement in Ireland, it was the proud and not undeserved boast that it 'brought a soul back into Eire, but before Fenianism arose that soul had fled'.[15] In England what spirit had been aroused in the 1840s was soon exhausted. For, more than anything else, the famine and post-famine immigration sapped the political libido. McAnulty could write from the Corn Market in Newcastle in June 1848 that 'The friends of Ireland have formed a club here, called the "No.1 Newcastle-on-Tyne Felon Repeal Club" and ... one hundred and twenty-four members were enrolled in almost twenty minutes', but clubland for the majority of Irish was precluded by poverty.[16]

Under these economic circumstances, the confessional not the political rostrum served Irish wants. Although the Church did not attempt to suppress the political aspirations of its Irish flock, it ensured that their first allegiance was to itself by denying the sacraments to Hibernians, Freemasons, Ribbonmen and Fenians. The Church never tired of reminding the Irish that 'the better the Catholic the better the Irishman'. And just as the enfranchised working classes took their cue from their employers or their landlords, so those Irish who secured the vote took their lead from the Church. They were encouraged to clamour for the rights of the Church: to oppose bills and administrations that were hostile or unsympathetic to Catholic claims, and to support Catholic endowments and Catholic education. Because Irish and Catholic interests were inextricably bound together in the Independent Irish Party between 1852 and 1859,[17] the Irish had no hesitation in supporting this cause, though before the enfranchisement of 1867 they were 'a dead weight, contributing little to the political strength of Catholicism, while demanding a large share of social services and of the attention of Catholic politicians'.[18] Not until much later in the century, when the Church became publicly allied with the Conservatives over the education issue, did Irish politics and Church politics come into conflict.[19]

Adherence to the politics of the Church excluded the Irish from the main social and political reform movements of the period. Consequently, they were further alienated from those who might have been their natural allies in the struggle for Ireland, the working class. In supporting the Pope against Garibaldi, for instance, the Irish proved themselves opposed to liberal reform. As Disraeli proclaimed of his party's non-intervention policy in Italy, Catholics and Tories were 'natural allies'. The Irish on Tyneside saw no rapport between their feelings for Ireland and those of Garibaldi for Italy. In accord with statements of Cardinal Wiseman, the battle in Italy was quite simply a war on the Pope. In Newcastle in January 1860 Father Suffield:

> spoke to a crowd of six thousand labourers, assuring them that though the Temporal Power might be mentced [sic], the Spiritual Power would last as long as the world itself. The Church was entering on a period of martyrdom than which nothing was more spiritually grand. He urged the Catholics to demand the expulsion from the

Pope's dominions of the insolent foreigner who held the Sardinian dagger in one htnd [sic], English gold in the other.[20]

Catholics in the Diocese of Hexham and Newcastle not only gave public support to the Pope, but attempted to counter the English 'republican gold' with a Papal Fund, amounting to £1,042. 0s. 3d by October 1860.[21] And in St. Mary's Sunderland, as in Catholic Churches throughout England, a solemn requiem mass was held 'for the Irish Volunteers who had lost their lives in defence of the Holy Father in Italy'.[22] To the politicised English working class, however, Garibaldi was the hero of social revolution. Upon his arrival in Tyneside in April 1854 he was presented with 'a magnificent sword, indicative of the future hope of successful revolution in Italy'.[23] In 1860 the *Newcastle Daily Chronicle* gave open support to Garibaldian recruiting and when the mayor of Gateshead took exception, the Newcastle magistrates could find no grounds for prosecution.[24]

The contrary Irish-Catholic take on Garibaldi in turn coloured the view of Fenianism by Tynesiders. The phenomenon reflected, they believed, a distressing flaw within the Irish character. This seemed confirmed by a melee that took place at Newcastle races in June 1866. During the disturbance 'supposed Fenians, numbering several hundreds' belonging principally to Jarrow and the neighbourhood of the shipbuilding yards on the river'[25] were heard by witnesses to have shouted '"Down with Garibaldi"' and "May the Pope get to heaven"'.[26] Whether the Irish were Fenians or militant Roman Catholics (quite possibly they saw no conflict in being both) it is obvious that through this event the public came to regard both Fenianism and Catholicism as absurd Irishness totally out of touch with English politics. As one justice stated at the trial of the 'Town Moor Rioters', 'the sooner the people gave up such folly as was set forth by the Fenians the better. It was folly of the grossest kind … [but] why the Irish people disliked Garibaldi he did not know'.[27] For many locals, the observation of Charles Booth that 'amongst the Irish, rebellious blood turns not against both Church and State as in Italy, but against the State alone',[28] summed up these seeming contradictions.

Until the Fenian disturbances in England in the 1860s the politics of the Irish remained largely Church-controlled and, as such, were seldom in alignment either with English liberalism or working-class radicalism. Thereafter, increasingly, Irish leaders emphasised that 'it was the duty of every Irishman to do his utmost to secure the independence of his native country'.[29] Although the Church as late as 1895 in the face of Irish Nationalist opposition could still influence the Irish-Catholic vote, after the Fenian disturbances the politics of the Irish became far more secular.[30]

******

By the 1860s the Irish in the North-east had escaped much of their earlier destitution, but their social place remained low. At St. Patrick's Day celebrations in Newcastle in 1862 one spokesman 'drew attention to what was necessary to be done to raise the social status of the Irish in this town. He thought that it was highly desirable that they should have a Catholic newspaper in Newcastle, where their body was so numerous'.[31] No Irish Catholic press was established in Newcastle until 1884,[32] but recognition preceded it. The shooting of Sergeant Brett during the forced escape of Colonel Kelly and Captain Deary from the police van in Manchester in 1867, the subsequent capture of these and other Fenian 'criminals', the execution of the 'Manchester Martyrs' in November of that year, and the Clerkenwell prison explosion in the following month, all served to give the Irish in England unprecedented notoriety – indeed, to put them for a time in the forefront of public interest. Local editorialists now became keenly aware of their Irish communities, and the first of the national tabloids, the *Pall Mall Gazette*, supplied them with frightening figures of their actual size from the 1861 census.[33] Police authorities debated wearing guns, army garrisons fortified their security, and municipal officials began to investigate the whereabouts and extent of stored explosives. Bloody-faced Irishmen turned up at police stations to report dastardly outrages that had been perpetrated upon them for not supporting their local Fenian organisation.[34] In the dark hours of the morning more than one pedestrian saw, or thought he saw,

Irish brigades drilling on barren field or moor. Even Her Majesty, while staying at Balmoral, was not spared shocking rumours of a Fenian attempt to kidnap her.[35] If the Irish had been the forgotten victims of English exploitation, with amazing swiftness they became the dreaded Fenians. With American funds and ammunition, they were bent, seemingly, on the overthrow of all that was sacred to Britain.

While the Irish in Manchester received the greatest amount of public attention and came under the most scrutiny by the authorities, the Irish in the North-east soon gave rise to considerable alarm. *The Times*, which noted the 'outbreak of Fenianism ... at Newcastle races a year and a quarter ago', reported in October, 1867, that:

> A good deal of anxiety prevails in the north of England with regard to the movements of the Fenians. A large number of the lower order of Irish are employed in the factories, ironworks, and iron shipbuilding yards of the Tyne and Tees, and in some of the pit districts of Durham and Northumberland, and of late midnight drillings and other such like movements have been observed among them. All the garrisons and barracks are now guarded by soldiers.... Fears, however, are entertained of street outrages, and if such were to occur they would be almost certain to bring conflict between the lower orders of English and Irish....[36]

In another article *The Times* quoted the Mayor of Middlesbrough as saying that while 'nothing like danger in the town from Fenianism was apprehended..., it was the duty of the council and the duty of everyone to be forearmed'.[37] It was also noted that both Hartlepool and Sunderland had increased the strength of their constabulary. When a letter was intercepted by London detectives which contained an accurate depiction of the plans of the garrison at Berwick, rumours were rampant of a threatened invasion 'by a party of Fenians who were to come from the south'.[38] The militia were put 'on duty day and night, and their arms... fully charged' and the coastguard were readied for action.[39] The 22nd Regiment was put to guard Tynemouth garrison while the nipples were 'removed from the rifles stored in the Armoury in Nelson Street, Newcastle'.[40] Alleged Fenian recruiting at Hartlepool, South Shields, Sunderland, Stockton and Middlesbrough in October brought about the enrolment of special constables from householders, shopkeepers and the Volunteer Corps.[41] After the Clerkenwell explosion these precautionary measures were stepped up in response to the circular from the Home Office to the mayors of some fifty towns 'requesting that special constables may be sworn in for the preservation of property and the suppression of any riotous proceedings'.[42]

Public reaction in the North-east was not dissimilar to that found in other areas of Irish settlement in England. The statement at the trial of the Town Moor rioters that the Fenians 'seemed to be people who, in the first place, must be fools... come from America to Ireland, hoping, with the assistance obtained from America, to overturn the English Government', was fairly typical of insular thinking on the subject.[43] That the Irish Revolutionary Brotherhood had been in existence in Ireland since the 1850s, and that it had been a growing concern of Dublin Castle, was little known. When the British did hear of Fenianism, during the period of its greatest strength in Ireland, in 1865,[44] most agreed with *The Times* that 'a more extravagant and chimerical idea never entered the head of an Irishman. ... It is entirely of exotic growth, an importation from America, and entirely out of harmony with real Irish sentiment'.[45] From 1865 onwards the Fenian 'threat' received sporadic public attention, occasionally being the subject of an editorial as, for example, when a shipload of arms was seized in Cork in November 1866. On this event the *Newcastle Daily Chronicle* commented that 'the Fenian conspiracy is once more raising its head, promising to create uneasiness in this country, and probably a great deal of alarm in Ireland'.[46]

That by the end of 1866 the Fenian 'scare' was part of every-day conversation in the North-east and that the Irish were being regarded with some suspicion is illustrated by the 'Fenian outbreak' that took place near West Hartlepool in December of that year.[47] The incident occurred when fourteen Irishmen, who had been issued with pike poles and boat hooks to retrieve some jettisoned cargo on the beach, entered the local public house and jokingly announced that they were 'Fenianism come to invade Seaton'. The barmaid, who later admitted that they 'looked like Fenians',[48] fled to the local constable and raised the alarm. 'The village was kept in pandemonium for nearly two hours', stated the *Durham Chronicle*, until 'a body of armed policemen from West Hartlepool could be called to quell the disturbance'.[49] The Irishmen, fleeing when the police were called, eventually gave themselves up rather than remain out in the cold night. They were subsequently charged 5s and costs and the matter became, according to a local writer, a huge joke among the local inhabitants. In the national press, however, the fourteen became an army of fifty Fenians, and the pike poles were pointed at policemen's breasts.

The events in Manchester in September of the following year temporarily turned local Fenianism into a deadly earnest issue. But the sheer number of false rumours about Kelly being spotted in Durham City and Weardale or his expected arrival in Newcastle,[50] together with abundant reports on local Fenian organisations, soon altered the public temper. There was a backlash against the police who were believed to be exaggerating the alarm. As a local wag put it:

> 'There has been a fearful outbreak' of the Fenian villains, exclaim a crowd of old women of both sexes, – O dear no, but of panic and fright amongst a good few people in authority, whom we generally expect to find with their heads tolerably well set on their shoulders ... in the north-eastern districts we hear of no 'movements' of an alarming character except among the police.[51]

In Sunderland, where the town council had become divided between 'Revolver and Anti-Revolver' factions, a level voice cautioned that 'the evil they all deplored had its origin, more or less, in the conviction ... that there was danger where there were a large number of Irishmen', but there was in fact no foundation to the many rumours 'except in the morbid imagination of those who circulated them'.[52] The *Newcastle Daily Chronicle*, which had earlier spoken of 'large numbers of Irishmen [who] are still madly bent upon any wild movement to which their leaders may summon them', was by the middle of October calling Fenianism so much humbug.[53] 'The farce succeeds the tragedy', ran one editorial which spoke of 'the public ... being entertained by the farce of constabulary alarm' and Fenianism as the 'scapegoat of every villain in England'.[54]

But the Clerkenwell explosion of 13 December 1867 was no farce and in its wake the aspersions cast on the local police came to a rapid halt. For a brief while the Fenian 'scare' became the Fenian 'panic' and the fear and anger that was provoked was by no means safely contained in London. It 'is quite clear', wrote the *Newcastle Daily Chronicle*, 'that a sufficient number of the disaffected can at any time be got together, ready to venture upon any enterprise, no matter how lawless and desperate its character .... Should such outrages become of frequent repetition, the Irishman in England will be regarded and treated as no better than a wild beast.'[55] Some doubtless already thought so, or always had. But local fears and whipped-up prejudices were soon allayed; only a week later the *Chronicle* was calling for sanity and level-headedness. To the proposal that the Irish workforce in England should be dismissed, it replied:

> There could not possibly be a more preposterous proposition. The idea ... is monstrous .... After what has happened, the metropolis had indeed cause for apprehension, but this cure for terror would be very quickly found worse than the disease ... If the respectable Irish workman, who has no feelings save those of execration and abhorrence for the machinations of misguided countrymen, is punished simply because he is Irish, it needs no prophet to predict that the latter end of Fenianism will be worse than the beginning ... to abandon ourselves to unreasoning suspicion is simply to awaken distrust .... Ours is a district where Irishmen have hitherto conducted themselves with eminent propriety, and what they have done we believe they will continue to do.[56]

Still, the fear of an outbreak and where it might next occur was uppermost in the public mind. When a massive explosion rocked Newcastle only five days after Clerkenwell, people rushed into the streets shouting incoherent statements about Fenians.[57] The explosion, which killed five senior officials of the Newcastle Corporation, was Fenian-inspired inasmuch as the Corporation was attempting to shift its stockpile of nitro-glycerine to more secure premises. But the local effect of the explosion was a salutary shifting of attention from the mania of Fenianism at precisely the time when the national press was never more full of it.

Throughout the Fenian disturbances, working-class opinion was largely in agreement with the establishment. The substantially working-class readership of the *Newcastle Daily Chronicle* was not allowed to forget the Irish opposition to Garibaldi. The paper felt that the Irish were deliberately 'putting the steadfastness of their friends to the test'. They had:

> ...by acts of culpable indiscretion, contrived to throw away much of the sympathy they would otherwise have had the right to claim ... What occurred nearer to home a few years ago? When a public discussion respecting Garibaldi was advertised to take place in Birkenhead, the Irish residents kept the town in an uproar for days and nights together.... Again, when the Pope wanted mercenaries to keep the Roman populace in bondage, it was Irishmen who furnished him with a contingent.[58]

Although a few radical labour leaders endorsed Fenianism,[59] and some spoke of Ireland being indisposed by conditions that 'we would not tolerate ourselves',[60] indeed, that 'Fenianism is nothing more than the sign and fruit of long existing wrongs',[61] for the most part, local working people had negligible engagement with the issues or were simply indifferent. Certainly there was little hostility. 'An Irish Row at South Shields' in late October 1867, was an exception which was not repeated during the course of the Fenian scare.[62] When J.W. Pease MP opened a new mechanics' institute in Crook on 16 October 1867 and 'could not help observing that the Government seemed to be making at the present moment unnecessary alarm with regard to the Fenian movement in this country', his audience (few of whom would have been Irish) heartily endorsed the statement.[63] Earl Derby's government, after all, was no favourite with the labourers of the North-east. Indeed, it is likely due to the lack of support for the Conservatives that the working classes, along with middle-class Liberals, maintained indifference to the political ramifications of Fenianism. As the judge at the trial of the Town

Moor rioters of July 1866 queried, 'why they [the Irish] came here and enforced these opinions on people who cared nothing about them, and who were peaceful people, he could not understand. ... No one wanted to tyrannise over the Irish; but there must be peace and quietness'.[64] Such warnings might also have sufficed to keep the Irish in check and thus provide the indigenous population with little opportunity for mass anti-Irish demonstration. *The Times*, in an article on Newcastle on 17 December, noted that the area 'has been remarkably peaceful, and no disturbances of any kind have taken place'.[65]

The lack of local hostility soon made Fenianism ephemeral. As Norman McCord has written of the press reaction generally, 'even in the crisis months there were many other topics like Reform and Government changes with which Fenianism had to struggle for attention'.[66] When in 1868 Fenianism faded from public view, it left few scars in Durham and Newcastle. The strongly liberal bias of the population also prevented the Tories from launching a campaign on the basis of anti-Irish feeling. Unlike Salford, for instance, where 'the Orangemen and home-bred militants were in no mood to let anti-Irishness die', and exploited those sentiments (with the help of William Murphy) to bring off Salford's 'Conservative Reaction' of 1868,[67] the North-east had neither the sympathies to exploit nor the exploiters. Thus if Fenianism at any level of British society 'failed to attract any large or influential body of support', in the North-east it also failed to serve as a platform for political advantage.[68]

To the local Irish, however, it was another (and enduring) matter. Although the number of Fenians was probably very small, few Irish wanted to confess non-allegiance to the Brotherhood.[69] For the recognition the Irish received through it was analogous to that received by the Catholic Church through No-Popery. And like the Church, the Irish were eager to sustain that kudos – though notoriety sometimes meant overacting. In Middlesbrough the Irish were 'reported to openly boast that they [had] plenty of arms hidden' and the police were given to know from 'one who had been there' that 'the Fenians drill secretly on the marshes in the vicinity of the town and that ... at one particular meeting ... it was decided that a number of persons in Middlesbrough should be shot, among others the superintendent of police'.[70] It seems fairly certain that such reports, most often made by the Irish themselves, were deliberately designed to keep the police and the public guessing. Like the 'mysterious' confessional, supposed secret societies were a perfect medium for social empowerment.

'That there are some members of the Fenian Brotherhood in Newcastle and Tyneside', wrote the *Newcastle Chronicle*, 'does not admit of doubt'.[71] In 1859 a branch of the National Brotherhood of St. Patrick – the public body of the Fenians – was established in the town and this probably served as a headquarters for a 'circle' of the Irish Republican Brotherhood (IRB).Certainly 'a large number of the labouring Irish were pronouncedly in favour of [secret oaths]',[72] and the Fenian journal *The Irish People* is reputed to have 'almost annihilated the circulation of *The Nation* in many places north and south of the Tweed'.[73] John Walsh of Middlesbrough was not only a Fenian organiser, but also one of the four representatives of Great Britain on the Supreme Council of the Fenian Brotherhood.[74] But the fact that no suspicious Irish activity was reported *before* the Fenian scare reached its peak (presuming that there was some substance to the many reports) suggests a late and perhaps superficial adherence. Which is not to say that many Irish in the region did not warmly and sincerely support the Fenian cause. In local Irish folklore, at least, 'many a hunted Fenian, escaping from English police, found a welcome and safe hiding in the home of a poor Tyneside worker, or in the fine house of a well-to-do compatriot, whose worldly success, wealth, and high social standing put him above all suspicion of Fenian sympathies'.[75]

Such sympathies provoked a good deal of Catholic reaction from the Pope downwards, but in the North-east the Church remained remarkably quiet.[76] Though making its position clear with respect to secret societies and violence, it was careful not to incite Irish patriotism against the Church. Not until after the Clerkenwell explosion did the bishop of the diocese feel compelled to speak out: 'If we have not before this taken occasion to address you', he stated, 'it is only because we did not feel ourselves called upon to do so ... we [now] feel that we cannot any longer remain silent'.[77] It was not specifically Fenianism that occasioned this, but the proposed funeral procession and capital punishment discussion to commemorate the memory of the 'Manchester Martyrs' who had been executed the month before. Even this event would likely not have resulted in the address from the bishop being 'freely posted throughout Newcastle ... and read in the Catholic chapels in that town and surrounding district after mass', had not the Clerkenwell disaster unfortunately taken place only two days in advance of the proposed procession. As it was, the bishop was probably only anticipating the discretion that the Irish themselves would have exercised. It is noteworthy too, that the bishop's address, though commanded 'by the virtue of our sacred office', took pains to show sympathy with 'your long-tried country'. It therefore 'affectionately entreat[ed]' the Irish not to take part in the procession because it would 'but only serve as an occasion to your opponents to inflict injuries both upon it [Ireland] and upon you'.

The proclamation doubtless contributed to the abandoning of the proceedings, for though they 'created considerable *curiosity* in the town and neighbourhood as to what would be the result should such a meeting be allowed to take place ... [this] curiosity was in no way gratified, for no one likely to be interested in discussing the question of 'capital punishment for political offences' attended the place of meeting'.[78] But the Church could hardly call this its victory over Fenianism or over the non-Catholic politics of the flock. With a shrewdness that surpassed that of the Church in Ireland, Catholic authorities in the North-east realised that their best course was to maintain just the right amount of aloofness in Irish affairs. In not forcing the Irish to make a decision between either their fidelity to the Church or their loyalty to Ireland, the Church retained the confidence of the Irish at that crucial moment. The Irish remained within the fold but did not feel the necessity to compromise their politics for those of the Church.[79]

Thus Fenianism, though a failure in Ireland and of no revolutionary significance in the North-east, was a catalyst for a secularist Irish political awakening. Whether the local Irish actually took part in Fenian activity, expressed sympathy or opposed a return to the ways of 1798, it was almost impossible for them not to be become involved with Irish nationalism. Particularly among the younger Irish, many of whom had never set foot in Ireland, the separatist ideal took root. It was something positive and something that no Englishman could share or remove. It marked the Irishman, if only in his own eyes, as someone special, someone perhaps even to be feared. What had previously been only a nationalistic pride thus became a political consciousness (in synchronicity with the lessening financial straights). Further, the Fenian scare demonstrated the Irish political potential in England at a time when the electorate was being enlarged.[80] Hence Fenianism could not have arrived at a more opportune moment. It removed much of the former apathy of the Irish and made them more aware of their strength and more eager to employ it in furthering Irish interests at the municipal and national levels. If Fenianism, then, was a failure in the use of force as a means of winning national salvation it was a conquest in 'the realm of the spirit' among Irish exiles in Britain and in the North-east in particular, enlivening nationalist ideals and alerting them to the potential of their political muscle.[81]

******

That the political infusion of Fenianism was not transitory is witnessed in the rise of many Irish political clubs in the late 1860s and 1870s. Both Newcastle and Consett established Irish Institutes and Gateshead and Hartlepool, along with many other towns, formed branches of the Irish National Foresters. The extent of these organisations and the political solidarity they expressed with Ireland was evident in an amnesty meeting for the release of the Fenian prisoners that took place in Newcastle in October 1872. Between 20,000 and 30,000 Irish congregated on the Town Moor. The press described them as coming:

from all parts of Tyneside – Sunderland, Consett, Middlesbrough, and other distant towns being well represented – and as a large majority of them wore green ribbons, sashes and scarves, their appearance was exceedingly attractive. Some of the most numerous bodies were headed by large silk banners; the prevailing tints being the much-revered emerald, the most conspicuous pieces of ornamentation the cross, the harp and the shamrock.[82]

Such a carnival parading through the streets of Newcastle on route to the Town Moor could have left little doubt as to the rising self-awareness of the local Irish, if not the finding of their political feet. As the chairman of the demonstration, Bernard McAnulty, told the crowd, 'The Irish were a formidable and powerful body in this country if they only exercised their power properly ... the day would fast approach when they would be able to make an impression on the legislature of this country'. The ostensible reason for the demonstration - amnesty for the Fenian prisoners – was genuine enough, but it also served as a convenient front for the more ambitious goal of welding all the Irish into one political force. The organisers of the meeting were probably aware of the article in *The Nation* only a week before that spoke of Newcastle as having:

> certainly the numbers that constitute power ... the highest patriotic spirit, and no lack of men capable of organising and directing the people. But there is want of community spirit – an absence of that sentiment which produces unity and the organisation which is absolutely essential to make the crude elements of political force a power to be exercised with effect.[83]

Thus the speakers implored the Irish to 'drop their religious distinctions, and cease to play their tomfooleries about the difference in their creeds'; rather, 'endeavour to get their names placed on the list of electors to let their weight be felt in the selection of Parliamentary representatives ... and not allow their differences on religious grounds to separate them into hostile factions'.[84]

A number of overtures to the English working class were also made at the demonstration. Perhaps the most effective of these was that by the Geordie who 'professed to be a cosmopolitan ... who believed in the brotherhood of all mankind'.[85] If, he said, 'the reforming working men of England combined with those of Scotland, and then lent a hand to their fellows across St. George's Channel, he was sure that the career of the country would be brighter and more glorious than it had ever yet been'. Though doubtless there was a good deal of wishful thinking by another speaker who believed that the 'working classes of England ... were beginning to examine the question for themselves, ... were beginning to ask the reasons for the unfriendliness which existed between the two important parts of their nation, and were beginning to see that the dust had been thrown in their eyes', nevertheless, his conclusion, that workers were beginning 'to say that if it were right to give sympathy to Italians, Poles, Frenchmen, Russians, Hungarians, and Germans, it could not be right to keep it from poor Paddy', was salutary and thought provoking.[86] It at least prevented the liberal press from dragging out the usual Garibaldi rhetoric.

In light of the later unofficial liaison between Liberals and Home Rulers, it is interesting to note the parliamentary expressions at this meeting. While the Irish were encouraged to register on electoral lists, they were not instructed how they should vote. 'They must make up their minds only to support the government which best served their turn;' stated one speaker, 'and then try to make England worth living in, and to give Irishmen Ireland for themselves'.[87] Since Gladstone was the culprit with regard to Irish political prisoners, the speakers could not profess much sympathy with the leader of the Liberals. Indeed, Gladstone was shown to be a hypocrite for having spoken in Lancashire 'about removing the wrongs of the country [Ireland] owing to the increase of Fenianism .... Was it not cruel, therefore of Mr. Gladstone, who vaunted of his great remedial acts to punish those men who were the first to open his eyes to what he should do for the country?'[88] Though there was definitely a desire for Gladstone to release the prisoners that the Irish could support the Liberals with impunity, the speakers were careful not to indict the whole of the Liberal Party. Nor was there any denunciation of Conservatives. In other words, the Irish were being instructed to cast their vote to the highest bidder, a practice that in parliamentary terms had fitting precedents in the Independent Irish

Party in the 1850s and the Catholic Stafford Club in the early 1860s. At an extra-parliamentary level, however, this non-partisan voting tactic – which would climax (and somewhat contradict itself) in the 'Parnell Manifesto' of 1885 – was a strategic innovation.

Although the amnesty demonstration gave a clear indication of the future political role of the Irish and was testimony to their increased politicisation, the local press was not encouraging. The Conservative *Newcastle Courant* believed that the meeting proved only that the Irish had 'become more resolute and headstrong than ever in their Fenian and rebellious tendencies'.[89] In complaining that the Irish were making the Sabbath 'at least in our own district ... the chosen time for almost all their demonstrations', the *Courant* was perhaps attempting to provoke religious animosities. One Sunderland paper, also interpreting the event as 'Fenian', so misconstrued a speech by John 'Amnesty' Nolan given the day prior to the Newcastle meeting as to have him say that 'Irishmen in England should at once possess themselves of bowie knives, swords, and pistols, carry these on their persons at all times, and in leisure hours learn how to use them'.[90] The *Newcastle Daily Chronicle*, which gave full coverage of the meeting, expressed no support. Significantly, in the *Chronicle's* next issue, two articles on Irish disturbances appeared in bold type.[91] One, a 'Serious Sequel to the Town Moor Amnesty Meeting' depicted the drunken return of 120 Consett Irishmen; the other, a 'Serious Irish Assault in Durham', was a trivial affair that would normally have been relegated to small print in the court column.

But if some still believed that Irish politics had not outgrown Fenianism or intemperance, such beliefs were soon dispelled with the formation of the Home Rule Confederacy in 1873. Again the Irish in the North-east responded eagerly to the call, and the fact that the first general meeting of Home Rulers was held in Newcastle in August 1873 is indicative of the recognised strength and potential of the Irish in the region.[92] Isaac Butt, MP acknowledged in a confidential letter at the close of the Newcastle Conference that 'we are wielding a tremendous power here in the north of England and I feel confident it will tell immensely at an election'.[93]

A good deal of Home Rule's success in the North-east was attributable to the influence and energy of the clergy. Not only Irish priests, of whom there were few, but the English priests as well gave the movement encouragement and leadership. Fenianism had taught the Church that opposition to Irish politics was futile; far better, if possible, to side with the aspirations of the flock. Hence Father Waterton in South Shields used the occasion of St. Patrick's Day, 1873 as a suitable time for establishing a branch of the Home Rule Association. He told his audience in St. Bede's:

> ... many people did not understand what it meant, and there were many who kept aloof from it because they thought some danger lurked in the name of Home Rule. That was a great mistake. Home Rule was the embodiment of the principle that the Irish nation was perfectly able to know what it required, and to legislate for that purpose; and that neither Scotch, English, nor Welsh could possibly have an adequate idea of the wants of Ireland. Some thought that Home Rule was Fenianism in disguise, but that also was a mistake. Home Rule was only an earnest appeal for justice.[94]

Long before Cardinal Manning gave his endorsement to the Irish Party in 1885, the clergy were deeply involved with Irish nationalism. On platforms alongside Irish politicians, the clergy were present in substantial numbers. 'There were a great many people who had objections to any Catholic clergyman, or any other clergyman, taking the chair on occasions when political matters were about to be discussed' stated Durham's Rev. Perrin, while seven other priests sat on the platform beside him at an anti-coercion meeting in 1881,

> ... but though this meeting did partake of a political nature, still there were other considerations which might warrant a clergyman taking part in it ... He had a notion that if clergymen could stand forth for the claims of the poor and starving foreigner, surely it could not be inconsistent for a clergyman to stand forth to stop the cruel starvation which was almost always at the heels of his poor unhappy fellow countrymen.[95]

But however the clergy might justify their involvement in order to maintain their positions in the Irish community, they were nonetheless effective in making Home Rule ubiquitous among the

Irish Catholics. From 1873, St. Patrick's Day celebrations lost much of their former sentimentality and, while still remaining religious, became occasions for hard-core political rallies.[96] Even the more solemn foundation stone ceremonies or church openings of 17 March could not escape spontaneous nationalist outburst. Thus Bishop Chadwick, laying the foundation stone for SS. John and Patrick's Church, Felling, in 1873, was forced to join in the 'vehement response' to a call for three cheers for 'the nation we belong to'.[97]

The quality of non-religious leadership and the attachment of some Irish politicians to the North-east further explains the success of the Nationalist movement in the area. Besides Bernard McAnulty, who was among the executive of the Home Rule Confederacy, there were Nationalist delegates from almost every town in Durham. Lewis Barry of Newcastle, brother of John Barry, the MP for County Wexford, was also on the executive (along with the local Irish leader, Edward Savage) and was responsible for organising much of the Irish vote in the region.[98] Timothy Healy, who came to Newcastle in 1873, acted as secretary of the local branch of the Home Rule Association and for a number of years was secretary of the Irish Institute in Newcastle. Throughout his political career, Healy retained a keen interest in Newcastle's Irish and was largely responsible for the repeated visits of Parnell, Joseph Biggar, John Francis, O'Donnell, A.M. Sullivan and O'Connor-Power to the North-east. It was Healy also who prevailed upon Michael Davitt, after his release from prison, to speak at the rally in Newcastle at which Davitt was nearly murdered by a local Fenian faction who resented his defection to constitutionalism.[99] As Parnell's secretary Healy assured the recognition of the area's Irish, and when he resigned his secretarial duties in 1880 to take the parliamentary seat for Wexford he used his influence to get another Newcastle-connected Irishman, Henry Campbell, to fill the vacancy. Although in the split between the National League and the Parnell Leadership Committee in 1890-91 Healy's reputation in the North-east suffered, he later came to be remembered as the 'life and soul of the National movement in Newcastle-on-Tyne'.[100] In light of these personalities and the efforts of the Church, it is not surprising that

Newcastle became the centre of the short-lived Northern Land League (1879-1881) when the Home Rule Confederation declined.[101]

The strength of Irish nationalism in the North-east meant that few politicians could ignore Irish issues or fail to make a play for the Irish vote in any electoral campaign. Particularly in those contests where Irish votes could determine the outcome, politicians were anxious to take the Home Rule pledge. Although in practice the Irish vote went mainly to the Liberal Party, there were occasions when Tory candidates could benefit from the non-partisan tactics. One such was the Newcastle Tory Charles Hammond who, good to his word, was one of the ten English members to support Isaac Butt's Home Rule motion of July 1874.[102] On the other hand the Sunderland Liberal John Candlish and the Hartlepool Liberal, Ralph Ward Jackson, were blacklisted by Home Rulers on the basis that 'the man who voted for coercion was not likely to support Home Rule'.[103]

The importance of the Irish vote was made clear in a municipal contest in Gateshead in 1877.[104] Unlike most other corporations in the region, Gateshead had come under the domination of a clique known as the Liberal Registration Association (LRA) which controlled the town council.[105] Benjamin Biggar, a dyed-in-the-wool Tory who represented the East Ward, had been expelled from the council by this clique shortly before the elections of November 1877. The LRA put forward their candidate for the East Ward, Mr. Robson, and conducted a vigorous campaign on his behalf. It was largely taken for granted that the Irish vote, upon which the ward was heavily dependent, would be in favour of Robson, especially since Gateshead's Irish spokesmen Messrs. Devine, Cassidy and Doyle were associated with the LRA. Considerable consternation was aroused, therefore, when Biggar announced that his radical nephew Joseph Biggar, MP for Cavan, alias the 'Belfast Pork Butcher', a Roman Catholic convert and one of the pillars of Home Rule in Westminster, was about to come to Gateshead in support of his 'Uncle Ben'. While Robson began avidly denouncing Benjamin

Biggar as 'the worst enemy of Ireland that Ireland ever had', the Gateshead Irish spokesmen sent a telegram to Joseph Biggar asking if the announcement was true.[106] Joseph Biggar replied: 'I intend to address a meeting in favour of Benjamin Biggar, but not against your interests'.[107] The LRA, not to mention the Irish voters, were dumbfounded. Meanwhile 'Uncle Ben', scarcely campaigning at all, awaited the arrival of his trump card.

Two days before the election Joseph Biggar arrived in town and was met at the station by Timothy Healy, who informed him of his uncle's great unpopularity. Healy recollected that:

> 'Ben' had sent Irishmen to jail after a St. Patrick's Day procession at Jarrow-on-Tyne, so Joe asked me to get our friends together that evening in order that he might talk to them. I yielded, but the gathering was a 'frost'. Joe, however, grimly earnest, went on the platform at the Gateshead Town Hall to face the opponents of 'me Uncle Ben.'[108]

According to Healy, Joseph Biggar seduced the Irish by telling them that 'Tory and all as my Uncle is, he was the only member of my family, except my sister, who did not disown me when I joined the Catholic Church (loud applause)'. In fact, Biggar made no such statement. He swung the Irish vote through an appeal to the non-partisan plank of the Home Rulers:

> Now what are the Irishmen of the east ward of Gateshead asked to do on this occasion? They are asked to follow the lead of the Liberal Registration Association of Gateshead. If we, in the House of Commons, were to act as you are asked to do here, we would immediately lose our individuality, with the result that we would be a mere cipher.... They [the LRA] wish to use the Irish vote, if possible, in this ward because the Irish vote is very important.... Mr. James, the member for Gateshead, is their mouthpiece for the time being ... and we know how he has voted on Irish questions.[109]

Despite cries of 'What has that to do with Benjamin Biggar', Joseph Biggar continued to expose Mr. James as an MP hostile to Home Rule, as well as opposed to equal facilities for Roman Catholic education in Ireland. 'Speaking as an Irish Roman Catholic

Nationalist', he concluded, and 'speaking as a Radical, because my sympathies are entirely in favour of Radicalism no matter where it is, I would implore you gentlemen here present to enter on Friday next your decided protest against this system of nomination by a small clique who affect to speak for the rate-payers of this community'. The rhetoric was effective: Tory 'Uncle Ben' defeated the LRA's Robson by a majority of 204 votes.[110]

******

By the mid-1870s Liberal politicians in the North-east were all Home Rulers. The fact that four of the ten English Members who voted with Butt in 1874 were from the region,[111] gives credence to political image of Tyneside and Durham as 'unsurpassed for strength of character, wealth of intellect, and ... of a sturdy outspoken democracy'.[112] The reasons for this political orientation were essentially those we have already touched upon in exploring the social and religious toleration toward the area's Irish: the nature of the economy, the strength of religious dissent and the weakness of High-Anglican/High-Toryism, and the predominance of a working-class population. To these factors must be added the long-standing Whig tradition as epitomised by Lords Grey and Durham. Largely undisturbed by the major Victorian radical movements – Chartism, anti-poor law, factory reform and free trade – the North-east was not provoked into reaction, and thus quietly slipped into ambit of Liberal Reform.[113]

At a parliamentary level Liberal reformism chiefly characterised the North-eastern politicians, who had little quarrel with the Nationalists. Indeed, three of the four Liberals in all of England for whom Parnell made exceptions in his anti-Liberal, anti-Radical manifesto of 1885 were Members for Durham and Newcastle: Joseph Cowen, Samuel Storey of Sunderland, and Thomas Thompson of Durham City.[114] Of these, Joseph Cowen was for the Irish their local spokesman in Westminster. 'His sympathy with Irish Tynesiders was extraordinary. They almost adored him for defending the obstructive tactics of Parnell and Biggar in the

House'.[115] While most other North-eastern Liberals who supported Home Rule were unwilling to endorse the Land League or oppose Gladstone's Coercion Bills of the early 1880s, Cowen consistently supported Irish claims and opposed coercion with as much vigour as he had earlier led the local opposition against the House of Lords' amendment to the Irish Church Bill.[116] In 1876 Cowen with his 'extraordinary gift of florid, impassioned, ingenious and overwrought rhetoric'[117] delivered a powerful speech in the House for the release of the Fenian prisoners and in 1883, when Healy and company were imprisoned for 'seditious speeches', it was Cowen's well-phrased questions in the House that resulted in the two-month sentences being remitted.[118]

Cowen had no vested interests in Ireland or the Irish, nor did he act out of any self-interest for the Irish vote; he scarcely required their support. He responded to what he believed to be purely democratic principles. A speech, delivered at an Irish conference in Newcastle in August 1881, for example, is typical of many of his addresses on behalf of the Irish:

> ... the Irish immigrant carries with him bitter memories; and with honourable devotion and commendable liberality he aids his countrymen to free themselves from laws that overmastered him or drove him into exile.
> But is it not a fact that movements both legal and rebellious have often been helped from the outside? The money with which the Greeks commenced their War of Independence was found by English sympathisers. Repeated funds have been raised in England during the last century for revolutionary efforts to secure the independence of Poland, Italy, and Hungary. Did we not send English legions to fight against Don Carlos, in Spain, and King Bomba in Naples? How can we consistently cry out against help being sent by Irishmen abroad to Irishmen at home to promote objects in which they are equally alike interested?[119]

Little wonder that the Irish idolised him. In October 1880 they presented him with a formal address of thanks and Alderman McAnulty, making the presentation, 'spoke the sentiments of every honest Irishman on the face of the globe [when] he wished that Mr.

Cowen might be spared [from his lingering illness] to be an honour to his country'.[120]

It is interesting to compare Cowen with Thomas Burt, MP, the Radical spokesman for Northumbrian pitmen. While Burt voted with Butt in 1872 and claimed like all Liberals that he did not endorse coercion, he nevertheless voted for coercion, justifying his position by arguing that the Land Bill should have been introduced before the Coercion Bill. As he saw it:

> The choice [in Ireland] was between anarchy and despotism; between the coercion of the Land League and the coercion of the Government; and, for my part, much as I detest coercion, if we must have it applied, I think it is much better to have it applied by a responsible representative government rather than by an irresponsible and ferocious mob.[121]

Cowen's principled radicalism strongly rebuked this argument and he lashed out at Burt for pandering to Gladstone.[122] It was perhaps in revenge that Cowen included the former president of Burt's own union (John Bryson of the Northumberland Miners' Association) in his fact-finding labour delegation to Ireland in 1881. When Bryson returned to Tyneside full of support for the Land League he did a lecture tour of the area, much to the chagrin of the normally dispassionate Burt.[123] This division between two of the area's leading labour MPs was ultimately to the detriment of local working-class support for the Land League (see below) but it clearly did damage to Burt's radical mystique while further promoting Cowen as a champion of Ireland.

Cowen, the owner of one of provincial England's largest circulating newspapers, the *Newcastle Daily Chronicle*,[124] was able to popularise the cause of Irish Nationalism and bid for its support among the non-Irish. By the time of the 1873 Conference, the *Chronicle* was already appealing for a 'fair hearing' for Butt and his coadjutors, stating that on the strength of liberalism in the area 'not here need any Irishman "fear to speak of ninety-eight"'.[125] But the immediate reaction to the conference was by no means favourable. The *Chronicle* did not take lightly to '*unmeasured invective against England'*[126] and declared as 'absurd'

> ..the notion that whenever a Liberal candidate for a seat in the House of Commons declines to accept the Home Rule platform in its integrity, a Tory should be supported quite independent of the Tory's opinion on the question .... Home Rule might be peculiarly advantageous, but Home Rule inspired by Ultramontane agency was the direst curse that could be inflicted upon Ireland.

Such a statement was little different from the *Newcastle Courant's* reaction to an earlier speech by McAnulty, that 'If the Pope were infallible, it is hard to see how devout Catholics can be Home-Rulers'.[127] The *Examiner's* comment on Home Rule a year later aptly summed up the enigma that it presented to Liberals and Conservatives alike:

> While the English Tory hates it because he believes that in two years after its establishment not an English landowner would be left in the country, there are English Liberals who distrust it because they see in it civil discord, the opportunity of Ultramontanism, and the triumph of a narrow, bigoted form of patriotism. It looks too much like the substitution of Cardinal Cullen for the Castle.[128]

Through Cowen's maturing radicalism, however, the *Newcastle Daily Chronicle* gradually outgrew its former fidelity to Gladstonian Liberalism. By the time of the Home Rule Conference of 1880, which was also held in Newcastle, the paper was speaking with pride about 'our good town' being 'the scene of the present conference' and about Ireland as 'the *CINDERELLA* sister, for whom a side table must be prepared'.[129] Well might one speaker proclaim that 'he had never seen in an English journal such a high tone of moral principle enunciated with regard to England's dealings with other nations, and particularly with the people of Ireland, than he had read that day and at other times in the columns of the *Newcastle Chronicle*'.[130] Nor was there any lack of sincerity in the 'prolonged cheers' which greeted this.

But how successfully Cowen, the *Chronicle,* and the other advocates of the Nationalist movement mustered working-class support is not readily ascertained. While at a grass-roots level it is probably correct that 'Irish questions were no more popular [in the North-east] than anywhere else in England',[131] at the same time it was impossible for local politicians to ignore Irish questions whilst casting for the Irish vote. Evidence would suggest that the working class generally recognised much of the political rhetoric as token overture to Ireland, while remaining themselves largely unmoved by Irish political questions. Workers' leaders such as William Crawford and John Wilson (both supporters of Irish Nationalism) were virtually forced to show sympathy with Ireland to thwart charges of hypocrisy, while Liberals who were not anxious to alienate either Irish voters or the Irish Party in the Commons, were similarly pressured. The only notable exception to this Irish befriending from a Member of Parliament who relied on working-class support was Thomas Burt. He may have spoken for the silent sentiments of many more conservative locals when he defended himself against the attacks of Cowen and Bryson, arguing that 'those persons do a poor service to Radicalism who make it a synonym for anarchy and violence'.[132] Burt's arguments also appealed to those who found it difficult to reconcile union aims with those of the Land League. Certainly, the following defence against endorsing the Land League could be readily understood by many workers:

> It has been said that they [the Land Leaguers] were fighting a great battle of the rights of labour, and that we should have joined our forces with theirs, and given our active sympathy and practical help in the severe struggle in which they were engaged. If they were actually a trade union, it does not necessarily follow that we should have rushed to their support until we knew something of their constitution, their aims, their methods, and the spirit by which they were animated. I suppose there is no doubt of the fact that, notwithstanding the tremendous and not always over-scrupulous efforts put forth on behalf of the League in this district, very few English working men have joined it. There is scarcely an accredited trade union leader who has boldly advocated the claims of the League ....[133]

Radical labour leaders and politicians like Crawford and Wilson, and platform Irish Nationalists like O'Connor-Power, could easily counter Burt's type of argument, but the communion of interests between the Irish Nationalists and the English workers was not easily translated.[134] The occasions were rare when evicted miners could be shown that the owners were doing 'nothing less than Boycotting' and that these owners were the same so-called Liberals who 'would pass the Coercion Bill to stop it [boycotting] in Ireland (applause)'.[135] While on this particular occasion – the strike at Seaham Colliery in 1881 – the colliers passed a resolution 'condemn[ing] the action of the House of Commons in passing the Coercion Bill', there were many more workers who were only too willing to agree with Liberals like Joseph Pease that the Land League was disgracing Ireland by invoking a 'reign of violence' or that the obstructionist policy in the Commons by the Irish Party was most definitely not in the interests of the working classes.[136]

There was also a good deal of annoyance among workers at the emphasis on Irish politics (particularly in the early 1880s) to the exclusion of their own. This was not unlike the local reaction to Fenianism. The *Newcastle Courant*, though hardly a working-class paper, expressed irritation over Irish affairs shared by many outside its circulation. The Irish 'settle themselves in increasing numbers in our midst', it complained:

> In the enjoyment of comfort, and an abundance of the good things of English life, they do not all of them forget the political whine and cant to which they had been trained in the land of their birth. ... And so we have Irish political deputations, Irish political oratory, and Irish organisations on English soil, with a view to action on English elections. The whole thing is purely Irish. It is Irish life in England.[137]

The *Durham Chronicle*, by the 1880s an organ for the Liberal working class, similarly regarded the local Irish as self-centred and not a little over-wearying. Discussing an 'Irish Distress Meeting at Willington' in 1883, the *Chronicle* remarked:

> Calling upon the Government to prevent distress in Ireland, after all that has been said and done on this painful subject during the past few years, can only be the merest piece of platform formality. ... if the Irish colony at Willington had subscribed but a single five

pound note for the furtherance of emigration, they would have done more for their fellow countrymen than all the speaking and resolutionising of Sunday last.[138]

While apathy, indifference or annoyance at Irish politics could often be found among the working classes, there was also a conservative element that openly repudiated Irish claims. Just as in times of prosperity there were those who opposed the formation of unions,[139] so, when the franchise was extended, there were some who, especially in times of depression, were attracted to associations such as the Conservative Working Men's Clubs.[140] Such places could be havens for workers who felt that Irish issues had a questionable relevance to their own interests and who were tempted, when times were tough, to lace their opinions with ethnocentric ones. As Welbourne noted in his study of the miners' unions of Durham and Northumberland, when jobs became scarce and wages fell,

> It was a common saying that prosperity would not return to the north until every Scotchman went home, bearing two Irishmen on his back. And jeer at him as his leaders might, the Conservative working man stuck firmly to his political faith, the more so as foreign policy was of absorbing interest. Not every miner was captured by the cry of 'Peace, Retrenchment, and Reform'.[141]

Thus, in part for his support of Irish politics in the 'bad days' of the mid-1880s John Wilson was defeated at the polls, despite his miners' constituency and his fine credentials in the Durham Miners' Association.[142]

******

Yet it would be wrong to infer from lack of indigenous working-class support for Irish nationalism that hostility to the Irish was an inevitable corollary. Overall, the political career of the region's Irish points to a high level of political toleration. The success of the local Nationalist movement and the recognition of its strength by leading Irish spokesmen says something for leniency at least. While a part of the 'acceptance' of these politics may have been only the result of public indifference and a certain apathy or psychological removal from things Irish, a large measure of the local toleration must be credited to the radical working-class spokesmen – best represented by Joseph Cowen and William Crawford – who recognised the principles involved in the Irish cause and were willing to stake their reputations in defence of them. The disproportionate amount of discussion on Irish affairs provoked by these disinterested spokesmen not only kept Irish issues alive in an area where they could easily have become the exclusive domain of the Irish, but also frustrated much of the potential for anti-Irishness. If we compare (though somewhat unfairly) the riots that resulted from the cry of Home Rule in Portract and Glasgow in August 1875[143] and again in Glasgow in 1880[144] with the calm that prevailed in the North-east, the propitious circumstances of the Irish in the area are sharply evident. It was, after all, extremely difficult for those who professed to be radical Liberals to react to the Irish in the manner that Lord Londonderry and the Tory clique did in calling for the suppression of the Land League tyranny.[145] The alternative, therefore, was to remain detached from Irish affairs – hence the appeal of Thomas Burt. We cannot, therefore, account for lack of anti-Irishness in the region by reference to the locals' fathoming of a Celtic mindscape. Nor can we simply endorse T.P. O'Connor's view that there existed a 'community of occupation, interest, and struggle' which accounts 'for the fact that in no part of Great Britain [were] the relations ... so friendly and intimate as on Tyneside'.[146] Rather, the political sentiments of the majority of the population and the stream of rhetoric that emphasised a radical tradition and spirit of liberalism made hostility to the Irish an inexorable contradiction. In light of almost enforced toleration, together with the strength of the Irish organisations, and the support of several political and labour leaders, it is not surprising that the North-east was one of the few areas that remained solidly behind Gladstone in 1886 after his endorsement of Home Rule.[147] Fittingly, Newcastle was the site for the elevation of Home Rule to the forefront of the Liberal platform in 1891.[148]

Conclusion

The composite picture of North-eastern society between 1840 and 1880 is made unique by the intensity of its detail. The rapid population growth in response to unprecedented industrial expansion, the strength of dissenting religion relative to the weakness of the Church of England, and the degree of allegiance to Whig, Liberal and Radical politics are features that together with the region's geographical isolation make it historically distinct.

Thus the extensive Irish population that emigrated to Durham and Newcastle after 1840 entered a place that, if not exactly open-armed, was not ill-disposed to them, and was remarkably free from the fears and insecurities that apparently fed religious and ethnic intolerance elsewhere. As a part of a larger influx to the area, the Irish were not overly conspicuous and were not therefore readily singled out as responsible for the social disruptions and economic ills so far as those existed. The substantial Irish contributions to North-eastern Catholicism did little to mar the relatively well-accepted place of that faith which, even at mid-century, was hardly affected by militant Protestantism. The ever-greater appreciation of the Irish in the local workforce and the lack of their occupational competition further diminished the potential for anti-Irishness at the same time as it facilitated the fairly rapid enhancement of their social and economic status. The Fenian rising, occurring when the Irish had escaped their earlier destitution, sparked a political interest that matured with the emergence of Home Rule and became increasingly viable after 1867 with the extension of the franchise. While Fenianism was greeted with only slightly less alarm and trepidation than elsewhere in the country, its local impact was short-lived and did not permanently embitter North-easterners to the Irish. Meantime, with the shift to constitutional means for the independence of Ireland, local Irish Nationalists gained the support and encouragement of many of the area's leading politicians.

Thus, unlike their compatriots in other parts of Britain, the Irish in Durham and Newcastle were rarely the victims of religio-ethnic hostility and economic scapegoating. For this reason, the written record of Irish life in the region is slender, being composed primarily of passing comments – even when Irishness was a burning public issue nationally. While there is evidence that North-easterners shared some of the popular Victorian prejudice against the Irish, the geographical separation of the area, its religious composition, social makeup, economic prosperity, and political traditions gave little scope for its inculcation. The proof lies in the speed, and the degree to which, the Irish were able to prosper locally in religion, economics and politics. Although only a few of the nineteenth-century national surveys of the Irish in England included the North-east, none for the later years would dispute that Paddy's meeting with Geordie was all in all an uncommonly smooth and fruitful affair.

Appendix

Appendix I

Churches and Missions in Co Durham and Newcastle to c.1880

Location	Church	Date of Mission or First Structure	Date of Church or Chapel	Remarks
Barnard Castle	St. Mary		1847	
Birtley	St. Joseph	1696	1842	Former Benedic. Mon.
Bishop Auckland	St. Wilfrid	1844	1846	
Blackhill	Our Lady	1856	1884	
Brooms	SS. Mary & J.	1745	1857	Former St. Cuth's
Byer-Moor [Burnopfield]	Sacred Heart		1869	School-chapel
Castle Eden [Hutton Henry]	SS. Peter & Paul	1740	1832	
Chester-le-St.	St. Barnabas		1875	School-chapel
Consett	St. Patrick		1870	School-chapel
Cornforth	SS. Patrick ...		1874	Served from Trimdon
Coxhoe	St. Patrick		1866	Served from Trimdon
Crook	St. Cuthbert	1853	1854	
Croxdale Hall	St. Herbert		1807	
Darlington	St. Augustine	1783	1827	
	SS. Mary & Pat		1859	Closed in 1872
	St. William		1871	School-chapel
Dunston	St. Philip	1880	1895	
Durham	St. Cuthbert	1685	1827	
	St. Godric	1860	1864	
Easington	St. Thomas	1863	1876	Room cum chapel
Esh Laude	St. Michael	1799	1832	Smyth estate
Gainsford	St. Osmund		1852	Chapel of ease
Gateshead	St. Joseph	1850	1859	Jesuit Mis. c. 1697
	St. Wilfred	185?	1904	
[Felling]	St. Patrick		1841	
Hartlepool	St. Mary	1834	1851	Priest in 1832
Hartlepool, W.	St. Joseph	1859	1867	Room; school 1873
Haverton Hill	SS. Michael..	1865		Room let
Hebburn	St. Aloysius	1871	1888	School-chapel
Houghton-le-S.	St. Michael	1832	1837	
Jarrow	St. Bede	1860	1861	School-church
Langley Moor	St. Patrick	1876	1883	

continued

176 Appendix

Monkwearmouth	St. Benet		1864		School-chapel
Newcastle	St. Andrew	1798	1841		New church, 1875
	St. Mary		1844		Had chapel of ease
	St. Patrick		1853		Closed in 1874
	St. Dominic	1860	1873		
	St. Michael		1873		School-chapel
Newhouse [Waterhouses]	Qn. of Martyrs		1871		Former ancient ch.
Port Clarence	St. Thomas	1865			Temp. mission
Sacriston	SS. Michael		1867		School-chapel
Seaham Harbour	St. Mary M.	1852	1870		
Sedgefield	St. Joseph	183?	1854		Served from Thornley
South Shields	St. Bede	1849	1876		Formerly St. Cuth's
Stanley	St Joseph		1872		School-chapel
Stella	SS. Mary...	1700	1832		
Stockton	St. Mary	c1693	1842		
Sunderland	St. Mary	1769	1844		
	St. Patrick	1860	1861		
	St. Joseph		1873		
Thornley	St. Godric	1850	1858		School-chapel
Tow Law	St. Joseph		1869		School-ch; Taylor - Smith fam.; served from Wolsingham
Trimdon	St. Williams	1861	1864		
Tudhoe	St. Charles	1858	1870		Salvin family
(New) Tunstall	St. Leonard		1873		
Tyne Dock	SS .Peter & P.		1884		
Ushaw Moor			1909		School from 1879
Washington	Our Lady		1861		School-chapel
Willington	Ly. of Perpetual Succour	1874	1877		School-chapel
Witton Park	St. Chad	1871			Room; served from Bishop Auckland
Wolsingham	Thomas of C.	1849	1854		

Sources: Bernard Kelly, *Catholic Missions* (London, 1906); *Whellan's Directory of Durham and Newcastle*, 1856; *Kelly's Directory of Durham*, 1890; *Catholic Directory*, 1800-1869; *Northern Catholic Calendar*, 1869-1910; Bishop Bewick, "List of Missions opened Since A.D. 1850," (written before 1884) in possession of Rev. W. Vincent Smith. None of these contains a complete or accurate list; by cross checking and with the help of Rev. Smith it is hoped that most of the errors have been removed, though name changes, churches being rebuilt and missions being abandoned and later reopened makes any such list contain some margin of error.

Appendix II

Diocesan Statistics, 1847-49

Mission	Est. Nos. of Caths.	Adults	Bapts.	Easter Commts.	Confirms	Converts
Barnard Castle	[260]		[36]			
Birtley	386	298	78	212	30	
Bishop Auckland	1,100	845	179	104	80	
Brooms	1,540	1,149	259		70	
Castle Eden	350	200	42	120	23	
Croxdale	220	135	24	124	37	
Darlington	400	320	90	280	80	
Durham	1,220	880	70	320	84	
Esh Laude	310	250	60	193	58	
Felling	850	550	320	400	117	21
Hartlepool	650	560	120	370		
Houghton	400	110	99			
Newcastle						
St. Andrews	5,500	3,500	1,020	1,170		
St. Mary	5,000	2,500	540	1,000		
Sedgefield						
Stockton	560	370	126	240	102	38
South Shields	1,000	800	180			
Sunderland	3,300	2,500	220	900		
Wolsingham	240	165		30		
	23,286	15,132	3,463	4,463	681	59

Source: Status Animarum, etc. for the diocese of Hexham and Newcastle, v.2, 1847-1912 (passim), pp.5-9. These are the extant statistics of the diocese as transcribed by Rev. J. Lenders, between January and March 1931. Where no figures are given, the returns were not made. The figures in parenthesis are taken from the *1st Annual Report of the Catholic Poor-Schools Committee,* 1848, pp. 91-93.

Appendix III

Diocesan Statistics, 1852

Mission	Est. Nos. of Caths.	Adults	Bapts. 49-52	Easter Commts.	Confirms 1849-52	Converts
Barnard Castle	414	281	14	101		11
Birtley	450	300	33	200	62	21
Bishop Auckland	750	600	70	280	80	17
Brooms	1,930	1,360	373	430	133	12
Castle Eden	221	191	54	126		5
Croxdale	280	196	33	127	30	6
Darlington	1,150	800	120	600	176	38
Durham	1,307	896	117	430	125	30
Esh Laude	530	260	57	192	68	25
Felling	1,106	756	236	370	180	56
Gateshead	1,948	1,062	276	543		21
Hartlepool	1,000	800	67	556	121	70
Houghton	830	478	165	400	31	30
Newcastle						
St. Andrews	8,500	8,000	360	1,000	330	94
St. Mary	6,500	6,000	285	1,600	376	50
Seaham Harbour						
Sedgefield	150	80	51	70		
South Shields	1,200	800	176	600	149	16
Stella	800	560	120	261	61	30
Stockton	740	570	139	233	30	18
Sunderland	8,000	4,000	297	2,000	257	115
Thornley	130	90	82	40		10
Wolsingham	700	620	157	250	55	70
	38,636	28,700	3,282	10,409	2,264	745

Source: Status Animarum, etc. v.2, pp.11-15.

Appendix IV

Diocesan Statistics, 1855

Mission	Est. Nos. of Caths.	Adults	Bapts. 52-55	Easter Commts.	Confirms 1852-55	Converts
Barnard Castle	372	245	63	112		2
Birtley	806	490	121	302		15
Bishop Auckland	1,295	841	240	255		18
Brooms	3,700	2,800	396	530		5
Castle Eden	123	101	20	130	49	7
Crook	1,120	880	112	181		13
Croxdale	500	430	59	140	30	15
Darlington	1,273	821	165	580	123	29
Durham	1,460	1,110	421	540	124	30
Esh Laude	550	290	54	208	69	24
Felling	1,505	915	270	400		30
Gateshead	2,000	1,100	300	600		20
Hartlepool	1,573	1,074	227	666	154	47
Houghton	1,080	605	195	400		28
Newcastle						
St. Andrews	8,700	8,000	434	1,500	230	73
St. Mary	8,000	6,000	1,100	10,000	219	75
Seaham Harbour			Included with Sunderland			
Sedgefield	140	64	43	71		
South Shields	1,750	1,219	245	650		20
Stella	1,100	770	133	300	81	18
Stockton	800	600	156	280		14
Sunderland	6,748	3,987	1,026	1,600		
Thornley	557	329	100	139		
Wolsingham	532	344	138	240		45
	45,684	33,015	6,018	19,824	1,079	528

Source: *Status Animarum, etc.* v.2, pp.19-25.

Appendix V

Diocesan Statistics, 1861

Mission	Est. Nos. of Caths.	Adults	Bapts. 58-61	Easter Commts.	Confirms 1858-61	Converts
Barnard Castle	496	330	32	168	46	11
Birtley	1,664	941	104	633		14
Bishop Auckland	2,324	1,924	160	1,200	546	60
Blackhill	2,760	1,915	165	1,340	508	30
Brooms	1,134	783	113	850	327	26
Castle Eden	557	307	40	242		
Crook	2,416	1,523	137	1,060	194	44
Croxdale Hall	700	376	32	202	97	22
Darlington	1,694	1,146	104	787	86	24
Durham	2,700	1,500	160	1,100	700	150
Esh Laude						
Felling	2,500	1,600	140	900	170	29
Gainsford	88	49		36	18	
Gateshead	3,570	1,774	220	1,000		
Hartlepool	1,856	837	163	1,300	167	200
Hartlepool, W.	1,127	600				
Houghton	1,520	927	94	1,070	45	
Jarrow	1,155	728		472		8
Newcastle						
St. Andrews	5,964	4,666	424			239
St. Mary	8,496	6,496	531	3,248	1,433	116
Seaham Harbour	799	473	43			11
Sedgefield	1,500	900	82	850	128	58
South Shields	1,330	874	472	541	590	72
Stella	1,270	825	65	540	240	40
Stockton	1,035	710	102	460		15
Sunderland	6,800	4,000	450	4,041		105
Thornley						
Tow Law & Wolsingham	590	249	39	275	50	9
Tudhoe	643	420	57	315		18
	56,688	35,999	3,929	22,630	5,345	1,301

Source: *Status Animarum, etc.* v.2, pp.27-33.

Appendix VI
Diocesan Statistics, [1874]

There are no extant statistics for the diocese between 1861-7. There is, however, one paper unsigned, undated and scribbled in pencil within the record book in the archives. Rev. Lenders has deduced that this must have been the rough draft for the *Elenchus Sacerdotum ...quo progressus Religionis Catholicae in Anglia ab Hierarchia restaurata a.d. 1850 usque ad annum 1875 indicantur*, which was to be presented to Rome in 1875. Lenders substantiates this claim by the following: "Langley Moor which started in 1876 is *not* in the list; Sunderland has three churches and St. Joseph's started in 1874; several of the Missions, the names of which have been inserted between the lines, date from 1874[1]" also, the titles were written in Latin and the milage from the seat of the bishop in Newcastle was listed in another column. We will assume this draft to have been written in 1874 and extract from it the estimated numbers of Catholics for those parishes in Durham and Newcastle for which figures were given.

Mission	Nos. of Caths.	Mission	Nos. of Caths.
Barnard Castle	350	Houghton	1,000
Benfieldside [Blackhill]	3,220	Hutton House [Castle Eden]	600
Birtley	1,093	Jarrow	4,100
Bishop Auckland	2,500	Monkwearmouth	2,000
Brooms	2,052	Newcastle	17,000
Burnopfield [Byer-Moor]	1,300	Newhouse	1,340
Crook	2,000	Sacriston	480
Croxdale	800	Seaham Harbour	1,000
Darlington	3,596	South Shields	3,500
Durham	1,950*	Stella	1,220
Easington	1,000	Stockton	2,500
Esh Laude	760	Sunderland	7,840
Felling	3,300	Thornley	1,300
Gainsford	150	Tow Law	1,050
Gateshead	5,000	Trimdon	1,862
Hartlepool	2,000	Tudhoe	1,965
Hartlepool, W.	2,000	(New) Tunstall	800
Haverton Hill	550	Washington	1,050
Hebburn	1,800	Total	86,052

*Since Durham listed 2,700 Catholics in 1861, this number must remain extremely suspect. It perhaps should read 2,950.

1. *Status Animarum, etc.*, v.2, p.121.

Appendix VII

Diocesan Statistics, 1875

Mission	Est. Nos. of Caths.	Baptisms	Easter Communicants
Barnard Castle	386	18	227
Birtley	1,130	55	502
Bishop Auckland	3,600	192	1,500
Blackhill	3,270	153	1,330
Brooms	1,800	121	850
Byer-Moor & Stanley	1,200	65	450
Castle Eden	700	25	220
Cornforth, Coxhoe & Trimdon	3,000	86	853
Crook	2,330	107	1,100
Croxdale	492	49	205
Darlington			
St Augustine	3,000	123	750
St. William	1,800	123	1,000
Durham			
St. Cuthbert	1,300	120	800
St. Godric	1,000	99	656
Easington	1,500	65	
Esh Laude	[680]	31	420
Felling	3,100	198	
Gainsford	149	7	107
Gateshead	[7,500]	381	1,500
Hartlepool	1,500	124	690
Hartlepool, W.	2,000	127	400
Hebburn	[2,282]		
Houghton	1,100	70	
Jarrow	4,000	283	1,200
Monkwearmouth	2,000	150	931
Newcastle			
St. Mary	8,000	424	2,534
St. Dominic	4,000	281	1,900
St. Michael	1,290	83	400
St. Andrews	3,000	121	300
Newhouse	1,600	72	970

continued

Port Clarence	600	34	110
Sacriston	560	35	208
Seaham Harbour	1,000	104	407
South Shields	3,500	176	1,200
Stella	1,445	84	631
Stockton	2,750	181	
Sunderland			
St. Mary	2,100	188	1,140
St. Joseph	1,500	92	
St. Patrick	4,000	170	1,200
Thornley & Sedgefield	1,800	92	400
Tow Law & Wolsingham	947	45	500
Tudhoe	1,800	125	600
(New) Tunstall	800	58	308
Washington	900	47	
	92,031	5,184	28,499

Source: Status Animarum, etc., v.2, pp.131-139. These figures are taken from a large master copy dated 1875. Of the original returns made by the priests only one is extant: Washington, whose figures are correctly copied onto the master sheet. The figures in parenthesis are calculated averages from the 1882 and 1874 statistics.

Appendix VIII

Diocesan Statistics, 1882

Mission	Est. Nos. of Caths.	Baptisms	Easter Communicants
Barnard Castle	300		140
Birtley	1,200	60	700
Bishop Auckland	2,265	159	1,663
Blackhill	3,600*	148	1,700
Brooms	1,800	95	850
Byer-Moor & Stanley	1,450	54	420
Castle Eden	1,200	40	330
Chester-le-Street	120(a)	15	84
Cornforth, Coxhoe & Trimdon	1,000	59	159
Crook	1,250	76	712
Croxdale	160	14	75
Darlington			
St Augustine	1,800*	106	950
St. William	950	58	
Dunston	547	31	[201](b)
Durham			
St. Cuthbert	1,231	71	
St. Godric	970	69	640
Easington	1,230	43	175
Esh Laude	600	48	620
Felling	3,200	155	1,050
Gainsford	150*	9	118
Gateshead	10,000(c)	406	3,000
Hartlepool	1,600	94	609
Hartlepool, W.	4,000*	140	1.050
Hebburn	2,764	102	1,200
Houghton	1,450*	92	500
Jarrow	5,800	327	2,537
Langley	800	40	600
Monkwearmouth	3,684	165	1,976
Newcastle			
St. Mary	9,000*	455	2,400
St. Dominic	4,800	299	1,700
St. Michael	2,520	95	450
St. Andrews	2,288	183	1,089
Newhouse	1,368	54	630

continued

Port Clarence	855	30	
Sacriston	900	89	450
Seaham Harbour	1,100	49	594
South Shields & Tyne Dock	4,300	168	1,338
Stella	1,496	73	625
Stockton	6,000	308	1,600
Sunderland			
St. Mary	2,000	138	1,200
St. Joseph	2,000	107	
St. Patrick	3,900	142	
Thornley & Sedgefield	900*	73	400
Tow Law & Wolsingham	1,100	50	398
Tudhoe	1,800	98	645
(New) Tunstall	1,500	66	448
Washington	1,300	71	563
Willington	825	57	454
Witton Park	1,100	56	775
	106,173	5,369	37,818

*Noted as approximations

a. 'The number *varies very much* on account of the number who leave the mines and go elsewhere'. Mission priest.
b. The figure for 1883; **a** house to house census gave a Catholic population for that year of 800.
c. 8,000 known; 2,000 unknown.

Source: Status Animarum, etc., v.2, pp.141-149.

References

Foreword by Donald MacRaild   pages ix-xvi

1. The term has become popular in Irish academic circles to describe part of the process of competition between different political traditions, Unionist, Nationalist, 'traditional', revisionist, counter-revisionist, and so on. For the scholarly debate, see two important studies: C. Brady (ed.), *Interpreting Irish History: the Debate on Historical Revisionism* (Dublin, 1994) and D.G. Boyce and A. O'Day (eds), *The Making of Modern Irish History: Revisionism and the Revisionist Controversy* (London, 1996).

2. John Rex, 'Immigrants and British Labour: the Sociological Context', in K. Lunn (ed.), *Hosts, Immigrants and Minorities: Responses to Newcomers in British Society, 1870-1914* (Folkestone, 1980), pp.22-38.

3. Although only the last of these titles remains in print: J.A. Jackson, *The Irish in Britain* (London, 1963); G. Davis, *The Irish in Britain, 1815-1914* (Dublin, 1991); D.M. MacRaild, *Irish Migrants in Modern Britain, 1750-1922* (Basingstoke, 1999).

4. *The Irish in the Victorian City* (Beckenham, 1985); *The Irish in Britain, 1815-1939* (London, 1989); *The Irish in Victorian Britain* (Dublin, 1999).

5. Apart from Cooter's work we can point to three other theses: L. Gooch, 'The Durham Catholics and Industrial Development, 1560-1850', MA, University of York, 1984; S. Doherty, 'English and Irish Catholics in Northumberland, 1745-1860', PhD, Queen's University, Belfast, 1984; and Caroline L. Scott, 'A Comparative Re-examination of Anglo-Irish Relations in Nineteenth-century Manchester, Liverpool and Newcastle-upon-Tyne', PhD, University of Durham, 1998. Shorter studies, mostly in article form and published in local history journals, have added to our knowledge of parts of the north-east. These include: P. Norris, 'The Irish in Tow Law, County Durham, 1851-1871', *Durham County Local History Society Bulletin*, 33 Dec. (1984); J Robinson, 'The Coming of the Irish to Jarrow and Hebburn', *Journal of the Northumberland and Durham Family*

History Society, 6, 3 (1981); M., McManus 'Folk Devils and Moral Panics? Irish Stereotyping in Mid-Victorian Durham', *Bulletin of the Durham County Local History Society*, 53 Dec. (1994). T.P. McDermott has also written two useful essays on the Tyneside Irish: 'Irish Workers on Tyneside', in N. Mc Cord (ed.), *Essays in Tyneside Labour History* (Newcastle, 1977) and 'The Irish in Nineteenth-century Tyneside' (Newcastle Polytechnic, 1982). Middlesbrough and the neighbouring industrial sector have been examined in M. Chase, 'The Teesside Irish in the Nineteenth-century', in P. Buckland & J.C. Belchem (eds) *The Irish in British Labour History* (Liverpool, 1993) and idem., '"Dangerous People"?: the Teesside Irish in the nineteenth-century', *Bulletin of North East Labour History*, 28 (1994). For census-based case-studies, see Frank Neal, 'Irish Settlement in the North-east and North-west of England in the Mid-nineteenth Century', in R. Swift and S. Gilley (eds), *The Irish in Victorian Britain: the Local Dimension* (Dublin, 1999) and his 'The Foundations of the Irish Settlement in Newcastle upon Tyne: the Evidence in the 1851 Census', in D.M.MacRaild (ed.), *The Great Famine and Beyond: Irish Migrants in Britain in the Nineteenth and Twentieth Centuries* (Dublin, 2000).

6. *Royal Commission on the Condition of the Poorer Classes in Ireland*, Appendix G., *Report into the State of the Irish Poor in Great Britain*, PP (1836).

7. J.H. Treble, 'The Place of the Irish Catholics in the Social Life of the North of England, 1829-1851', PhD, University of Leeds, 1969.

8. Michael Anderson, *Family Structure in Nineteenth Century Lancashire* (Cambridge: Cambridge University Press, 1971).

9. Most notably, Lyn Hollen Lees, *Exiles of Erin: the Irish in Victorian London* (Manchester, 1979); and Frances Finnegan, *Poverty and Prejudice: The Irish in York*, c.1840-1880 (Cork, 1982).

10. C.G. Pooley, 'Migration, Mobility and Residential Areas in Nineteenth-century Liverpool' (PhD, University of Liverpool, 1978); J.D. Papworth, 'The Irish in Liverpool, 1835-1871: Family Structure and Residential Mobility', PhD, University of Liverpool, 1982.

11. For example, Donald M. MacRaild, *Culture, Conflict and Migration: The Irish in Victorian Cumbria* (Liverpool, 1998), which examines five census decades (1851-91).

12. E.G. Mary E. Daly, *Dublin: the Deposed Capital, 1860-1914* (Cork, 1984); A.C.Hepburn, *A Past Apart: Studies in the History of Catholic Belfast* (Belfast, 1996); Cormac Ó Gráda, 'Did Ulster Catholics Always Have Larger Families?', *Irish Economic and Social History*, 12 (1985), 79-88.

13. Mike Barke, 'The People of Tyneside: a Demographic History', in R. Colls and W. Lancaster (eds), *Newcastle: a Modern History* (Chichester, 2001). Barke is a graduate of both Liverpool and Glasgow.

14. The political issues are analysed particularly well in Joan Hugman, 'Joseph Cowen of Newcastle and Radical Liberalism', PhD, University of Northumbria, 1993. A useful sketch is also found in N. Todd, *Militant Democracy: Joseph Cowen and Victorian Radicalism* (Whitley Bay, 1991). See also Donald M. MacRaild, *Faith, Fraternity and Fighting: The Orange Order and Irish Migrants in Northern England*, c.1850-1920 (Liverpool, 2005), ch.6.

15. F. Neal, 'English-Irish conflict in the north-east of England', in J. Belchem and P. Buckland (eds), *The Irish in British Labour History* (Liverpool, 1992).

16. For further discussion of these issues concerning north-east Orangeism, see MacRaild, *Faith, Fraternity and Fighting*, esp. ch.2 and ch.5.

Author's Preface pages xvii-xxii

1. R.J. Cooter, 'On Calculating the Nineteenth Century Irish Catholic Population of Durham and Newcastle', *Northern Catholic History*, No.2 (1975), 16-25; idem, 'Hibernians and Geordies in the Nineteenth Century', *Northern Catholic History*, No.4 (1976), 20-9; idem, 'Lady Londonderry and the Irish Catholics of Seaham Harbour: "No Popery" Out of Context', *Recusant History*, 16 (1976), 288-98.

2. Of this I was made acutely aware many years later when a researcher in the archives at Ushaw College reported back that I had become renowned for always wearing pyjama bottoms – in fact, a pair of rather trendy flared striped trousers from west-coast America!

3. *The Making of the English Working Class* (London, 1963), p.480.

4. In fact that possibility was just emerging in 1972 during the last few months of my time in Durham when a group of us under Peter Barham's inspired guidance engaged in a weekly reading of Foucault's *Madness and Civilization*.

5. Walter Arnstein, 'The Murphy Riots: a Victorian dilemma', *Victorian Studies*, 19 (1975), 51-71.

Introduction pages 1-6

1. A partial exception is J.H. Treble, 'The Place of the Irish Catholics in the Social Life of the North of England, 1829-51', PhD Thesis, University of Leeds, 1969. However, this includes only minimal information on the North East and is in this respect typical of studies on the 'north of England'.

2. The Crowe Collection of Pastorals, Circulars and Miscellanea, and four volumes of Pastorals and Circulars of the Vicars Apostolic and Bishops of the Northern Division and Diocese of Hexham and Newcastle.

3. J.G. Bell Collection: Forming a General History of Coal, Collieries, Colliery-Engineering and Mining, 20 vols.

4. A partial exception is Felix Lavery (ed.), *Irish Heroes in the War* (London, 1917) which contains some undocumented background on the Tyneside Irish.

5. 'Themes in Northern History', *Northern History*, 1 (1966), p.4.

Chapter 1 pages 7-20

1. *Third Report From the Select Committee on Emigration From the United Kingdom*, 1827, PP, 1826-27, V, p.231.

2. Robert Rawlinson, *Report to the General Board of Health on the Municipal Borough of Sunderland* (London, 1851), p.33.

3. David Dougan, *The History of North East Shipbuilding* (London, 1968), p.63.

4. *Population Census of Great Britain*, 1851, Appendix, Table 17, p.cvi.

5. *Kelly's Directory of Durham* (1890), p.419 and 55.

6. Ellen Wilkinson, *The Town That Was Murdered: the Life Story of Jarrow* (London, 1939), pp.71-2.

7. *Whellan's Directory of Durham and Newcastle* (1856), p.640.

8. Bernard C. Sharratt, *The Catholic Church in Hartlepool and West Hartlepool: 1834-1964* (West Hartlepool, 1964), p.27.

9. J.W. House, *North Eastern England Population Movements and the Landscape Since the Early 19th Century* (Newcastle, 1954), p.3. This is the only comprehensive demographic study of the North East. While invaluable, its uses are restricted, its figures reflecting regional rather than political boundaries.

10. The majority of these had simply migrated across the River Tyne from County Durham.

11. For a detailed study of the stages of population growth in relation to local coal mining, see, Arthur E. Smailes, 'Population Changes in the Colliery Districts of Northumberland and Durham', *Geographical Journal*, 91 (Jan. 1938), 220-32.

12. For the whole of the North East, the natural population increase was as follows 1851-61: 140,995; 1861-71: 175,104; and 1871-81: 252,508: House, *North Eastern England,* Table 1, p.56.

13. In 1841 only Northumberland and Cumberland had sizeable Scottish populations but, as the Census noted, 'even in these two counties they do not rise above 4 per cent on the total numbers enumerated': *Census of Great Britain,* 1841, p.223.

14. George Grey, Assistant Overseer for the Poor Law in Newcastle, stated that the Irish 'mostly land at Whitehaven ... [and] so far as I have learned, they make their way directly to Newcastle': *Select Committee on Poor Removals,* 1855, PP, 1854-5, XIII, q.425-27, p.31.

15. *Census of Great Britain, 1851*: Enumerator's Manuscript returns for the parish of All Saints, Newcastle. Newcastle Central Library. The total Irish community has been calculated here by adding to Irish-born all those children who were still within the family yet not born in Ireland. Non-Irish lodgers and visitors living with Irish families have been excluded. Only the Irish actually on Wall Knoll Street have been included; not those in adjoining 'closes', lanes, alleys and entries. The number of non-Irish has been similarly calculated.

16. *Census of Great Britain, 1851*: Enumerator's returns for the Ecclesiastical District of Thornley, Parish of Wolsingham, South Durham. Durham County Record Office. Both Wall Knoll Street and Thornley had Irish populations in the 1840s; thus the ratio of Irish-born to non-Irish-born children is distorted by the number of them born in Durham and Newcastle. For Wall Knoll Street there were 39 such children; for Thornley, 29.

17. John A. Jackson, *The Irish in Britain* (London, 1963), map p.12.

18. *Newcastle Daily Chronicle,* 10 Oct. 1867, p.4.

19. 'Irish in England', Letter XV, *Nation,* 19 Oct. 1872, p.662.

20. See, B.M. Kerr, 'Irish Seasonal Migrations to Great Britain 1800-1838', *Irish Historical Studies,* 3 (1942-43), 365-80.

21. 9 Nov. 1831. Edward Hughes (ed.), *The Diaries and Correspondence of James Losh,* vol. 2: 1824-33, Surtees Society, vol. l74 (London, 1963), pp.200-1.

22. William Fordyce, *The History and Antiquities of the County Palatine of Durham* (Newcastle and London, 1851), vol. 1, p.183.

23. 'Appendix', *First Report of the Commissioners for Inquiring into the Employment and Condition of Children in Mines and Manufactories,* Mines, Pt. I: Report by James Mitchell, PP, 1842, XX, q.201, p.142.

24. Evidence of Robert Rawlinson, *Select Committee on Railway Labourers*, 1846, PP, 1846, XIII, q.1043, p.501.

25. Thomas Richmond, *Local Records of Stockton-on-Tees and the Neighbourhood* (London, 1868), 17 Feb. 1833, p. 165.

26. Thomas Carlyle, *Chartism* (2nd edn., London, 1842), pp.25-29, quoted in James E. Handley, *The Irish in Modern Scotland* (Cork, 1947), p.9.

27. *Report of the Poor Inquiry (Ireland) Commission*, 'Appendix G: Report of the State of the Irish Poor in Great Britain', PP, 1836, XXXIV, p.427 (hereafter, 'Appendix G', 1836).

28. 'Appendix G', 1836, p.433.

29. Eric Strauss, *Irish Nationalism and British Democracy* (London, 1951), pp.l03-4; George O'Brien, *The Economic History of Ireland from the Union to the Famine* (London, 1921), pp.231-32.

30. 'Appendix G', p.452.

31. *Ordo and Catholic Directory* (1842), p.38.

32. Ibid., p.39.

33. J.H. Treble draws attention to earlier references to Catholic missions at Birtley and Houghton-le-Spring where the congregations were described as consisting of colliers, ('The Place of the Irish Catholics in the Social Life of the North of England', PhD thesis, University of Leeds, 1969, p.67). While we cannot be certain of the nationality of these congregations, evidence presented in Chapter 3 will suggest that these Catholics were unlikely to have been Irish.

34. The late arrival of the Irish in the area was also commented on by the correspondent to the *Nation* in 1872: 'Irish in England', Letter XV, 19 Oct. 1872, p.662.

35. On Wall Knoll Street and St. Mary Street (alias Sandgate) between 1841 and 1871 there were on average 2.7 children per set of Irish parents *with* children. It is interesting to note the gradual increase in this average over the decennial periods. 1841: 2.2; 1851: 2.7; 1861: 2.8; and 1871: 3.1. There were, of course, many fatherless children but these were nearly equally offset by the number of couples with no children. Thus, as one clergyman pointed out, 'I am convinced that the fallacy of the Irish being more prolific arises from the fact that they live in small houses, often several families in a house, the houses frequently packed in long courts, whence the children swarm into the main streets for a breath of air and for a sight of life, and hence passers-by are astounded at the number of children'. Quoted in Rev. John Morris, *Catholic England in Modern Times* (London,

1892), p.95. To this must be added that infant mortality was always higher in the slum areas where many Irish resided, and that there was no easily accessible birth-control for non-Catholics either.

36. Morris, *Catholic England*, p.79. Morris was secretary both to Cardinal Wiseman and Archbishop Manning, 1861-67.

37. *Newcastle Courant*, Pt. II, 17 May 1850, p.4.

38. John Wilson, *Memoirs of a Labour Leader: the Autobiography of John Wilson, J.P., M.P.* (London, 1910), p.90. There does not appear to have been the same amount of interest in either the California Gold Rush of 1849 or that in British Columbia in 1858.

39. See, for example, 'Important to Miners Intending to Emigrate', *Durham Chronicle*, 13 Aug. 1869, p.5; 'The Ironmasters and Emigration', *Durham Chronicle*, 24 Mar. 1865, p.5.

40. It has been estimated that by 1881 some 3,000 miners left Durham for the United States: G.H. Metcalf, 'A History of the Durham Miners' Association 1869-.1915', MA thesis, Durham University, 1947, p.386; E. Welbourne, *The Miners' Unions of Northumberland and Durham* (Cambridge, 1923), p.213.

41. Robert Pashley told the *Select Committee on Poor Removals* (1854) that 'the number of removals of the Irish [from all England] is about 10,000, that is, two per cent', but the Commissioner for the Poor Law in Ireland insisted that 'no inference can safely be drawn as to the whole number of removals in each year': PP, 1854, XVII, q.645, p.473 and q.471, p.45 respectively.

42. *Poor Law Removals*: PP, 1860, LVIII, p.79l; PP, 1863, LII, p.267; PP, 1864, LII, p.305.

43. Rev. Hardcastle's speech, 9 Mar. 1840, in Henry French Etherington, *Full Report of ... a Public Meeting Held in the Wesleyan Chapel, Hartlepool ... to Establish an Auxiliary in Aid of the British Reformation Society* (Sunderland, 1840), p.18.

44. *Census of Great Britain, 1871*: Enumerators' Manuscripts for the Parish of All Saints, Newcastle. Public Records Office.

45. R. Samuel, 'The Catholic Church and the Irish Poor', paper presented to the Past and Present Conference, July 1966, p.36.

46. 'Irish in England', *Nation*, Letter XV, 19 Oct. 1872, p.662.

47. *Kelly's Directory of Durham* (1890), p.1. David Dougan, *The History of North East Shipbuilding* (London, 1968), p.63.

Chapter 2 pages 21-44

1. *Glasgow Argus*, quoted in *Newcastle Chronicle*, 20 Jan. 1847, p.8.
2. *Select Committee on Poor Removals*, 1855, PP, 1854-5, XIII, q.425, p.31.
3. *Tablet*, 24 May 1851, p.325.
4. Ibid., p.325.
5. The growth of Catholicism in Gateshead suggests that the majority of Irish were Catholic. In 1852 the *Catholic Directory* (p.48) listed upwards of 3,000 Catholics for the Borough while citing the Census figure of 1,544 for the Irish-born. A typical comment on their condition was given by *The Tablet* (21 June 1851, p.388) when it spoke of the 'indefatigable Pastor of the new Mission at Gateshead [who] ... continues to breast the difficulties common to the establishment of most all Missions, but in the case of St. Edmond's difficulties (owing to the almost entire absence of affluent persons) of more than ordinary character. The work proposed to be accomplished in such a locality is fit only for a priest who counts every thing worthless as compared with the salvation of souls'.
6. Evidence of Thomas Hedley before the *Select Committee on the Irremovable Poor*, 1860, PP, 1860, XVII, q.2840, p.149.
7. 'Report of the Committee Appointed to Act in Conjunction with the Board of Guardians During the Prevalence of Cholera', in *Proceedings of the Newcastle Common Council*, 12 Oct. 1853, p.137. Newcastle City Archives. For an impression of conditions in the eighteenth century, see George Balmer's painting, 'Grey Horse Inn, Quayside', Laing Gallery, Newcastle.
8. *Inquiry into the Condition of the Poor of Newcastle-Upon-Tyne* ([reprinted from *Newcastle Weekly Chronicle*], Newcastle, 1850), p.23.
9. 'Condition of our Chief Towns – Newcastle-Upon-Tyne', *Builder*, 19 (13 April 1861), p.242.
10. Henry Armstrong, *Report of the Medical Officer of Health* (Newcastle, 1877), p.22. Newcastle Central Library, Local Tracts Collection.
11. *Newcastle Courant*, 6 Aug 1875, on the occasion of Newcastle having the highest death-rate of the 18 large towns listed in the Register-General's returns.
12. Newcastle first gained this distinction in 1866 with an overall death rate of 36.7 per 1,000. Liverpool, Manchester and Leeds were next with 33.1, 29.6, and 28.4, respectively. 'Report of the Public Health', 1866, presented to Council, 6 Mar. 1867, p.193. The average death rate for the city between 1851 and 1871 was 35.5.

13. *An Account of the Great Fire and Explosion Which Occurred in Newcastle and Gateshead on the 6th of October 1854* (Newcastle, 1854), p.4.

14. *Inquiry into Newcastle Poor*, p.47.

15. 'What the horse is to the Arab, or the dog to the Green-lander, the pig is to an Irishman. He feeds it quite as well as he does his children, assigns to it a corner in his sitting-room, shares his potatoes, his milk, and his bread with it, and all these favours, he confidently expects, the pig will in due time gratefully repay. Upon the pig it is that the best hopes of the poor peasant often repose. J.G. Kohl, *Ireland: Dublin, The Shannon, Limerick ... O'Connell and the Repeal Association* (London, 1844), p.25.

16. *Proceedings of the Newcastle Common Council*, 4 Oct. 1848, p.202.

17. Twenty-four cases were brought before the magistrates in 1866. *Proceedings of Council*, 6 Mar. 1867, p.213.

18. D.B. Reid, *Report on the Sanitary Conditions of Newcastle, Gateshead, North Shields, Sunderland, Durham and Carlisle. Appendix II, Second Report of the Commissioners on the State of Large Towns and Populous Districts*, PP., 1845, XVIII, p.529.

19. Ibid., p.563.

20. Ibid., p.533.

21. Ibid., p.549.

22. Medical Officer's Report Book for July 1851, quoted in *Public Health Report to the General Board of Health on Darlington* (1850), John Smith (ed.) Durham Local History Society (1967), pp.10-11.

23. *The History and Description of Fossil Fuel, the Collieries and Coal Trade of Great Britain* (London, 1835), p.292. See also, *Report of the Commissioner ... to Inquire into the State of the Population in the Mining Districts*, PP, 1846, XXIV, pp.383-446; and 'Aspects of the Working Classes', *Newcastle Chronicle*, 7 Mar. - 16 May 1851.

24. *Whellan's Durham Directory* (1856), p.98.

25. *Durham Chronicle*, 21 July 1865, p.6.

26. *Durham Chronicle*, 6 Jan. 1882, p.7.

27. *Newcastle Courant*, 4 Mar. 1853, cited in J.F. Clarke, 'Labour Relations in Engineering and Shipbuilding on the North East Coast, 1850-1900', MA thesis, University of Newcastle, 1966, p.28.

28. *Newcastle Daily Chronicle*, 13 May 1865, quoted in Ellen Wilkinson, *The Town That Was Murdered: the Life Story of Jarrow* (London, 1939), pp.73-

74; see also, 'Launch of the Hudson', *Newcastle Chronicle*, 18 June 1858, p.6.

29. 'History and Progress of the Consett Iron Works', *Newcastle Chronicle*, 9 July 1858, p.6.

30. Ibid., p.6.

31. For example, Consett Iron Co. Ltd., *Description of the Works* (Newcastle, 1893).

32. Minutes of the Nuisance Removal Committee, Feb. 1861, quoted in George Neasham, *History and Biography of West Durham* (n.p., 1881), p.25n.

33. B.S. Rowntree, *Poverty: A Study of Town Life* (4th edn., London, 1902), pp.86-7.

34. Enumerator's prefatory note for St. Mary Street ('Bearing the assumed name of Sandgate') for the above described places. Manuscript Returns for the parish of All Saints, 1861.

35. *Select Committee on Poor Removals*, 1855, q.4ll, p.30.

36. 'Report of the Newcastle Committee to D.B. Reid', Second *Report... on the State of Large Towns* (1845), p.526.

37. George Grey, evidence before the *Select Committee on Poor Removals*, q.411, p.30.

38. Manuscript Returns for the parish of All Saints, 1861, for the north side of St. Mary-Sandgate from the White House entry to Johnson's entry.

39. 'Ghetto' is meant here as a loose containment of Irish within the larger slum area. In Newcastle the Irish never entirely dominated one whole area of the slum, but rather, formed numerous pockets of settlement primarily in the Sandgate area. Certain entries or closes such as 'Nags Head' off Sandgate and 'Mount Pleasant' or 'Craig-alley Stairs' were inhabited entirely by Irish, while others like 'Young's Entry' were nearly void of Irish.

40. See, for example, K. Boyle, 'The Irish Immigrant in Britain', *Northern Ireland Legal Quarterly*, 19 (Dec 1968), pp.4l8-45. *Cf* J. Augustine O'Gorman, 'The Irish Ghetto Originated in Ireland, Not in the United States', *Éire-Ireland*, 3 (1969), pp.147-50.

41. Engels, *The Condition of the Working Class in England* (1845; repr. London, 1969), p.123.

42. 'Report of the Medical Officer of Health to Council', 1874, cited in S. Middlebrook, *Newcastle Upon Tyne, Its Growth and Achievement* (Newcastle, 1950), p.273.

43. James C. Street, *The Night-side of Newcastle: A Lecture Delivered in the Church of Divine Unity* (Newcastle, 1865), p.14. Northumberland County Record Office.

44. *Tablet*, 20 Mar. 1852, p.180. St. Giles was a notorious slum in London's West End.

45. It is not possible to discern the exact proportions of Catholic to Protestant Irish. Evidence presented in the following two chapters points to a low percentage of Protestant Irish.

46. 'Newcastle, St. Andrews – A Rev. gentleman is expected shortly to join this mission from Ireland, who, it is understood, is well acquainted with the Irish language, and who will in consequence be more adapted to a district in which such vast numbers of the Faithful are natives of the sister country': *Tablet*, 16 Aug. 1851, p.517.

47. J. Hickey, *Urban Catholics* (London, 1967), p.57.

48. R. Samuel, 'The Catholic Church and the Irish Poor', paper presented to the Past and Present Conference, July 1966, p.48.

49. *A Few Brief Observations, Illustrations and Anecdotes Respecting Pitmen in a Northern Colliery Village by an Incumbent in the Diocese of Durham* (Sunderland, 1862), p.4.

50. *Durham Chronicle*, 21 July 1865, p.2.

51. Street, *The Night-side of Newcastle*, p.6.

52. *Whellan's Directory of Durham* (1865), p.90.

53. John C. Kirk, 'The History of Thornley', *Northern Daily Mail*, 24 Mar. 1970, p.12.

54. Francis Mewburn, *The Larchfield Diary: Extracts from the Diary of the Late Mr. Mewburn, First Railway Solicitor* (London, 1876), entry for 25 Mar. 1863, p.186.

55. 'An Appeal to the Catholic Laity on the Present Condition of the Poor', *Rambler*, 2 (Oct. 1854), pp.279-80.

56. Rev. R. Belaney, *The Reign of Sin and the Reign of Grace, A Sermon Preached at St. Wilfrid's Church, Bishop Auckland* (13 Dec. 1863), p.13. Ushaw Pamphlets Collection.

57. The only prominent Catholic to attend a public meeting to raise funds to help Father Mathew was Rev. Dr. Riddell. *Newcastle Chronicle*, 1 Jan 1841. Cited in W. Donald Cooper, 'The Teetotal Movement with Particular Reference to the North-East of England: 1835-1860', History Honours Paper (Durham, 1968), p.35.

58. Rev. Patrick Rogers, *Father Theobald Mathew: Apostle of Temperance* (Dublin, 1943), pp.149-50.

59. See, for example, 'South Shields Retreat', *Tablet*, 1 July 1854, p.446.

60. 'Irish Riot at Southwick [near Sunderland]', *Newcastle Daily Chronicle*, 19 July 1867, p.2. The town was described as having a population 'from 5,000 to 6,000, and one-half of them Irish'.

61. Kirk, 'The History of Thornley', 24 Mar. 1970, p.12.

62. *Durham Chronicle*, 17 Mar. 1865, p.8.

63. Ibid., 23 Mar. 1866, p.5.

64. Ibid., 23 Mar. 1883, p.5.

65. A similar conclusion was reached by the commissioners for 'Appendix G: Report of the State of the Irish Poor in Great Britain' in the *Report of the Poor Inquiry (Ireland) Commission*, PP 1836, XXXIV, p.446.

66. *Criminal and Miscellaneous Statistical Returns of the Newcastle Police for the Year Ending 29th Sept., 1861* (Newcastle, 1861), Table 1.4, p.4. Newcastle Central Library, Local Tracts Collection. The specifying of 'Irish-born' does not necessarily reflect on the attitude of the Newcastle police towards the Irish, for other towns (Bradford for example) had earlier implemented this analytical category.

67. Borough of Newcastle, *Criminal and Miscellaneous Statistical Returns of the Constabulary for the Year Ending 29th Sept., 1869* (Newcastle, 1869), Table 9, p.11. Newcastle Central Library, Local Tracts Collection.

68. W.G. Lumley, 'The Statistics of the Roman Catholic Church in England and Wales', *Journal of the Statistical Society of London*, 27 (Sept. 1864), pp.317-18.

69. On Bradford, see, C. Richardson, 'The Irish in Victorian Bradford', unpublished paper delivered to the conference at Durham University 16 Sept. 1969, pp.15-16. The criminal statistics are not reproduced in the published version of this paper in the *Yorkshire Bulletin of Economic and Social Research*, 20 (May 1968), 40-57.

70. *Tablet*, 19 Oct. 1867, p.669.

71. 'The Temperance Reformation, the United Kingdom Alliance and Local Option', 4 Sept. 1882, quoted in Vincent A. McClelland, *Cardinal Manning, His Public Life and Influence, 1865-1892* (London, 1962), p.200.

72. *The League of the Cross and Crusade Against Intemperance: Official Report of the Conventions of [12 July] 1875 and [11 October] 1876* (Manchester, 1877), p.16.

73. Quoted in Rev. J. Lenders, *History of the Parish of Sacriston* (Minsteracres, 1930), p.22. Ushaw Pamphlets Collection.

74. *Tablet*, 30 May 1874, p.693.

75. Neasham, *History and Biography of West Durham*, p.75.

76. *Tablet*, 7 Mar. 1885, p.391.

77. *Newcastle Daily Chronicle*, 12 Aug. 1887, quoted in *Northern Catholic Calendar* (1888), p.10.

78. As distinct from the London Hibernian Society, a Protestant evangelical society which for a short time in the 1830s had auxiliaries in Newcastle and Stockton. See, 'Report Of the Hibernian Society Meeting on Monday, the 11th October 1830', *John Bull*, unpaginated. Newcastle Central Library, Local Tracts Collection.

79. James A. McFaul, 'Hibernians', *Catholic Encyclopedia* (New York, 1910) vol.7, pp.320-21.

80. Such were the instructions issued by the Society of Hibernians in Ireland to the Irish in New York (c.1830): *Lecture on the Ancient Order of Hibernians* (Chicago, 1904), quoted in McFaul, 'Hibernians', pp.320.

81. John O'Leary, *Recollections of Fenians and Fenianism* (London, 1896), vol. 1, p.111. O'Leary, when in America, also supposed that the Ancient Order of Hibernians was a Ribbon organisation 'but neither then nor since could I at all gather ... what business they had there'.

82. John Denvir, *The Irish in Britain from the Earliest Times to the Fall and Death of Parnell* (London, 1892), pp.128-29.

83. J.H. Treble, 'The Place of the Irish Catholics in the Social Life of the North of England', PhD thesis, University of Leeds, 1969, p.223.

84. *Tablet*, 27 Mar. 1852, p.197.

85. Pastoral, 22 Mar. 1852, Ushaw Collection, vol. 3.

86. *Newcastle Chronicle*, 24 Mar. 1854, p.4.

87. *Tablet*, 1 July 1854, p.466.

88. Hogarth to Clergy, 3 April 1857, Ushaw Collection, vol. 4.

89. Hogarth, Pastoral, 9 Feb. 1858, Ushaw Collection, vol. 4.

90. Ibid., 1 May 1858.

91. Ibid., 23 Feb. 1859. An example of this 'zeal' and the methods used by some clergy to eliminate Hibernians can be seen in Rev. F. Betham of Gateshead who in 1851 nailed on his chapel door statements by the Holy Pontiff condemning secret societies, adding: 'I earnestly call upon these misguided men [in secret societies] to seek pardon and reconciliation with the Church, lest perhaps the Lord in His anger overtake them and they cry out for mercy when there is no longer mercy to be found; but if they neglect this invitation, then it will be my painful duty to collect the names of the contumacious, and to post them on the doors of the church, as persons excommunicated, and to be avoided by the Faithful': *Tablet*, 13 Dec. 1851, p.790.

92. Holy Guilds were established in Newcastle and Stockton in 1844 and in Bishopwearmouth in 1845 in order to 'withdraw individuals from the societies of Odd-Fellows, Hibernians, et.hoc. genus omne'. *Tablet*, 19 April 1845, p.247.

93. 'Hibernicus to editor', *Tablet*, 16 Dec. 1854, p.790.

94. Bishop Bewick, Pastoral, *Tablet*, 28 Oct. 1880, p.713. The two evils were often cited side-by-side in order that it appear that, as Dr. Cullen stated, 'Drunkenness is encouraged by the meeting of such societies'. Pastoral, 1 Dec 1861, quoted in *The Times*, 5 Dec. 1861, p.4.

95. M.C. Bishop, 'The Social Methods of Roman Catholicism in England', *Contemporary Review*, 39 (Mar. 1877), p.611.

96 William G. Todd, *The Irish in England* (London, 1857), p.2, reprinted from the *Dublin Review* 31 (Dec. 1856).

97. Ibid., p.3.

98. 'Appendix G: Report of the State of the Irish Poor in Great Britain' in the *Report of the Poor Inquiry (Ireland) Commission*, PP 1836, XXXIV, p.456.

99. Edwin Chadwick, *Report on the Sanitary Conditions of the Labouring Population* (1842), M.W. Flinn (ed.) (Edinburgh, 1965), p.199.

100. 'Appendix G: Report of the State of the Irish Poor in Great Britain', p.438.

101. Charles Booth, *Life and Labour of the London Poor*, 3rd series, vol. 7, pp.243-4, quoted in Samuel, 'The Catholic Church and the Irish Poor', p.23.

102. *Public Health Act Report to the General Board of Health on Darlington* (1850), pp.10-11.

103. *Inquiry into the Condition of the Poor of Newcastle-Upon-Tyne* (Newcastle, 1850), p.43. The author had lived in Ireland and maintained strong Protestant views.

104. T. Fordyce, *Local Register of Remarkable Events of Northumberland, and Durham, Newcastle-Upon-Tyne and Berwick-Upon-Tweed* (Newcastle, 1867), vol. 3, 14 Mar. 1844, pp.182-83.

105. L. P. Curtis Jr., *Anglo-Saxons and Celts: A Study of Anti-Irish Prejudice in Victorian England* (New York, 1968).

106. *Durham Chronicle*, 25 Aug. 1865, p.5.

107. S. Baring-Gould, *The Church Revival: Thoughts Thereon and Reminiscences* (London, 1914), p.277.

108. Quoted in T.S. Ashton, *Economic and Social Investigations In Manchester*, I (London, 1934), pp.52-3.

109. George Robinson, *Lecture on the Sanitary Condition of Newcastle delivered before the Literary and Philosophical Society, 10th Feb., 1847* (Newcastle, 1847), p.5. Newcastle Central Library, Local Tracts Collection.

110. Cited in W. Young, 'Public Health in Newcastle 1845-54 With Special Reference to the Cholera Epidemic of 1853', History Honours Paper (Newcastle, 1965), p.19.

111. J. Kitching, 'The Catholic Poor Schools 1800 to 1845: The Catholic Poor: Relief, Welfare and Schools', *Journal of Educational Administration and History*, 1 (June 1969), p.3.

112. J. Gillow, *Bibliographical Dictionary of English Catholics* (London, 1885-98), vol. 5, pp.418-49.

113. *Durham Advertiser*, 7 Sept. 1849, p.4.

114. Mewburn, *The Larchfield Diary*, entry for Sept. 1853, p.121.

115. Rev. J. Davies, *Sermon on Public Thanksgiving Day October 27, 1853* (Gateshead, 1853), p.7. Newcastle Central Library, Local Tracts Collection.

116. *Report of the Commissioners Appointed to Inquire into the Causes which have led to or have Aggravated the Late Outbreak of Cholera in the towns of Newcastle-Upon-Tyne, Gateshead, and Tynemouth*, PP, 1854. XXXV, 131, p.vi.

117. Ibid., q.19, p.2.

118. Ibid., q.56, p.3.

119. *Sunderland Herald*, 8 Sept. 1854, quoted in T.J. Nossiter, 'Elections and Political Behaviour In County Durham and Newcastle, 1832-74', D.Phil. thesis, Oxford University, 1968, p.98.

120. Committee's 'Report' to D. B. Reid for the *State of Large Towns*, 1845, p.527.

121. Ibid., p.527; Edward Hughes (ed.), *The Diaries and Correspondence of James Losh*, vol. 2: 1824-33, Surtees Society, vol. 174 (London, 1963), pp.200-1.

122. Arthur Redford, *Labour Migration in England, 1800-1850* (Manchester, 1926), pp.159-60.

123. 'Irishmen in England', editorial, 24 Dec. 1867, p.2.

124. *Select Committee on Poor Removals*, 1854, Appendix 17, p.664.

125. *All Saints Parish: Guardians Meeting 1840-48*. Newcastle City Archives.

126. Removal Warrant Papers, 1849, 20/75/1249. Newcastle City Archives. The papers appear to be complete for 1849; they also record eight removals to Scotland.

127. Ibid., 16 May 1844, p.206.

128. *Minutes of the Newcastle Board of Guardians*, 15 Aug. 1844, p.2. Newcastle City Archives.

129. Ibid., p.2.

130. *All Saints Parish: Guardians Meeting*, 11 Mar. 1847, pp.365-70.

131. *Inquiry into Newcastle Poor*, p.73.

132. *All Saints Parish: Guardians Meeting*, 1 July 1853, p.157.

133. *Gateshead Observer*, 24 Jan. 1852, p.5.

134. *Durham Chronicle*, 16 July 1875, p.6 (my italics).

Chapter 3 pages 45-72

1. See Appendices 1-5. Except where indicated all tables and figures in this chapter are drawn from the appendices.

2. Return of Rev. Edward O'Dwyer of Cockermouth, Cumberland, 1865, for the 'Status of Baptisms and Marriages 1850-65', in *Status Animarum etc. for the Diocese of Hexham and Newcastle*, vol. 2, (1847-1912), p.51. Catholic Diocesan Archives.

3. A.C.M. Forester, 'Catholicism in the Diocese of Durham in 1767', *Ushaw Magazine*, 72 (Mar. 1962), p.91.

4. W.H.D. Longstaffe, *History of Darlington* (Darlington, 1854), p.250.

5. R. Surtees, *History of Durham* (London, 1816-1840), cited in *Northern Catholic Calendar* (1885), p.47.

6. A rural exception is Brooms where in 1836 a 'singular and unlooked for change took place' by the opening of 'the Railroad and a new Colliery' (John Smith to Miss Taylor of Cornsay, Brooms, 11 Mar. 1836). Smith, calling it an extraordinary case, makes no reference to any Irish, and in speaking of the increased number of 'children from the rails' at Sunday school, states that '1/3 at least of the 54 children are of Protestant parents.' Ushaw MSS. I am grateful to Rev. W. Vincent Smith for drawing this letter to my attention.

7. 'Four Catholic Congregations in Rural Northumberland 1750-1850', *Recusant History*, 9 (April 1967), 88-119; idem, 'More Northumberland Congregations', *Recusant History*, 10 (Jan. 1969), 11-34.

8. 'No official government estimates of the size of the [Irish] migration are available until 1841, when the first census revealed 289,404 Irish people living in England and Wales, a figure within a few hundred of the Catholic population calculated by the vicar apostolic over 20 years before!' J. Kitching, 'The Catholic Poor Schools 1800-1845: Pt. II, The Schools: Development and Distribution', *Journal of Educational Administration and History*, 2 (Dec. 1969), p.2.

9. Ibid., p.3. The number is that given by Vicar Apostolic Briggs.

10. 'A Statement of the Number of Seats in the Several Churches and Chapels ... Within the Parish of All Saints ... in the Month of August, 1838', *Journal of the Statistical Society of London*, 1 (Oct. 1838), p.379.

11. John Denvir, writing at the end of the 19th century, might be read as confirming the rather late arrival of the Irish in the area: 'In our days, since the Catholic Hierarchy was re-established, the See of Hexham and Newcastle has been filled by men of the same race as St. Cuthbert, the patron of the diocese. Dr. Chadwick, the second bishop, was a native of Drogheda, and Dr. O'Callaghan, the fourth bishop, was born in London of Irish parentage'. *The Irish in Britain from the Earliest Times To The Fall and Death of Parnell* (London, 1892), p.444.

12. *Catholic Directory* (Dublin, 1843), p.43.

13. Cited in *Northern Catholic Calendar* (London, 1936), p.97. From the 1870s the *Calendar* published brief histories of the missions, most of which were written by local priests.

14. *Tablet*, 19 April 1845, p.247.

15. Ibid., p.247; see also, C.H. Blair, *The Mayors and Lord Mayors of Newcastle, 1216-1940* (Newcastle, 1940).

16. *Tablet*, 8 June 1844, p.358.

17. *Tablet*, 24 Aug. 1844, p.533.
18. Ibid., p.533.
19. J.A. McEvoy to Rt. Rev. Dr. Penswick of Liverpool, 26 Oct. 1835. The letter is included among those transcribed and bound into 10 volumes by Rev. W. Vincent Smith in the Diocesan Archives, vol. 1, p.244.
20. *Northern Catholic Calendar* (1885), pp.47-8.
21. The estimates provided in Table 3.1 are compiled from returns provided by priests and do not appear to have been calculated merely from the baptisms. In some instances the priests indicated that they had undertaken door-to-door census. In general, the smaller the area, and/or the later the date of the return, the greater the accuracy.
22. On the development of schools and Catholic education, see, John F. Hayes, 'Roman Catholic Education in County Durham, 1580-1870', M.Ed. thesis, University of Durham, 1969. In the early 1840s there were no Catholic poor schools in the area; by 1876 there were 77: *Northern Catholic Calendar* (1876), pp.43-44.
23. *Northern Catholic Calendar* (1885), p.49.
24. 'An Ecclesiastical Census', editorial, *Newcastle Daily Chronicle*, 26 Oct. 1872, p.2. The *Census of Great Britain, 1851: Religious Worship: England and Wales*, PP, 1852-3, LXXXIX, p.cclxix, puts the first figure at 80. This is clearly wrong, and should be borne in mind when examining Map 4.3.
25. *Catholic Magazine* (1832), cited in *Northern Catholic Calendar* (1886), p.47.
26. Compiled from information contained in Appendix I.
27. McEvoy to Penswick, 26 Oct. 1835, p.244.
28. S. W. Gilley, 'Evangelical and Roman Catholic Missions to the Irish in London 1830-1870', Ph.D. thesis, University of Cambridge, 1970, p.11.
29. *Tablet*, 6 Aug. 1853, p.501.
30. Father Elzear Torregiani, *Franciscan Missions Among the Colliers and Ironworkers of Monmouthshire* (London, 1876), p.44.
31. Hogarth, Pastoral, 4 Oct. 1848, Crowe Collection, Ushaw.
32. *Tablet*, 5 June 1852, p.358; see also, K.S. Inglis, *Churches and the Working Classes in Victorian England* (London, 1963), p.125.
33. J. Lenders, *History of the Parish of Sacriston* (Minsteracres, 1930), pp.11-12.

34. *The Church of Our Lady of Mercy and St. Godric* (Durham, 1964), p.4. Ushaw Pamphlets Collection.

35. Bernard C. Sharratt, *Catholic Church in Hartlepool and West Hartlepool: 1834-1964* (West Hartlepool, 1964), p.27.

36. *Northern Catholic Calendar* (1885), p.49.

37. *Tablet*, 4 Nov. 1854, p.695.

38. Hogarth, Pastoral, 2 Jan. 1852. Ushaw Collection, vol. 3; *Northern Catholic Calendar* (1939), pp.100-1.

39. Pastoral, 4 July 1836. Ushaw Collection, vol. 2.

40. McEvoy to Penswick, 26 Oct. 1835, p.243.

41. *Northern Catholic Calendar* (1938), p.110.

42. Public Appeal of Rev. James Worswick, 1796, quoted in Rev. W. Vincent Smith, *Catholic Tyneside 1534-1860* (Newcastle, 1931), p.74.

43. Bishop of Abydos (Francis Mostyn) and *cum successione* Bishop of Longo (William Riddell), Pastoral, quoted in *Tablet*, 19 Oct. 1844, p.661.

44. 'Ecclesiophilist' to the editor, *Tablet*, 26 Oct. 1844, p.681.

45. *Tablet*, 2 Nov. 1844, p.693.

46. L.E.O. Charlton, *Recollections of a Northumbrian Lady [Barbara Charlton] 1815-66* (London, 1949), p.244; see also the comments of Mrs Beckwith to Lady Londonderry, cited below, Chapter 4.

47. *Tablet*, 19 July 1845, p.455.

48. 'Pray for the Good Estate of Henry Silvertop', reads the inscription below one of the windows in St. Patrick's, Consett, for example.

49. The sympathies of the rich were 'justly excited' by the distress in Ireland in 1847, but for the most part only after Pope Pius IX directed the clergy to remind the wealthy 'that the value of riches lies not in the money-bags of the rich, but in the food of the poor' etc. 'Encyclical Letter of our most Holy Lord Pius IX ... to all Primates, Archbishops, and Bishops, To Implore the Divine Help for The Kingdom of Ireland', 1847, Crowe Collection, Ushaw. Another exception to the general parsimony of the rich came shortly before the passage of the Educational Act of 1870 when, provoked by Government action, the Catholic gentry subscribed £40,000 towards Catholic schools, facilitating the rapid erection of some '30 or 40 schools' in the diocese of Hexham and Newcastle. *Northern Catholic Calendar* (1934), p.90.

50. 'To the Clergy', 14 Dec. 1846, Ushaw Collection, vol. 2.
51. 'Where Does Our Strength Lie?' *Rambler,* 14 (May 1849), p.4.
52. 'To the Clergy', 24 Sept. 1849, Ushaw Collection, vol. 3.
53. Pastoral, Feb. 1850, Ushaw Collection, vol. 3.
54. Pastoral, 14 Nov. 1850, Ushaw Collection, vol. 3.
55. Ibid.
56. *Tablet,* 1 Feb. 1851, p.68.
57. *Tablet,* 13 Dec. 1851, p.790.
58. Pastoral, quoted in *Gateshead Observer,* 24 Jan. 1852, p.5.
59. Ibid., p.5.
60. Pastoral, 13 Feb. 1853, Ushaw Collection, vol. 3.
61. *Tablet,* 29 Jan. 1853, p.67.
62. Pastoral, 16 Feb. 1857, Ushaw Collection, vol. 4.
63. Pastoral, 19 Feb. 1862, Ushaw Collection, vol. 4.
64. See, Hogarth et al. on Poor Schools, 15 Feb. 1848, Crowe Collection, Ushaw; and *Annual Reports of the Catholic Poor-School Committee* (1848 *et passim*).
65. Pastoral, 10 Feb. 1853, Ushaw Collection, vol. 3.
66. 'To the Clergy of the Diocese of Liverpool', 4 June 1852, Crowe Collection, Ushaw.
67. Cited in J.F. Clarke, 'Labour Relations in Engineering and Shipbuilding on the North East Coast, 1850-1900', MA thesis, University of Newcastle, 1966, p.28.
68. Robert Belaney, *The Reign of Sin and the Reign of Grace: A Sermon Preached at St. Wilfrid's Church, Bishop Auckland. December 13th, 1863* (Bishop Auckland, 1863), p.16. *Cf.* Archbishop Manning, *Ireland: A Letter to Earl Grey* (London, 1868), p.12: 'There can hardly be found in Great Britain a population poorer than those who are driven by poverty from Ireland .... Nevertheless, in all parts of England the same spirit of generosity and of piety, in everything which relates to the Church and the clergy, is to be found'. Ushaw Pamphlets Collection. Similar opinions were expressed by William G. Todd, *The Irish in England* (London, 1857), p.11, and in the 'Irish in England', *Nation,* Letter IV (27 July 1872), p.470.
69. Belaney, *The Reign of Sin,* p.16.

70. This normally applies only to persons over the age of 12 or 13. The very aged or sick, while excused from attendance, were usually visited by the priest and included in the list of Easter communicants.

71. Most of this leakage occurred between 1849-52, for over the next three years the adult Catholic population increased by 15 percent, while Easter communicants rose by 15.6 percent. Omissions in the returns for 1861 prevents worthwhile comparisons, and since adults are not listed for 1875 and 1882, it is difficult to estimate the extent of leakage. That the whole Catholic population increased by 15 percent between 1875 and 1882 and Easter communicants rose by only 3.2 percent suggests some leakage, but the difference between the two percentages is due mainly to the number of births in that period.

72. According to Rev. J. Lenders, 'at Bishop Auckland, non-Catholics were in astonishment, when they saw Sunday after Sunday a great number of Irish on their way to Tudhoe': *The History of the Parish of Prudhoe on Tyne* (n.d.), pp.7-8. Ushaw Pamphlets Collection.

73. *Northern Catholic Calendar* (1935), pp.95-6.

74. Anon., *A Few Brief Observations, Illustrations and Anecdotes Respecting Pitmen in a Northern Colliery Village by an Incumbent in the Diocese of Durham* (Sunderland, 1862), p.4; see also, Appendix VIII.

75. *Northern Catholic Calendar* (1893), p.56.

76. *Northern Catholic Calendar* (1935), p.94.

77. Spiritual provision for Catholics in the workhouse drew a great deal of attention from the Catholic Institute and from the bishops. Because most Irish paupers in the North East were given outdoor relief, the *Returns on Religion of Workhouse Inhabitants*, PP, 1854, LV, pp.461-78 only reveal an average of 147 Catholics in the poor houses of Newcastle and Co. Durham at the dates of the inquiry. It was ascertained in 1868 that for all the union workhouses in the four northern counties there were only 300 Catholic children. 'Circular of Catholic Poor-School Committee', April 1868, Ushaw Collection, vol. 4. Provision was made for church attendance of Catholics in the area's workhouses and for visitations by priests. It is also worthy of note that Newcastle's workhouse was the second in England to allow special Catholic services on Sundays. *Tablet,* 7 Oct. 1882, p.591.

78. Bishop Hogarth wrote on 20 April 1858: 'We deeply regret the rapidly increasing numbers of mixed marriages in our Diocese, and ... earnestly exhort you, Dearly Beloved Brethren, to discourage them by every prudent means in your power'. Ushaw Collection, vol. 4. In an effort to discourage mixed marriages yet retain those Catholics who might find them unavoidable, the following note appeared in the *Northern Catholic Calendar*

for the first time in 1875 (p.46): 'Though the Church most strongly condemns mixed marriages knowing full well the miseries in time and eternity generally following such unions, and to show her abhorrence of such unions refuses to give the Bride the Nuptial Blessing, still for grave and weighty reasons the bishop can grant a dispensation on application of the priest'.

79. *Census of Great Britain, 1851: Religious Worship*, p.42l.

80. John Morris, *Catholic England in Modern Times* (London, 1892), p.95.

81. Ibid., p.81.

82. *Catholic Directory* (1843), p.43.

83. Quoted in *Tablet*, 19 Oct. 1844, p.661.

84. *Northern Catholic Calendar* (1853), p.53.

85. *Tablet*, 5 June 1852, p.358.

86. 'The Progress of Catholic Poverty', *Rambler*, 5 (Mar. 1850), p.204.

87. Hogarth, Pastoral, quoted in *Gateshead Observer*, 24 Jan. 1852, p.5.

88. S.W.Gilley, 'Evangelical and Roman Catholic Missions to the Irish in London', p.5.

89. Mostyn and Riddell to the clergy, 'The Letter Intimating the Gracious Approval of the Bishops of the District on the formation of the Newcastle Conference', 1846. Copy in possession of Rev. W. V. Smith.

90. *Report of the Conference of Newcastle-On-Tyne of the Brotherhood of St. Vincent De Paul, from its establishment, 15th February, 1846, up to Christmas, 1848* (Newcastle, 1849), p.7. Copy in possession of Rev. W. V. Smith.

91. Ibid., p.8.

92. *Catholic Magazine*, 3rd ser., 3 (Jan. 1844), p.1.

93. *Report of the ... Brotherhood*, p.9.

94. Ibid., p.10.

95. Philip Hughes has remarked of the priests who ministered to the 'famine fever' victims in Liverpool in 1845, that they 'may be pardoned if they were less interested than the young Dr. Wiseman thought becoming, about the niceties of ecclesiastical deportment': 'The English Catholics in 1850', in George A. Beck (ed.), *The English Catholics, 1850-1950* (London, 1950), p.56. While this may have been true for some of the urban priests, there were many others in rural parishes in 1845 very much concerned with such niceties. Manning, much later in the century, could still bitterly

refer to the comfortable laity: 'What are our people doing? Oh, I forgot; they have no time. They are examining their consciences or praying for success in finding a really satisfying maid'. Maurice Rickett, *Faith and Society: a study of the structure, outlook and opportunity of the Christian Social Movement in Great Britain and the U.S.A.* (London, 1932), p.101, quoted in Inglis, *Churches and the Working Classes*, p.l32.

96. S.W. Gilley, 'Heretic London, Holy Poverty and the Irish Poor, 1830-1870', *The Downside Review*, 89 (Jan. 1971), pp.76-7.

97. Obituary of Rt. Rev. Provost Consitt in *Catholic Fireside*, quoted in *Northern Catholic Calendar* (1888), p.43.

98. 'Where Does Our Strength Lie?' *Rambler*, 14 (May 1849), p.4.

99. 'Progress of Catholic Poverty', *Rambler,* new series, 5 (Mar. 1850), p.204.

100. James C. Street, *The Night-side of Newcastle: A Lecture Delivered in the Church of Divine Unity* (Newcastle, 1865), p.4.

101. *Tablet*, 18 Sept. 1869, p. 506.

102. *Northern Catholic Calendar* (1876), p.44.

103. Quoted in Edmund S. Purcell, *Life of Cardinal Manning* (London, 1895), vol. 2, p.678.

104. Manning, Pastoral, 8 June 1866, quoted in Vincent Alan McClelland, *Cardinal Manning, His Public Life and Influence, 1865-1892* (London, 1962), p.33. The spirit of diocesan independence is well recorded in a letter from the bishop of Liverpool 'To the Clergy Only', 23 May 1853, when he complained about Wiseman's appeal for central funds, stating that 'it is my duty to look to the salvation of my own flock, I have to be answerable for them, and not for those who are many hundreds of miles distant, and who have their own canonically appointed Pastors to watch over them'. Crowe Collection, Ushaw.

105. Obituary of Rev. Michael Thomas D. Bourke, *Northern Catholic Calendar* (1906), p.103.

106. One might even challenge calling Chadwick 'nominally Irish', for his father had apparently only been briefly stationed in Ireland when the future bishop was born.

107. Report on the *Conventu Ecciesiatico* held in St. Andrew's presbytery 20 April 1852, Ushaw Collection, vol. 3. The five Irish-born priests were Philip and Francis Kearney, J. and E. Kelly, and Robert Foran.

108. Todd, *The Irish in England*, pp.7-8.

109. Ibid., p.8.

110. Morgan V. Sweeney, 'Diocesan Organization and Administration', in Beck, *The English Catholics*, p.136.

111. *Tablet*, 13 Aug. 1853, p.516.

112. Obituary of Rev. James Foran, *Northern Catholic Calendar* (1901), p.121.

113. J.P. Baterden, 'Stella', *Northern Catholic Calendar* (1914), p.l24.

114. Obituary on Rev. Consitt, *Northern Catholic Calendar* (1888), p.43.

115. Torregiani, *Franciscan Missions Among the Colliers*, p.3.

116. Lenders, *History of Sacriston*, pp.15-26.

117. Ibid., p.29.

118. Obituary of Rev. Jeremiah Foran (who was unrelated to Robert or James), *Northern Catholic Calendar* (1905), pp.117-18.

119. Belaney, *The Reign of Sin*, pp.12-13.

120. R. Samuel, 'The Catholic Church and the Irish Poor', paper presented to the Past and Present Conference, July 1966, p.27; see also, S.W. Gilley, 'The Roman Catholic Mission to the Irish in London, 1840-1860', *Recusant History*, 10 (Oct. 1969), p.141.

121. Obituary of Rev. Mother Zavier O'Connell, *Northern Catholic Calendar* (1903), pp.l30-31.

122. Bernard W. Kelly, *Historical Notes on English Catholic Missions* (London, 1907), p.41.

123. *Newcastle Chronicle*, 29 Aug. 1851, p.5.

124. *Sunderland Times*, 20 Mar. 1860, reported in *Tablet*, 31 Mar. 1860, p.198. On the new church throwing the Protestant one 'into the shade' see *Tablet*, 29 Sept. 1860, p.613.

125. *Newcastle Courant*, 15 Nov. 1872, p.5, pp.8 and 5; the *Courant* saw enough significance in this event to include it in its annual résumé of remarkable events, 3 Jan. 1873, p.5.

126. *Durham Chronicle*, 18 Nov. 1864, p.8.

127. Ibid., 29 May 1863, p.8.

128. Henry Edward Manning, *Truth Before Peace: A Sermon Preached at the Opening of S. Godric, in Durham, November 15th, 1864* (Dublin, London and Durham, 1865). Ushaw Pamphlets Collection.

129. *Durham Chronicle*, 18 Nov. 1864, p.8.

130. *The Church of Our Lady of Mercy and St. Godric*, p.7.

Chapter 4 pages 73-110

1. 'Lord John Russell's Letter to the Bishop of Durham', *The Times*, 7 Nov. 1850, reprinted in E.R. Norman, *Anti-Catholicism in Victorian England* (London, 1968), pp.159-61.

2. Direct mention of the Irish was rarely made in ecclesiastical arguments. Even for an anti-papist writing in 1877 there was only 'a curious correspondence in date between the organization of the Catholic hierarchy ... and the influx of starving exiles from Ireland'. M.C. Bishop, 'The Social Methods of Roman Catholicism in England', *Contemporary Review*, 39 (Mar. 1877), p.611.

3. 'Bishop Maltby of Durham to the Venerable the Archdeacon of Lindisfarne', *The Times*, 17 Jan. 1851, p.5.

4. *Durham Advertiser*, 17 April 1835, p.43.

5. Ibid., editorial, 30 Aug. 1833, p.3.

6. William G. Todd, *The Irish in England* (London, 1857), p. 5

7. 21 Mar. 1851, p.2.

8. *Newcastle Courant*, 21-28 Mar. 1851.

9. *Tablet*, 3 April 1852, p.213.

10. *Gateshead Observer*, 27 Mar. 1852, p.3.

11. *Tablet*, 24 May 1851, p.342.

12. See, T.M. Healy, *of Letters and Leaders of My Day* (London, 1928), vol. 1, p.23; Norman, *Anti-Catholicism in Victorian England*, pp.17-18; and G.F.A. Best, 'Popular Protestantism in Victorian Britain', in Robert Robson (ed.), *Ideas and Institutions of Victorian Britain* (London, 1967), pp.133-34. Murphy was the author of *The Photograph of the Great Anti-Christ, Awful Disclosures of New Hall Convent*, and *The Confessional Unmasked*, which was declared 'obscene' by the Queen's Bench in 1865. He made at least one visit to North Shields before his death in 1872, and it is likely that he did the North-Eastern circuit at some time, though I have found no evidence in either the local press or *The Tablet*.

13. *Tablet*, 13 Dec. 1851, p.790.

14. *Newcastle Courant*, 21 Mar. 1851, p.2.

15. During debate in the House of Commons, 23 Mar. 1851, quoted in *Newcastle Courant*, 28 Mar. 1851, p.3.

16. *Tablet*, 6 Nov. 1852, p.710.

17. Ibid., p.710.
18. 22 Mar. 1851, p.5.
19. *Inquiry into the Condition of the Poor of Newcastle-Upon-Tyne* ([reprinted from *Newcastle Weekly Chronicle*], Newcastle, 1850), p.34.
20. *Allan's Illustrated Tyneside Songs and Readings* (Newcastle, c.1860, revised edn. 1891), p.381.
21. *Tablet*, 24 May 1851, p.324.
22. Quoted in the above account, p.324. Transl. 'Look to your end, look to the rope's end'.
23. 16 May 1851, p.6.
24. 17 May 1851, p.5.
25. *Tablet*, 24 May 1851, p.325.
26. J. Lenders, *History of the Parish of Sacriston* (Minsteracres, 1930), pp.17-18.
27. See, for example, the references to Rev. Howel Marries' sermon at Trinity Church, Darlington: *Tablet*, 2 Oct. 1852, p.632.
28. *Newcastle Courant*, 28 Mar. 1851, p.3.
29. *Gateshead Observer*, 27 Mar. 1852, p.3: *Tablet*, 3 April 1852, p.213.
30. *Durham Chronicle*, 26 Mar. 1852, p.6; *Durham Advertiser*, 26 Mar. 1852, p.4.
31. *Tablet*, 30 Oct. 1852, p.693.
32. Ibid., 27 Mar. 1852, p.197. Two years later the *Newcastle Chronicle* commented on the St. Patrick's Day proceedings in an almost identical manner, stating that their appearance 'speaks favourably for the improved condition of the Irish labouring class, and affords an instance of their perfect ability to improve their social state, when they are favoured by happy auspices': 24 Mar. 1854, p.4.
33. 24 Mar. 1837, Lambton MSS, cited in T.J. Nossiter, 'Elections and Political Behaviour In County Durham and Newcastle, 1832-74', D.Phil. thesis, Oxford University, 1968, p.99.
34. Landers, *History of Sacriston*, p.18.
35. *Catholic Directory* (1842), p.39. Unfortunately, we are not informed of the reason for this munificence. Quite possibly it was to bring some priestly control to the Irish.
36. 'New Church and Mission at Gateshead', *Rambler*, 6 (1850), pp.558-59.

37. See, 'Address of Bishop Bewick', *Tablet*, 4 Nov. 1982, p.753.
38. *Tablet*, 20 Dec. 1851, p.806.
39. *Newcastle Chronicle*, 12 Nov. 1847, p.8.
40. 13 Nov. 1847, p.3.
41. 6 Nov. 1847, p.3.
42. Quoted in *Tablet*, 8 Jan. 1853, p.19.
43. Todd, *The Irish in England*, p.6.
44. *Newcastle Chronicle*, 20 Mar. 1857, p.6.
45. *Northern Catholic Calendar* (1903), p.129.
46. Larchfield Diary: entry for Feb. 1866, p.206. In the selection of Bishop Chadwick as Hogarth's successor, the *Durham Chronicle* noted that 'the appointment gives universal satisfaction': 2 Nov. 1866.
47. Quoted in *Tablet*, 28 April 1860, p.263.
48. *Newcastle Chronicle*, 27 Mar. 1857, p.3.
49. Ibid., editorial, 27 Mar. p.4.
50. *Newcastle Daily Chronicle*, 22 Mar. 1862, p.5. Tadini was no doubt drawing his material from a vast array of No-Popery literature dealing with Auricular Confession and Jesuits and nunneries, the most incredible of which was the American, W. Hogan's *Auricular Confession and Popish Nunneries*, referred to in Best, 'Popular Protestantism in Victorian Britain', p.131.
51. *British Protestant or Journal of the Religious Principles of the Reformation*, published by the London based British Society for Promoting the Principles of the Reformation.
52. For example, Mrs Pardiggle in Dicken's *Bleak House* (London, 1852), or Miss Clack in Wilkie Collins' *The Moonstone* (London, 1868).
53. *Record*, 17 April 1861, p.3.
54. 'Annual Meeting of the Home Missionary and the Irish Evangelical Society', *Record*, 15 May 1857.
55. '17th Annual Meeting of the Church Pastoral-Aid Society', *Record*, 15 May 1852.
56. *5th Annual Report of the British Reformation Society* (1852). Its mission was 'To treat the Roman Catholics as those who are without a saving knowledge of the true Christ – to address them as such with kindness and forbearance, but with uncompromising faithfulness – to give them and their children

the knowledge of the Scriptures, in opposition to the system of Rome': 'Anniversary Meeting of the Irish Church Missions to the Roman Catholics', *Record*, 5 May 1852. The British Reformation Society was originally set up to operate 'particularly in "the Sister Kingdom"'. *First Annual Report of the British Reformation Society* (1828), p.13. It was not until 1851 that 'a Church Mission to Roman Catholics in Great Britain' was established with 'trained' missionaries: 'it is their duty, 'by *Visitation, Lectures* (where desirable), and *Classes*, to enlighten both Protestants and Roman Catholics': *Ecclesiastical Developments in the Churches of Rome and England and Missionary Efforts by the Protestant Reformation Society* (London, 1872), pp.11-12.

57. 'Annual Meeting of the English Church Mission', *Record*, 8 May 1857. See also S.W. Gilley, 'Protestant London, No-Popery and the Irish Poor: Pt. II, 1830-1860', *Recusant History*, 11 (1971), p.27.

58. *2nd Annual Report of the Protestant Alliance* (London, May 1853), p.1.

59. 'Romish Efforts in England: The Annual Sermon of the Protestant Reformation Society, 8 May 1864', *British Protestant*, 20 (1864), p.17.

60. *3rd Annual Report of the British Reformation Society* (1830), pp.16-17. From a publication of the Newcastle Catholic Tract Society (July. 182?) it appears that the British Reformation Society had come to Newcastle shortly after its founding, for Rev. William Riddell 'then alluded, amidst cheers and laughter, to the proceedings of the itinerant fanatics of the Reformation Society ... and expressed his obligation to the Rev. Mr. Curr ... for the drubbing he had given to the 'unprincipled vagrants' (laughter)'. Ushaw Pamphlets Collection.

61. The remittances to London were printed at the back of every annual report.

62. *4th Annual Report of the British Reformation Society* (1831), p.20.

63. *5th Annual Report of the British Reformation Society* (1832), pp.23-24.

64. S. W. Gilley, 'Evangelical and Roman Catholic Missions to the Irish in London 1830-1870', Ph.D. thesis, University of Cambridge, 1970, Appendix II, p.381.

65. *8th Annual Report* (1835), p.23.

66. Ibid., p.23.

67. *13th Annual Report* (1840), p.12.

68. H. F. Etherington, *Full Report of the Proceedings ... to Establish an Auxiliary in Aid if the British Reformation Society* (Sunderland, 1840), p.4.

69. Ibid., p.10.

70. Ibid., p.18. See also, Rev. W. Knight, *Reply to the Rev Brabazon Ellis and A Sermon on True Christian Charity* (Hartlepool, 9 Mar. 1840). Ushaw Pamphlets Collection.

71. *16th Annual Report of the British Reformation Society* (1843), p.14.

72. *Tablet*, 27 June 1844, p.417.

73. In 1850 Townsend, dressed in full canonical robes, secured an interview with the Pope and endeavoured to 'induce his Holiness to do away with the bickerings, animosities, and polemical discords which keep the various denominations of Christians separate and at enmity .... The Pope was upon the whole very tolerant, as may be imagined from his having ... listened with calmness to Dr. Townsend's arguments in favour of releasing the Roman Catholic Clergy from their vow of celibacy': *Newcastle Journal*, 18 May 1850, p.5.

74. *Tablet*, 10 April 1852, p.230.

75. By 1858 the income of the English Church Missions had been reduced by such an extent that all but two of its missionaries were disbanded: Gilley, 'Protestant London, No-Popery and the Irish Poor, Pt II', p.28.

76. *British Protestant*, No.134, 16 (Oct. 1859), pp.3-4.

77. Ibid., No.135, 16 (Jan. 1860), p.10.

78. Ibid., No.136, 16 (April 1860), pp.7-8.

79. Ibid., p.8.

80. *British Protestant*, No. 142, 18 (Sept. 1861), pp.8-9.

81. Ibid., No.154, 18 (April 1862), pp.15-16.

82. *34th Annual Report of the Protestant Reformation Society* (1861), p.22.

83. *35th Annual Report of the Protestant Reformation Society* (1862), pp.22-23.

84. *36th Annual Report of the Protestant Reformation Society* (1863), p.19.

85. The very first object of the Society was 'to revive Protestant zeal'. *1st Annual Report of the British Reformation Society* (1828), p.1.

86. 4 July 1851, p.4.

87. *Tablet*, 24 April 1852, p.260.

88. Ibid., p.260.

89. *Newcastle Courant*, 21 Mar. 1851, p.3.

90. *Protestant Aggression: Remarks on the Bishop of Durham's Letter to the Archdeacon of Lindisfarne by a Catholic Clergyman Resident Within the Diocese of Durham* (Newcastle, 20 Jan. 1851), p.5. Newcastle Central Library, Local Tracts Collection.

91. Ibid., p.10.

92. *Tablet*, 27 Mar. 1852, p.197.

93. *Tablet*, 25 June 1853, p.405.

94. Who was actually countering whom depended on your sympathies. The British Reformation Society claimed in 1840 that *their* tracts were 'to neutralize the poisonous tracts of the Roman Catholic Institute, which are stereotyped and circulated throughout the kingdom with a perseverance and energy worthy of a better cause'. *13th Annual Report* (1840), p.13.

95. 'The Clifton Tracts' began to be issued from London in 1851 'with a view of supplying a want, long and generally felt ... a plain and simple statement of Catholic doctrines, principles, and practices, together with an exposure of Protestant errors'. Advertisement on cover of first issue. Ushaw Pamphlets Collection. For the scope of the 'paper war' from the Catholic point of view, see, 'Catholic and Protestant Missionary, Book and Education Societies', *Rambler*, 10 (1858), pp.268-79.

96. 'How to Convert Protestants', *Rambler*, 1 (1854), p.1.

97. *Tablet*, 8 Feb. 1851, p.83.

98. Ibid., 17 April 1852, p.246.

99. Ibid., 24 May 1851, p.325.

100. *33rd Annual Report of the British Reformation Society*, (July 1860), pp.18-19.

101. 'The Works and Wants of the Catholic Church in England', *Dublin Review*, 1 (1863), p.147.

102. Hogarth, June 7, 1852, Ushaw Collection, vol. 3.

103. Ibid.

104. 'History and Progress of the Consett Iron Works', 9 July 1858, p.6.

105. For example, 'The real strength of Rome consists in our weakness. The public temper, though it has shown itself able to resent, is utterly unfit to deal with aggression'. R.H. Cheney, 'Papal Pretensions', *Quarterly Review*, 89 (1851), p.484.

106. As outlined for London, see Gilley, 'Protestant London', pp.31-2.

107. By 1857 Rev. Beamish at the Annual Meeting of the English Church Missions was complaining that 'that Society, the Irish Church Mission Society, and the Protestant Reformation Society, met with less support than almost any other religious institution, whether as regarded their income or the number of persons who attended their anniversaries'. *Record,* 8 May 1857.

108. *Ecclesiastical Developments in the Churches of Rome and England ... by the Protestant Reformation Society,* p.9.

109. '6th Annual Meeting of the Protestant Alliance', *Record,* 18 May 1857.

110. All too often the final result was, to paraphrase Dr Johnson, that a Roman Catholic, in changing his religion, would pass, not from one form of Christianity to another, but from Catholicism to infidelity.

111. W. Todd, *The Irish in England,* p.8; R. Samuel, 'The Catholic Church and the Irish Poor', paper presented to the Past and Present Conference, July 1966, pp.45-6.

112. *Record,* 20 July 1854; 8 May 1857.

113. 'On the Statistical Position of Religious Bodies in England and Wales', *Journal of the Statistical Society of London,* 18 (1855), p.147.

114. Durham, 46.5 percent; Northumberland, 48.8 percent; while Lancashire was lowest with 40.0 percent.

115. The index of attendance for Maps 4.1 and 4.3 is the percentage attending on Census Sunday as it varied over each county. Churches that failed to submit returns have been incorporated according to a method devised by John Gay, *The Geography of Religion in England* (London, 1971), pp.51-54.

116. 'Religious Census of England', *Rambler,* 1 (1854), p.186.

117. Rev. J. Davies, *Sermon on Behalf of the Church Building Society, March 12th, 1843* (Gateshead, 1843), p.44. Newcastle Central Library, Local Tracts Collection.

118. K.S. Inglis, 'Patterns of Religious Worship in 1851', *Journal of Ecclesiastical History,* 11 (1960), pp.81-2.

119. Ibid., p.82.

120. Ibid., p.85.

121. Calculated from 'Table C', Horace Mann, 'On the Statistical Position of Religious Bodies in England and Wales.' *Journal of the Statistical Society of London,* 18 (1855), p.157.

122. Anglican sittings-to-population for the Diocese of Durham for each decade from 1841 to 1881, respectively, went from 1:6,268 to 1:6,251 to 1:7,571 to 1:8,656. Archdeacon Watson, 'Our Churches And Our Schools', *Durham Diocesan Magazine* (Oct. 1884), pp.113-15.

123. 'An Ecclesiastical Census', editorial, 26 Oct. 1872, p.2.

124. Cited in J.F. Clarke, 'Labour Relations in Engineering and Shipbuilding on the North East Coast, 1850-1900', MA thesis, University of Newcastle, 1966, p.29.

125. Evan R. Jones, *The Life and Speeches of Joseph Cowen, M.P.* (London, 1885), p.331.

126. *Sunderland Herald*, 4 Oct. 1850, cited in Clarke, 'Labour Relations', p.28.

127. See, Joseph Cowen, *Speech Delivered at the Unveiling Ceremony of the Memorial Fountain Newcastle to Dr. Rutherford*, Sept. 12, 1894, p.8; and Dr. Rutherford, *Meeting for the Proclamation of the Gospel* (April 2 [n.d.]), both in Newcastle Central Library Local Tracts Collection.

128. *Report of the Commissioners ... to Examine into the Spiritual Wants...of Certain Parishes in the Diocese of Newcastle* (Newcastle, 1883), p.7. Newcastle Central Library, Local Tracts Collection.

129. Jones, *Joseph Cowen*, p.329.

130. 'Methodism and the Church', *Durham Chronicle*, 13 Aug. 1869, pp 4-5.

131. See, R.F. Wearmouth, *Methodism and the Struggle of the Working Classes, 1850-1900* (Leicester, 1954), pp.210-42.

132. Wesleyan Methodist Conference Minutes, Methodist Archives, 1850-1851.

133. The exception was the anti-Catholicism of the Methodists in 1851 over the Ecclesiastical Titles Bill. As E.R. Norman has pointed out, however, the dissenters generally enjoyed the spectacle of No-Popery without contributing much to it themselves. For their outcry in 1851, they were chastised by their leaders, who reminded them of their own struggle against the Church of England and the Queen's supremacy in matters of faith and worship: *Anti-Catholicism in Victorian England*, pp.65-7.

134. *Rules of the First Select Friendly Society of Orangemen*, instituted Nov. 4th, 1814 (Newcastle, 16 July, 1821), revised altered and amended, 1830. British Museum.

135. *Newcastle Chronicle*, 4 June 1858, p.6; T. Fordyce, *Local Register, 1833-1866*, vol. 3 (Newcastle, 1867), p.342.

136. *Rules of the Rose of Consett Lodge of the Grand Protestant Association of Loyal Orangemen, District Sick and Burial Society* (Consett, 1868). Durham County Record Office: D/X274/1.

137. *Durham Chronicle*, 14 July 1882, p.5.

138. Ibid., 15 July 1881.

139. *Northern Catholic Calendar* (1885), p.47.

140. *Tablet*, 29 Sept. 1860, p.613.

141. 30 Dec. 1867, p.2.

142. Sir Timothy Eden, *Durham*, vol. 2 (London, 1952), p.604. The five were Maltby (1836-56), a right-wing Whig; Charles Thomas Longley (1856-60), a supporter of Russell after 1851; Henry Villiers (1860-61), a Tory; Charles Baring (1861-79), a Conservative; and Joseph Lightfoot (1879-89), a Conservative.

143. M.C. Bickersteth's description of what the Papacy meant to his father (the Bishop of Ripon): *A Sketch of the Life and Episcopate of the Rt. Rev Robert Bickersteth D.D.* (London, 1887), p.48.

144. *Tablet*, 17 May 1851, p.324.

145. *Durham Chronicle*, 22 Dec. 1882, p.5.

146. John C. Kirk, 'The History of Thornley', *Northern Daily Mail*, 24 Mar. 1970, p.12.

147. *Larchfield Diary*: entry for Oct. 1854, p.133.

148. *Tablet*, 7 Oct. 1854, p.630.

149. Belaney was born in Scotland of wealthy parents in 1804; educated at Edinburgh and Cambridge where he received his MA in 1846. After holding various curacies in Northumberland he became the Vicar of Arlington, Sussex, 1843-52. Being denounced as a Jesuit he brought a lawsuit against one of his own church wardens in 1852, the year in which he converted to Catholicism. He became one of the most indefatigable workers for Catholicism in England, introducing the Jesuits to Glasgow and the Servite Fathers to London. He spent his entire income on the church and died a pauper on August 24th, 1899. At his death he was the oldest priest in England. *Tablet*, 9 Sept. 1899, p.363; and J.A. Venn, *Alumni Cantabrigienses*, Pt. II, 1752-1900 (Cambridge, 1940).

150. 'Seaham Harbour', *Newcastle Daily Chronicle*, 2 Aug. 1862, p.4. This perception of Lady Londonderry was based on her heavy expenditure on churches, infirmaries and reading rooms in Seaham Harbour, her annual dinner and speeches to her tenantry, etc. William Fordyce, for example,

wrote of her and her husband: they 'employed thousands of workpeople, and both take a lively interest in their social and moral improvement, and in the establishment of schools for the education of the children': *History of Coal, Coke, Coal Fields [and] Iron* (London, 1860), p.92.

151. Alison, *Lives of Lord Castlereagh and Lord Stewart* (London, 1861), vol. 3, p.213.

152. Blake, *Disraeli* (London, 1966), p.126; Disraeli to Lady Bradford, 1874, quoted in Edith Londonderry (ed.), *Letters from Benjamin Disraeli to Frances Anne Marchioness of Londonderry, 1837-1867* (London, 1938), p.193.

153. Belaney to Francis Anne Vane Londonderry, Seaham Harbour, 2 Nov. 1860. Reprinted in *Tablet*, 24 Nov. 1860, p.740.

154. Francis Anne to Rev. G. Wilkinson, Seaham Hall, 9 Nov. 1860, *Tablet*, 24 Nov. 1860, p.740.

155. Thomas H. Ward, *Men of the Reign* (London, 1885), p.145.

156. *Whellan's Directory of Durham and Newcastle* (1856), pp.640-42.

157. See, Benefice Files of the Church Commissioners (Seaham) 40453, 23 Dec. 1842. Lord Londonderry had corresponded with the Archbishop of Canterbury in order that he might secure a perpetual curacy in his name. I am grateful to Mr. B. Maynard for this reference.

158. Benefice Files of the Church Commissioners (Seaham) 40453, 23 Dec. 1842.

159. Wilkinson to Lady Londonderry, Seaham Harbour, 12 Nov. 1860, *Tablet*, 21 Nov. 1860, p.740.

160. Francis Anne to Rev. Belaney, Seaham Hall, 15 Nov. 1860, *Tablet*, 24 Nov. 1860, p.740. Adolphous Vane was the third son of the Third Marquis (1825-64). The first son, of the Third Marquis, by a former marriage, was Fredrick William (1802-72) who became the 4th Marquis in 1854 but had few connections with the Durham estates. The first son of Frances Anne was Henry, Viscount Seaham (1821-84), later Earl Vane who became the 5th Marquis in 1872. *The Londonderry Papers: Catalogue* (Durham County Council, 1969), p.150.

161. *Record*, 30 Nov. 1860, p.4.

162. Belaney to Lady Londonderry, London, 19 Nov 1860, *Tablet*, 24 Nov. 1860, pp.740-41.

163. He sent £300 to Bishop Hogarth from Ireland in January 1860: *Tablet*, 7 Jan. 1860, p.4.

164. The article is quoted verbatim in a press cutting (undated, untitled) marked 7 Dec. 1861, contained in the Londonderry Papers, Durham County Record Office: D/LO/C-216.

165. Vicar of Christ's Church, New Seaham (1860-189?); his church was also paid for and endowed by the Marchioness. See, Durham County Record Office: D/LO/C-201.

166. Robert Anderson to Lady Londonderry, 6 Jan. 1862, Durham County Record Office: D/LO/C-216.

167. Rev. Scott to Lady Londonderry, 6 Jan. 1862, Durham County Record Office: D/L0/C-216, the figures included women and children. The Census taken by the Catholic Church in 1861 showed Seaham with a population of 799 Catholics, 473 of whom were adults. See Appendix V.

168. Lord Adolphous to [?*Hull Advertiser*], copy, 18 Jan. 1862, Durham County Record Office: D/LO/C-216(7).

169. Pemberton to Lady Londonderry, 7 Mar. 1862, Durham County Record Office: D/LO/C-216.

170. Robert Anderson to Lady Londonderry, 10 Mar. 1862, Durham County Record Office: D/LO/C-216(3).

171. Adolphous to Lady Londonderry, undated, Durham County Record Office: D/LO/C-216(4).

172. W. Gordon Gorman, *Converts to Rome, 1850-1910* (London, 1910), p.18.

173. Priscilla M.A. Beckwith to Lady Londonderry, 9 Dec. 1862, Durham County Record Office: D/LO/C-216(8). *Cf.* L.E.O. Charlton, *Recollections of a Northumbrian Lady [Barbara Charlton] 1815-66* (London, 1949), p.244.

174. Beckwith to Lady Londonderry, date illegible, Durham County Record Office: D/LO/C-216(2).

175. Lady Elizabeth Francis Charlotte Jocelyn; wife of the 4th Marquis and daughter of the 3rd Earl of Roden: Gorman, *Converts to Rome*, p.175.

176. *Tablet*, 7 Aug. 1869, p.314.

177. Pastoral, 25 Jan. 1854, Ushaw Collection, vol. 3.

178. 'Address of Bishop Bewick', *Tablet*, 11 Nov. 1882, p.753.

179. Pastoral, quoted in *Tablet*, 28 Oct. 1880, p 713.

Chapter 5 pages 111-142

1. 'Irish in England', Letter XV (19 Oct. 1872), p.662.

2. *Census of Great Britain*: Abstracts on Occupation, 1841 to 1881; J.W. House, *North Eastern England Population Movements and the Landscape Since the Early 19th Century* (Newcastle, 1954), Tables 5 and 6, pp.59-60.

3. Raymond Challinor and Brian Ripley, *The Miners' Association: A Trade Union in the Age of the Chartists* (London, 1968), p.146.

4. *Our Coal and Our Coalpits: the People in Them and the Scenes Around Them* by a Traveller Underground (London, 1853), p.208.

5. John Daglish to Lord Londonderry, 19 Sept. 1866, Durham County Record Office: D/LO/C-292.

6. According to a newspaper article, 'The Distress in Cornwall', send to Londonderry by his agent John Daglish, 22 Sept. 1866. By 10 Dec. 1866, Daglish had secured ninety Cornish miners.

7. H.R. Trevor-Roper, 'The Bishopric of Durham and the Capitalist Reformation', *Durham University*, 3 (1945-46), p.46.

8. J.H. Morris and L.J. Williams, *The South Wales Coal Industry 1841-1875* (Cardiff, 1958), pp.236-37.

9. J.T. Gleave, 'The Teesside Iron and Steel Industry', *Geographical Journal*, 91 (May 1938), p.454.

10. Questionnaire returned by the North of England Iron Manufacturers' Association to the *First Report of the Royal Commission appointed to inquire into the Depression of Trade and Industry*, 1886, PP 1886, XXI, Appendix B, p.117.

11. Bishop Hogarth, Pastoral, 25 Jan. 1854, Ushaw Collection, vol. 3.

12. House, *North Eastern England Population*, p.45.

13. *Newcastle Courant*, 12 Jan. 1866, cited in David Dougan, *The History of North East Shipbuilding* (London, 1968), p.37.

14. J.F. Clarke, 'Labour In Shipbuilding on the North-East Coast, 1850-1900', *North East Group for the Study of Labour History*, Bulletin No.2 (Oct. 1968), p.3.

15. Ibid.

16. Charles Palmer, *Industrial Resources of the Tyne, Wear and Tees* (1863), cited in Dougan, *Shipbuilding*, p.51.

17. Quoted in Dougan, *Shipbuilding*, p.36.

18. Denvir, *The Irish in Britain from the Earliest Times To The Fall and Death of Parnell* (London, 1892), p.443.

19. *Northern Catholic Calendar* (London, 1885), p.50.

20. J.H. Treble, 'The Place of the Irish Catholics in the Social Life of the North of England, 1829-51', PhD thesis, Leeds University, 1969, pp.52-3.

21. The rebuilding of Newcastle within the old city walls under the direction of Richard Grainger and the architect John Dobson came to a rapid halt shortly after the passage of the Municipal Reform Act of 1835. See, Norman McCord, 'Some Aspects of Mid-Nineteenth Century Newcastle', unpublished paper presented to the Urban History Conference April 1972.

22. *Whellan's Directory of Durham* (1856), p.650.

23. *Tablet,* 5 June 1852, p.358. The increase of Irish youths for this occupation, the author stated, could be verified by examining the Register of Seamen.

24. Ibid., p.358.

25. *Census of Great Britain, 1851*: Enumerator's manuscripts for South Shields between Market Place and Westoe Lane.

26. J.R. Boyle, *The County of Durham* (London, 1892), p.82.

27 *Census of Great Britain, 1851*: Abstracts, p.274n.

28. *The Church of Our Lady of Mercy and St. Godric* (Durham, 1964), p.4. Ushaw Pamphlets Collection.

29. See also, Arthur Redford, *Labour Migrations in England, 1800-1850* (Manchester, 1926), pp.150-51; R. Lawton, 'Irish Immigration to England and Wales in the Mid-Nineteenth Century', *Irish Geography,* 4 (1959-63), p.34; and Robert Rawlinson, *Select Committee on Railway Labourers,* 1846, PP, 1846, XIII, q.1043, p.501.

30. *The Railway Navvies* (London, 1965), p.83.

31. Calculated from *Census of Great Britain*: Abstracts on Occupation. This information is reproduced in R.M. Gard, 'Labour History of Railways in Durham and Northumberland to 1900: an introduction to sources and bibliography', *North East Group for the Study of Labour History,* Bulletin No.3 (Oct. 1969), p.17.

32. J.A. Patmore, 'A Navvy Gang of 1851', *Journal of Transport History,* 5 (1962), cited in Treble, 'Place of the Irish Catholics', p.62.

33. *Larchfield Diary:* entry for 1830, pp.22-23.

34. Pamela Horn, 'The National Agricultural Labourers' Union in Ireland, 1873-9', *Irish Historical Studies,* 17 (1971), pp.340-41.

35. 'Condition of our Chief Towns – Newcastle-upon-Tyne', *The Builder*, 13 April 1861, p.242.

36. Contained in Grainger's 'Report' in the *Report of the Commissioners Appointed to Inquire into the Causes which have led to or have Aggravated the Late Outbreak of Cholera in the towns of Newcastle-Upon-Tyne, Gateshead, and Tynemouth*, PP, 1854. XXXV. 131, p.55.

37. *Census of Great Britain*: Education, England and Wales, Reports and Tables, PP, 1852-53, XC, p.xxiii, quoted in Treble, 'Place of the Irish Catholics', p. 386.

38. 'Memorial Presented to Sir James Graham by the Rt. Rev. Dr. Wiseman', 1843, respecting the formation of the new factory schools. Ushaw Pamphlets Collection, vol.4.

39. George F. Shaw, 'The Irish Labourers in Liverpool', *Transactions of the National Association for the Promotion of the Social Sciences* (London, 1862), p.684.

40. John Stephens, 'Abstract of a Return of Prisoners coming under the Cognisance of the Police of Newcastle', *Journal of the Statistical Society of London*, 1 (Oct. 1838), p.362.

41. It was noted in 1913 that 'the extreme north is not an area in which the woman worker is in great request, differing in that respect from the Lancashire districts where she is so important a factor'. 'Social Problems in Newcastle-upon-Tyne and District', in Charles E. B. Russell, *Social Problems in the North* (London, 1913), p. 149.

42. *Report of the Select Committee on Poor Removals*, PP, 1854-5. XIII. 1, 1855, q.411, p.30.

43. 'Employment of Women', *Newcastle Courant*, 13 Dec. 1861, p.2. The information came from questionnaires sent to several local factories. The returns also showed that 'a large number of women' were employed in manual labour in shops, at wages ranging from 6s-14s per week. The article concluded that the scarcity of positions for women could only be relieved 'if women could be induced to emigrate in considerable numbers'.

44. In Sandgate 'the proportion of prostitutes to the whole female population is little more than one to seven, and [to] the male population rather more than one to six …. Prostitution is emphatically the traffic of the district': *Inquiry into the Condition of the Poor Of Newcastle-Upon-Tyne* (reprinted from the *Newcastle Weekly Chronicle:* Newcastle, 1850), p.33.

45. Evidence of Mr. Hedley, *Report of the Select Committee on the Irremovable Poor*, PP. 1860. XVII. 1, q.2791, p.146.

46. 'Irishmen in the North', *Newcastle Daily Chronicle*, 12 Oct. 1867, p.3.

47. *Durham Chronicle*, 12 Oct. 1865, p.5.

48. *The Nine Hours Movement Conference between C.M. Palmer, and the Workmen of Jarrow, Feb. 22, 1866*, p.3. Newcastle Central Library, Local Tracts Collection.

49. T.J. Nossiter, 'Elections and Political Behaviour In County Durham and Newcastle, 1832-74', D.Phil. thesis, Oxford University, 1968, pp.70-71.

50. Rev. William Hickey, 'On the Social Condition of the Labouring Population in Ireland', *Transactions of the National Association for the Promotion of the Social Sciences* (London, 1862), p.609. The following average rates per 10-hour day could be found in Dublin and neighbourhood in 1860: boys, 7d-8d; young men, 1s-1s 4d; labourers, 1s 8d; skilled men, 2s -3s 4d.; mechanics, 5s. *Labour statistics: Return of Wages Published between 1830 and 1886*, PP, 1887, LXXXIX, p.336.

51. 'Irish in England', *Nation*, Letter XV (19 Oct. 1872), p.662.

52. George Neasham, *History and Biography of West Durham* (Durham, 1881), p.30.

53. Belaney to the Marchioness of Londonderry, 2 Nov. 1860, *Tablet*, 24 Nov. 1860, p.740.

54. *Church of St. Godric*, p.8.

55. *First Report of the Royal Commission of Inquiry into the Housing of the Working Classes*, PP, 1884-5, XXX, q.740l, p.331.

56. John Bell Simpson, *Capital and Labour in Coal Mining During the Past 200 Years* (Newcastle, 1900), p.34. Wage rates in all the industries also varied according to location. The *Return of Wages*, (1887), p.656 reported that labourers at Masons in Darlington were receiving twice as much as those in South Shields. Wages in Newcastle were usually slightly lower than those in the industrial centres of Durham.

57. Return of the Sunderland Chamber of Commerce to the *First Report on the Depression of Trade*, 1886, Appendix A, p.88.

58. *2nd Report on the Depression of Trade*, PP, 1886, XXI, Pt.I, Appendix B, p.629.

59. Borough of Newcastle, *Report of the Public Health During the Year 1866*, p.9. Newcastle Central Library, Local Tracts Collection.

60. Rev. Robert Belaney, *The Reign of Sin and the Reign of Grace: A Sermon Preached at St. Wilfrid's Church, Bishop Auckland. December 13th, 1863* (Bishop Auckland, 1863), p.12.

61. *Larchfield Diary*: entry for 1866, p.210.

62. *Tablet*, 15 Dec. 1877, p.755.

63. 'Do you mean to say that rents in Newcastle are higher than they are in London? – Yes, I should think they are very often. I should call 3s a usual price for one of these kitchens'. *First Report into the Housing of the Working Classes*, q.7481, p.332.

64. Ibid., p.332.

65. Quoted in 'Appendix G: Report of the state of the Irish Poor in Great Britain' in the *Report of the Poor Inquiry (Ireland) Commission*, PP, 1836, XXXIV, p.459.

66. C.S. Parker, *Sir Robert Peel* (2nd edn, 1899), vol.2, p.117, quoted in Eric Strauss, *Irish Nationalism and British Democracy* (London, 1951), pp.122-23.

67. *Report of the Select Committee of the House of Lords on Colonization From Ireland*, 1847, PP, 1847, VI, p.xiii.

68. *Select Committee on Poor Removals*, 1854, Appendix 17, p.668.

69. *Newcastle Courant*, 30 Aug. 1850, p.4.

70. Ibid., p.4.

71. *Larchfield Diary*: entry for 1830, pp.22-23.

72. Morton to Durham, 15 Jan 1837, Lambton MSS., quoted in Nossiter, 'Elections and Political Behaviour In County Durham and Newcastle, 1832-74', p.98.

73. 'Appendix G', 1836, p.462.

74. *Larchfield Diary*: entry for 1861, p.170.

75. Were the Irish 'not here', wrote Belaney, 'labourers would be wanting in your Ladyship's works, and labour would cost your Ladyship more'. Belaney to Frances Anne Vane Londonderry, Seaham Harbour, 2 Nov. 1860, reprinted in *Tablet*, 24 Nov. 1860, p.740.

76. The number of importations from Ireland was probably few. The Commissioners noted in 'Appendix G', 1836, p.460, that there was little foundation to the claims that Irish labourers were imported into England: 'The great majority – so great as to form nearly the entire number – left

their own country spontaneously, and at their own expense'. This was even more so during the famine and immediate post-famine period.

77. According to *The Times* 'agents are appointed in many districts in Ireland to provide free passages to Newport, where it is promised them, the men will find employment on the South Wales railway at 4s. a day, and women to be engaged in whatever numbers they please at 2s and 2s 6d per day, at washing and other domestic work'. This 'delusive cajolery' was reported to have brought the Irish 'like locusts'. Quoted in *Newcastle Chronicle*, 26 Feb. 1847, p.6.

78. J. Hickey, *Urban Catholics* (London, 1967), pp.53-5, and 128-29.

79. When asked if there had been any migration from the country into Newcastle, a local spokesman replied 'There has been a little recently, but there has been a great deal in times past'. *First Report on Housing of the Working Classes*, q.7402, p.331.

80. Hickey, *Urban Catholics*, p.15.

81. In Newcastle 4,000 Irish were reputed to have 'worked upwards' into the skilled trades by 1872, but 'there is still in the rank and file of labour, or dependent on it, 25,000': 'Irish in England', *Nation*, Letter XV (19 Oct. 1872), p.662.

82. 'Irishmen in England', editorial, *Newcastle Daily Chronicle*, 24 Dec. 1867, p.2.

83. *Newcastle Daily Chronicle*, 10 Oct. 1867, p.4.

84. See, Coleman, *Railway Navvies*, pp.83-4; and almost any official report on railway labourers.

85. Robert Wood, *West Hartlepool: The Rise and Development of a Victorian New Town* (West Hartlepool, 1967), p.113.

86. 'History and Progress of the Consett Iron Works', 9 July 1858, p.6.

87. T. Fordyce, *Local Register*, vol.3, 8 Feb. 1846, p.204; G. Neasham, *West Durham*, p.72.

88. The majority of fights had nothing to do with the Irish. John Wilson characterised the local pitmen as maintaining a 'running fight, commencing at the Market Place, Durham and extending to the gate at the top of Gilesgate' every Saturday night after pub closing: *Memories of a Labour Leader, The Autobiography of John Wilson, J.P., M.P.* (London, 1910), p.91.

89. *The Making of the English Working Class* (London, 1963), p.480.

90. *Durham Chronicle*, 17 Mar. 1865; and 20 July, 31 Aug., 12 Oct., 19 Oct., 30 Nov., and 7 Dec. 1866.

91. J.F. Clarke, 'Labour Relations in Engineering and Shipbuilding on the North East Coast, 1850-1900', MA thesis, University of Newcastle, 1966, pp.94-98.

92. E. Allen, J.F. Clarke, N. McCord, and D.J. Rowe, *The North-East Engineers' Strikes of 1871: The Nine Hours' League* (Newcastle, 1971), pp.131-48.

93. *Irish Nationalism and British Democracy*, p.l24.

94. *Tyne Mercury*, 23 April 1844, p.2.

95. 'The Pitmen's strike', *Tyne Mercury*, 28 May 1844, p.2.

96. 'Public Meeting of Pitmen', *Tyne Mercury*, 28 May 1844, p.3.

97. *Northern Star*, in Bell Collection, vol.12, p.446.

98. *Durham Chronicle*, 5 July 1844, p.1; Durham County Record Office: D/LO/B-2.

99. *Tyne Mercury*, 4 June 1844, p.3.

100. Ibid., 16 July 1844, p.3.

101. George Grey, *Select Committee on Poor Removals*, q.598, p.40.

102. 'Arrival of Welsh Miners', *Durham Advertiser*, 2 Aug. 1844, p.2.

103. For an account of the 1832 strike and its forerunners see Richard Fynes, *The Miners of Northumberland and Durham: A History of their Social and Political Progress* (Blyth, 1873).

104. *Tyne Mercury*, 9 July 1844, p.3; for another example see, *Durham Advertiser*, 23 Aug. 1844, p.3.

105. The agents often promised inflated wages to secure outside labour. In one case, at Redcliffe Colliery, thirty-two Cornish blacklegs joined the strikers when the promised 4s per day turned out to be from 2s 6d to 3s. Fynes, *Miners of Northumberland and Durham*, p.91; Challinor and Ripley, *The Miners' Association*, p.132. Such deceits were 'at once an appeal to the cupidity of the men and an imposition on the credulity of the public': E. Welbourne, *The Miners Unions of Northumberland and Durham* (Cambridge, 1923), p.74.

106. A.J. Taylor, 'The Third Marquis of Londonderry and the North-East Coal Trade', *Durham University Journal*, 48 (1955-6), pp.21-27; David Large, 'The Third Marquis of Londonderry and the End of the Regulation, 1844-5', *Durham University Journal*, 51 (1958-59), pp.1-9.

107. Large, 'Londonderry and the End of the Regulation', p.2.

108. In his speech in the House of Lords, 7 April 1829, Londonderry 'expressed a hope that hereafter an arrangement might be made to connect the Roman Catholic clergy with the government, by giving them what the Presbyterians in Ireland had at present – a provision, which was called the *Regium Donum*'. *Hansard*, 2nd series, XXI, p.50l. Londonderry was one of the peers who voted in person in favour of the 3rd reading of the Emancipation Bill on 10 April 1829 (Ibid., p.694). In Ireland, Londonderry had allowed his tenants 'to accumulate up to three years unpaid rents, without evicting them, and whose estates were described by the tenant-rights radical Sharman Crawford as the most flourishing in Ireland'. Alan J. Heesom, 'The Third Marquis of Londonderry as an Employer', unpublished paper presented to the North East Group for the Study of Labour History, May 1972, p.34. The *Hull Advertiser*, while castigating Lady Londonderry, spoke of the late Third Marquis as 'a good Irish Landlord': 7 Dec. 1861, Durham County Record Office: D/LO/C-216.

109. *Tyne Mercury*, 23 April l844, p.3; Hindhaugh to Londonderry, 6 and 7 April 1844, quoted in Large, 'Londonderry and the End of the Regulation', p.5.

110. Large, 'Londonderry and the End of the Regulation', p.6.

111. 28 June 1844, Durham County Record Office: D/L0/C-326(23).

112. George Hunter to Londonderry, 30 June 1844, Durham County Record Office: D/LO/C149(265).

113. Ibid., 30 June 1844, Durham County Record Office: D/L0/C-149(266).

114. Ibid., 2 July1844, Durham County Record Office: D/LO/C-l49(264); Hindhaugh to Londonderry, 4 July 1844, Durham County Records Office: D/L0/C.-148(19).

115. Hunter to Londonderry, 2 July 1844, Durham County Record Office: D/LO/C-149(263).

116. Copies of the original broadsheet are in the Wigan Collection, Wigan Public Library, and in the Bell Collection, vol.12, p.336.

117. Heesom, 'Londonderry as an Employer', p.35.

118. Reprinted by the *Miner's Advocate* in the broadsheet 'Lord Londonderry and the Irish Press'. Wigan Collection; Bell Collection, vol.12, p.415; Fynes, *Miners of Northumberland and Durham*, pp.86-88.

119. Londonderry to Hindhaugh', 5 July 1844, Durham County Record Office: D/L0/C-326(24).

120. John Andrews to Hunter, 6 July 1844, Durham County Record Office: D/L0/C-.149(261).

121. Hunter to Londonderry, 5 July 1844, Durham County Record Office: D/L0/C-149(262).

122. Ibid., 10 July 1844, Durham County Record Office: D/LO/C-149(261).

123. Hunter to Londonderry, 19 Aug. 1844, Durham County Record Office: D/LO/C-149(253).

124. PP, 1846, XXIV, p.397. The agent, Ralph Elliot, told Tremenheere, 'It cost us 30s per man to bring the men from Ireland; then we gave them all 3s. a-day and their food for five months, and they were so awkward at the work at first that they could scarcely earn what their food cost us'.

125. Hunter to Londonderry, 31 July 1844, Durham County Records Office: D/LO/C-149(258).

126. W. Fordyce in his *History of Coal, Coke, Coal Fields [and] Iron*, cites the 'statistical Account of the Various Collieries on the River Tyne, Wear, and Tees', 25 Mar. 1843, given in the *1st Report of the Midland Mining Commission*. This account, listing only four of Londonderry's pits, numbers the men and boys employed as 1,497.

127. Cited in Challinor and Ripley, *The Miners' Association*, p.164, and Frank Machin, *The Yorkshire Miners* (Barnsley, 1958), vol.1, p.61.

128. Hunter to Londonderry, 31 July 1844, Durham County Record Office: D/LO/C-. 149(258); Londonderry to Hindhaugh, 3 Aug. 1844, Durham County Record Office: D/LO/C-326(25).

129. Ibid., D/LO/C-326(25).

130. See Hunter's apologetic letter of 8 Aug. 1844, Durham County Record Office: D/LO/C-149(257).

131. 'Great Meeting of Pitmen', *Tyne Mercury*, 31 July 1844, p.3.

132. Beginning in June the local press reported weekly on coal output and men who had left the union.

133. W. Baily (Hetton Colliery) to the *Report of the Commissioner ... State of the Population in the Mining Districts*, 1846, p.402.

134. Evidence of the colliery overviewers in the *Report of the Commissioner...to Inquire into the Operation of 5 and 6 Vict. And the State of the Population in the Mining Districts*, PP, 1845. XXVII, 197, pp.394-446. The only extant returns of the Coal Trade Office's circular of 17 Aug 1844 are those from the Haswell and Shotton collieries. Both reported that no 'strangers' had been imported.

135. Hunter to Londonderry, 4 Sept. 1844, Durham County Record Office: D/L0/C-.149(247).

136. Ibid., 1 Oct. 1844, Durham County Record Office: D/LO/C.-149(24O).

137. Hunter to Londonderry, 25 Oct. 1844, Durham County Record Office: D/LO/C-149(232).

138. Morris and Williams, *The South Wales Coal Industry*, pp.236-37; Hickey, *Urban Catholics*, p.55.

139. This is clear from the miner's journals and contemporary pamphlets. See Challinor and Ripley, *The Miners' Association*, p. 149; *The Miners Unions of Northumberland and Durham*, pp.80-81.

140. 'Appendix G', 1836, p.449.

141. Clarke, 'Labour in Shipbuilding', p.4; on the relationship between the helpers and the platers see, *Royal Commission on Labour Group 'A'*, vol. III, PP, 1893-4, XXXII, q.20,449-20,634, pp.25-31.

142. See, for example, the tirade on Lord Londonderry's importation of Irish for the 1844 strike by Rev. Hearne of Manchester, quoted in Treble, 'The Attitude of the Roman Catholic Church Towards Trade Unionism in the North of England, 1833-1842', *Northern History*, 5 (1970), pp.93-113.

143. K.S. Inglis, *Churches and the Working Class* (London, 1963), pp.313-4.

144. One manifestation of the New Unionism that also demonstrated Catholic influence was 'Local Assembly 3,504' of the Knights of Labour, which was established in November 1884 as the organisation of the English Window Glass Workers, with headquarters in Sunderland at Hartley's Glass Works. It sent delegates to Pittsburgh in July 1885. An Independent Order of the Knights of Labour was established at Jarrow in 1889. See 'Directory of Trade Union Secretaries', *7th Annual Report on Trade Unions*, 1893, PP, 1895, CVII, Appendix III, p.305, and again in the *8th Annual Report*, PP, 1896, XCIII, Appendix B, p.478. To judge by its rules, the Jarrow Order 'was expected to become a nation-wide organisation with "lodges" in all the principal towns of the country': Henry Pelling, 'The Knights of Labour in Britain, 1880-1901', *Economic History Review*, 9 (1956-7), pp.3l5-3l. But the Order had only 82 members in 1891 and lasted as a sick benefit society only until 1901.

145. *Royal Commission on Labour: Group 'A'*, 1893-94, q.26,344, p.414.

146. An example of the workings and difficulties of the NAUL can be found in the Minutes of the Executive Council Meetings, 6-27 April 1894. Newcastle Central Library, Local Tracts Collection. In the *7th Annual Report on Trade Unions*, 1893, p.110, the NAUL is listed as having 142

branches with 21,634 members; see also, *Royal Commission on Labour: Group 'A'*, 1893-94, q.20,425, p.24.

147. Durham Miner's Association (DMA) Minutes, 4 April 1885. Durham County Record Office.

148. In this he worked closely with Joseph Cowen, MP, placing the Irish cause before the English workers of the North East. At a meeting at Brandon on 21 Oct. 1885 the audience was told that if Crawford was sent to Parliament he would vote for coercion in Ireland. Crawford strongly refuted the charge, quoting from his DNA monthly circulars from 1881 to prove his support for nationalism. DMA Minutes, Oct. 1885.

149. E. Allen, *The Durham Miners' Association, A Commemoration* (Durham, 1969), pp.60-61. DMA Pamphlet.

150. Quoted in Sidney and Beatrice Webb, *The History of Trade Unionism* (London, 1896), p.280.

151. O'Connor, 'The Irish in Great Britain', pp.442-43.

152. A brief account of the strike in the context of the history of miners' associations is given in Welbourne, *The Miners Unions of Northumberland and Durham*, pp.214-20.

153. *Durham Chronicle*, 6 Jan. 1882, p.7.

154. Ibid., 6 Jan. 1882, p.7.

155. DMA Minutes, Jan. 1882; Welbourne, *The Miners Unions of Northumberland and Durham*, p.2l4.

156. *Durham Chronicle*, 17 Feb. 1882, p.2.

157. Ibid., 24 Aug. 1883, p.5.

158. Ibid., 10 Feb. 1882, p.6; 3 Feb. 1882, p.7.

159. Ibid., 15 Sept. 1882, p.3.

160. Ibid., 31 Mar. 1882, p.5.

161. Ibid., 31 Mar. 1882, p.8.

162. Ibid.,14 July 1882, p.3.

163. Welbourne, *The Miners Unions of Northumberland and Durham*, p.215.

164. *Durham Chronicle*, 10 Feb. 1882, p.6.

165. Ibid., letter to the editor signed 'Fairplay', 7 April 1882, p.8.

166. *Northern Catholic Calendar* (London, 1902), Obituary of Father Fortin, p.125: 'His sympathies were for the most part with the miners of the

district, and amongst these the whole of his missionary life was spent. He espoused their cause without fear of consequences when he considered that their just rights were in question'.

167. On 16 Dec. 1882, Fortin was presented with a purse of gold and a watch and chain by the DMA. At the presentation, Crawford stated, 'Whether the strike ends to-day or twelve months to-day, that strike had been a complete success. ... the name of Rev. Philip Fortin has become a household word among the miners of Durham, and a name which will long be cherished and sincerely honoured by them ... in after life you may remain, as you are now, in the broadest and truest sense, an ambassador of Christ amongst those over whom God has appointed you'. Fortin's reply to the presentation illustrates the leanings of the Church and its guarded pronouncements: 'If it is right and not wrong for workmen to combine together and form a union as it is now ... if it is lawful even in the eyes of the law of the land for men to combine together, and appoint officers in their union, it is surely right and lawful for them to defend those officers'. *Durham Chronicle*, 22 Dec. 1882, p.3.

168. Rev. A.D. Shafto, *Durham Chronicle*, 22 June 1883, p.3.

169. Cited in Welbourne, *The Miners Unions of Northumberland and Durham*, p.218.

170. *Durham Chronicle*, 22 Sept. 1882, p.8.

171. Ibid., to editor, 15 Dec. 1882, p.8.

172. Ibid., W.M. Hill (the agent to Robinson) to editor, 8 Dec. 1882, p.6.

173. Other titles included: 'Where are our Friends When Our Money is Gone', 'No Irish Need Apply', 'Exiles of Erin', 'Boys From Donegal', and 'Toils in the Mine'. *Durham Chronicle*, 29 Dec. 1883, p.7.

174. *Durham Chronicle*, 24 Aug. 1883, p.5.

175. Welbourne, *The Miners Unions of Northumberland and Durham*, pp.219-20.

176. Ibid., p.220.

177. The whereabouts of the portrait were proudly pointed out to me by a retired Irish miner in South Shields.

178. T.P. O'Connor, 'The Irish in Great Britain', in F. Lavery (ed.), *Irish Heroes in the War* (London, 1917), p.21.

Chapter 6 pages 143-172

1. E.P. Thompson has argued for 'a clear consecutive alliance between Irish nationalism and English Radicalism between 1790 and 1850', but admits that in the north of England this alliance was not explicit: *The Making of the English Working Class* (London, 1963), p.482.

2. Donald Read and Eric Glasgow, *Feargus O'Connor, Irishman and Chartist* (London, 1961), pp.49-50.

3. *Nottingham Mercury*, 1 Oct. 1847, quoted in Read and Glasgow, *Feargus O'Connor*, p.5.

4. There is little to suggest that the communications gap that existed between them and Chartists was ever effectively bridged. Rachel O'Higgins speculates that Ribbonmen strengthened Chartism in northern England, and points to the 'unusually high proportion' of Irish labourers involved with local radicalism wherever Ribbon Lodges were formed: 'The Irish Influence in the Chartist Movement', *Past and Present*, No.20 (1961), pp.85, 93. For the North East this is difficult to substantiate in the absence of evidence on Ribon Lodges and their membership.

5. J. Hickey, *Urban Catholics* (London, 1967), pp.137-145.

6. Donald Read, 'Chartism in Manchester', in Asa Briggs (ed.), *Chartist Studies* (Toronto and New York, 1959), p.51; Read and Glasgow, *Feargus O'Connor*, pp.93-4.

7. 'No local Chartists actually went to the polls either in 1841 or 1847; and although there was an active Chartist movement in the area in 1839, it virtually disappeared after the purge of Chartist leaders in the second half of the year. 1842 produced ripples, and 1848 virtually nothing': T.J. Nossiter, 'Elections and Political Behaviour in County Durham and Newcastle 1832-74', D.Phil thesis, Oxford University, 1968, p.112.

8. *Newcastle Courant*, 3 Feb. 1843, p.4.

9. T. Fordyce, *Local Register of Remarkable Events of Northumberland and Durham, Newcastle-Upon-Tyne and Berwick-Upon-Tweed, 1833-1875* (Newcastle, 1876), vol.3, for 31 Jan.1843, p.173.

10. *Report of the Poor Inquiry (Ireland) Commission: Appendix G, Report of the State of the Irish Poor in Great Britain*. 1836. XXXIV. 427 p.441.

11. In Newcastle the Act meant virtually household suffrage, and in the first year of its operation the electorate increased by 81 percent to nearly 8,000. Nossiter has described the Act as having 'brought about the biggest change in Newcastle local politics between 1835 and 1888, and drastically altered both the composition of the electorate and the council: 'Elections and

Political Behaviour in County Durham and Newcastle', p.181. The fact that the Liberal candidate for Newcastle in 1852 made reference to the 100 Roman Catholic voters there (*Gateshead Observer*, 27 March 1852, p.3) suggests that few Irish were immediately enfranchised by the Act. It was not until 1885 that any significant number of Irish county voters became eligible.

12. William G. Todd,. *The Irish in England*. Reprinted with additions from the *Dublin Review*, LXXXI (Dec. 1856), 470-521.

13. McAnulty (1818-1894) moved to Newcastle in the late 1830s and developed a prosperous bedding and drapery business. John Denvir described him as 'one of the best types of Irish in Britain that we have.... Working his way by the sheer force of ability and integrity into the very front rank of life in the town of his adoption, there has been no more ardent champion of his native land for over half a century ... [this] son of the northern province of Ireland, like so many of our people who have settled on the banks of the Tyne, his once powerful frame, bright cheery face, racy mother wit, and keen judgment, are familiar to all who have ever taken anything like a prominent part in the various Irish movements on this side of the channel': John Denvir, *The Irish in Britain* (London, 1892), p.141.

14. His obituary in the *Irish Tribune*, 15 Sept. 1894, claimed that he had organised local branches of the Precursor Society (1842), Repeal Association (1843), Young Ireland Confederate Club (1845), Tenant League (1850), and National Brotherhood of St. Patrick (1859): E.P.M. Wollaston, 'The Irish Nationalist Movement in Great Britain 1886-1908', MA thesis, University of London, 1958, p.51n. The list is suspect if only because Denvir, *Irish in Britain*, pp.140-41, quotes a letter of McAnulty's showing the formation of a Repeal Club in June 1848.

15. John O'Leary, *Recollections of Fenians and Fenianism* (London, 1896), vol.2, p.243.

16. Denvir, *Irish in Britain*, pp.140-41.

17. J.H. Whyte, *The Independent Irish Party 1850-59* (Oxford, 1958).

18. Josef Altholz, 'The Political Behaviour of English Catholics, 1850-1867', *Journal of British Studies*, 4 (1964-65), pp 89-90.

19. J.J. Dwyer, 'The Catholic Press, 1850-1950', in G. Beck (ed.), *The English Catholics, 1850-1950* (London, 1950), p.484. In the wake of Lord John Russell's turning to No-Popery in 1850, the Church flirted with the Conservative Party. The English Catholic elite were divided, however; John Wallis, the editor of *The Tablet* after 1855 was Tory, but Lord Acton remained a Liberal.

20. Quoted in Miriam B. Urban, *British Opinion and Policy on the Unification of Italy 1856-1861* (Pennsylvania, 1938), p 352.

21. *Tablet*, 13 Oct. 1860, p.645. No other diocese in England was reported as having a Papal Fund.

22. Ibid., 29 Sept. 1860, p.613.

23. Ibid., 29 April 1854, p.262.

24. Urban, *British Opinion*, p.506.

25. *Newcastle Courant*, 29 June 1866, p.5.

26. Ibid., 6 and 13 July 1866, p.5.

27. *Newcastle Courant*, 20 July 1866, p.5.

28. *Life and Labour of the London Poor*, 3rd Series, vol.7, p.246, quoted in R. Samuel, 'The Catholic Church and the Irish Poor.' Presented to the Past and Present Conference July 1966, p.24.

29. Peter Flannigan (a minor Irish figure) at the St. Patrick's Day speeches in Newcastle, *Newcastle Daily Chronicle*, 22 Mar. 1862, p.6.

30. The Irish in Sunderland were influenced to vote for the Tory candidate by the church promoting the schools issue while claiming that Home Rule was a dead issue. Wollaston 'The Irish Nationalist Movement in Great Britain 1886-1908', p.135.

31. Flannigan, *Newcastle Daily Chronicle*, 22 Mar. 1862, p.6.

32. The *Irish Tribune* was established by Charles Diamond in March 1884, later to become the *Tyneside Catholic News* which was syndicated in Irish districts throughout England. For a biographical note on Diamond, see, Wollaston, 'The Irish Nationalist Movement in Great Britain 1886-1908', p.244.

33. 'Irishmen in the North', *Newcastle Daily Chronicle*, 12 Oct. 1867, p.3.

34. See, for example, 'Alleged Recruiting at Hartlepool', *Newcastle Daily Chronicle*, 14 Oct. 1867, p.3.

35. In mid-October 1867, every English paper was discussing the suspected seizure of the Queen, though there was likely no foundation to the rumours. After the Clerkenwell explosion, the Queen was surrounded with 200 Guardsmen at Osbourne.

36. *The Times*, 8 Oct. 1867, p.9.

37. Ibid., 10 Oct. 1867, p.10.

38. *Newcastle Daily Chronicle*, 7 Oct. 1867, p.3.
39. Ibid.
40. *The Times*, 11 Oct. 1867, p.8; *Newcastle Daily Chronicle*, 8 Oct. 1867, p.3.
41. *Newcastle Daily Chronicle*, 9-15 Oct. 1867.
42. Ibid., 28 Dec. 1867, p.3. Most major towns in the North East received such instruction.
43. *Newcastle Courant*, 20 July, 1866, p.5.
44. For a perspective on Fenianism in Ireland see, Kevin B. Nowlan, 'The Fenian Rising of 1867', in T.W. Moody (ed.), *The Fenian Movement* (Cork, 1968), p38.
45. 18 Sept. 1865, quoted in Norman McCord, 'The Fenians and Public Opinion in Great Britain', in Maurice Harmon (ed.), *Fenians and Fenianism* (Dublin, 1968), p.38.
46. *Newcastle Daily Chronicle*, 30 Nov. 1866, p.8.
47. A more detailed account is given in Robert Wood, *West Hartlepool: The Rise and Development of a Victorian New Town* (West Hartlepool, 1967), pp.191-93.
48. *Newcastle Daily Chronicle*, 11 Dec. 1866, p.3.
49. *Durham Chronicle*, 7 Dec. 1866, p.7.
50. Ibid., 20, 26, and 28 Sept. 1867.
51. *Newcastle Daily Chronicle*, 14 Oct. 1867, p.2.
52. 'Sunderland Council Meeting', *Newcastle Daily Chronicle*, 10 Oct. 1867, p.4; on the 'unwarranted nervousness' of Sunderland's Mayor and Chief Constable in purchasing arms without the Council's consent, see *Newcastle Daily Chronicle*, 6-8 Nov. 1867.
53. 'The Fenian Outrage in Manchester', editorial, *Newcastle Daily Chronicle*, 20 Sept. 1867, p.2.
54. 'The Arming of the Police', *Newcastle Daily Chronicle*, 11 Oct. 1867, p.2.
55. *Newcastle Daily Chronicle*, 16 Dec. 1867, pp.2-3.
56. 'Irishmen in England', editorial, *Newcastle Daily Chronicle*, 24 Dec. 1867, p.2.

57. *Newcastle Daily Chronicle*, 18 Dec.1867, p.3. Similarly, an explosion in 1854 was immediately assumed to be the feared Russian invasion of Tyneside: *An Account of the Great Fire and Explosion, Which Occurred in Newcastle-Upon-Tyne and Gateshead on the 6th of October, 1854* (Newcastle, 1854), p.3.

58. 'The Fenian Alarm', editorial, *Newcastle Daily Chronicle*, 9 Oct. 1867, p.2.

59. McCord, 'The Fenians', p.46.

60. 'The. Church of Ireland', editorial, *Newcastle Daily Chronicle*, 21 Sept. 1867, p.2.

61. 'Fenianism: Its Causes and Cure', editorial, *Newcastle Daily Chronicle*, 2 Oct. 1867, p.2.

62. *Newcastle Daily Chronicle*, 28 Oct. p.3; the riot was not attributed to Fenianism.

63. Ibid., 17 Oct. 1867, p.3.

64. *Newcastle Courant*, 20 July 1866, p.5.

65. *The Times*, 17 Dec. 1867, p.10.

66. McCord, 'The Fenians', p.44.

67. R.L. Greenall, 'The Rise of Popular Conservatism in Salford,1868 to 1874', unpublished paper presented to the Urban History Conference, Canterbury, April 1972, pp.7-8.

68. McCord, 'The Fenians', pp.47-48.

69. The only recorded case of an Irishman disavowing any connection with the Fenians was that of Digby Seymour, Recorder of Newcastle. *Newcastle Daily Chronicle*, 24 Dec. 1867, p.2.

70. 'The Fenian Alarm', from the *Daily Telegraph*, reprinted in *Newcastle Daily Chronicle*, 9 Oct. 1867, p.3.

71. 'Irishmen in England', *Newcastle Daily Chronicle*, 24 Dec. 1867, p.2.

72. D.M. O'Connor, 'The Irish in Countries Other than Ireland: IV: In Great Britain and Wales', *Catholic Encyclopedia* (New York, 1910). vol. 8, p.152.

73. Denvir, *Irish in Britain*, p.182.

74. Joseph Keating, 'The Tyneside Irish Brigade', in Felix Lavery (ed.), *Irish Heroes in the War* (London, 1917), p.59.

75. Ibid., pp.49-50.

76. On the Pope see, *The Times*, 24 Oct. 1865, p.10; on Cardinal Cullen see, *Record*, 6 Dec. 1861, p.4; on Manning and priests in London see, Purcell, *Life of Manning*, vol. 2, pp.274-5; on the attitude of the church in Ireland see, O'Leary, *Recollections*, vol.2, pp.41-2; T.W. Moody, 'The Fenian Movement' in Moody (ed.), *The Fenian Movement*, pp.108-9; D. McCartney, 'The Church and the Fenians', in Harmon, *Fenians and Fenianism*, pp.11-23.

77. Quoted in *The Times*, 17 Dec. 1867, p.10; *Newcastle Daily Chronicle*, 16 Dec. 1867, p.2.

78. *Newcastle Daily Chronicle*, 16 Dec. 1867, p.3 (italics mine).

79. A rare instance of a Catholic leader having 'dangerous' Fenian connections is that of Michael J. Kelly, the master of a Catholic boys school, and later headmaster of St. Cuthbert's Grammar School, Newcastle. Kelly has been described as an 'ardent Fenian'. It was possibly his political views that forced his emigration to America in 1881. Father Charles Hart, *The Early Story of St. Cuthbert's Grammar School, Newcastle* (London, 1941), p.2.

80. The parish of All Saints, Newcastle saw an increase in its electorate between 1865 and 1868 of 215 percent. Nossiter, 'Elections and Political Behaviour in County Durham and Newcastle', p.526, see also, pp.123-l31 on the significance of the second Reform Bill in the area.

81. T.W. Moody, 'The Fenian Movement', p.111.

82. 'Great Amnesty Demonstration on Newcastle Town Moor', *Newcastle Daily Chronicle*, 28 Oct. 1872, p.3.

83. 'Irish in England', *Nation*, Letter XV (19 Oct. 1872), p.662.

84. *Newcastle Daily Chronicle*, 28 Oct. 1872, p.3. The speakers were Dr. Mallen (Gateshead's Irish spokesman) and Mr. Johnson, of Kanturk, Co. Cork.

85. Ibid., (Mr. George Tweddle of Newcastle).

86. Henry Campbell of Co. Down. He was involved with the Nationalist movement on Tyneside and, in 1880, became private secretary to Parnell.

87. Mr. George Hill of Newcastle; honorary organiser for Tyneside of the National League in the 1880s.

88. Mr. John Nolan, secretary of the Amnesty Committee, who became known as John 'Amnesty' Nolan. David Thornley, *Isaac Butt and Home Rule* (London, 1964), p. 94.

89. 'The Amnesty Orators and Their Aims', editorial, *Newcastle Courant*, 1 Nov. 1872, p.3.

90. Quoted by Nolan in his speech at the demonstration.

91. *Newcastle Daily Chronicle*, 29 Oct.1872, p.3.

92. The earlier Home Rule Conferences of 18 Jan. and 24 Feb. in Manchester and Birmingham were mainly executive meetings which had a much smaller attendance and received no comment in the local press. At the conference of 21 Aug. there were representatives from Consett, South Shields, Gateshead, Newcastle, Tunstall, Sunderland, Durham and Jarrow. Six priests were present as was the self-styled miners' historian, Richard Fynes. *Newcastle Daily Chronicle*, 22 Aug. 1873, p.3.

93. Butt to Mitchell-Henry, 23 Aug. 1873, quoted in Wollaston, 'The Irish Nationalist Movement in Great Britain 1886-1908', p.54.

94. *Newcastle Daily Chronicle*, 18 Mar. 1873, p.3.

95. *Durham Chronicle*, 4 Mar. 1881, p.6.

96. See, for example, the local St. Patrick's Day proceedings of 1875, *Durham Chronicle*, 19 Mar. 1875, p.8.

97. *Newcastle Daily Chronicle*, 18 Mar. 1873, p.4.

98. An official of the North Eastern Railway Company and local Irish leader, Savage had been hailed as a possible Nationalist MP at the time of his death in 1887.

99. T.M. Healy, *Letters and Leaders of My Day*, (London, 1929),vol.1, pp.55-57; J. Keating, 'The Tyneside Irish Brigade', p.62. Davitt was apparently spared his life by a platform priest who beat the mob back by wildly flailing his walking stick.

100. Denvir, *Irish in Britain*, p.275.

101. Charles Diamond was honorary secretary. Wollaston, 'The Irish Nationalist Movement in Great Britain 1886-1908', pp.60-62.

102. Healy, *Letters and Leaders,* vol.1, p.36.

103. Speech by the Home Rule MP for Dundalk, Philip Callan: 'Home Rule For Ireland – Great Meeting in Newcastle', *Newcastle Daily Chronicle*, 22 Aug. 1873, p.3.

104. *Newcastle Daily Chronicle*, 16-24 Nov. 1877.

105. For background on the politics of Gateshead see Norman McCord, 'Gateshead Politics in the Age of Reform', *Northern History*, 4 (1969), pp.167-83.

106. *Newcastle Daily Chronicle*, 19 Nov. 1877, p.4.

107. Ibid., p.4.

108. Healy, *Letters and Leaders*, vol.1, p.42.

109. *Newcastle Daily Chronicle*, 22 Nov. 1877, p.4.

110. Biggar, 778, Robson, 574. *Newcastle Daily Chronicle*, 24 Nov. 1877, p.4.

111. Charles Hammond, Edward T. Gourley (L.), Joseph Cowen (L.), and Thomas Burt (L).

112. Evan R. Jones, *The Life and Speeches of Joseph Cowen, M.P.* (London, 1885), pp.3-4. The only radical representing the North East before 1865 was the outsider John Bright, who obtained a seat in Durham City in 1843 as a result of Lord Londonderry having split the Tory vote.

113. For a brief summary of the area's Liberalism see, Nossiter, 'Elections and Political Behaviour in County Durham and Newcastle', pp.514 et passim.

114. The other was Henry Labouchere, standing for Northampton. C.H.D. Howard, 'The Parnell Manifesto of 21 November, 1885, and the Schools Question', *English Historical Review*, 62 (1947), pp.42-51.

115. J. Keating, 'The Tyneside Irish Brigade', p.55.

116. Jones, *Cowen*, pp.63-4; *Durham Chronicle*, 16 July 1869, p.5.

117. John Morley, *Recollections*, (London, 1918), vol.1, p.185.

118. Healy, *Letters and Leaders*, vol.1, p.186.

119. Jones, *Cowen*, pp.196-200.

120. Held in the Irish Literary Institute, Clayton St., 27 Oct.: Jones, *Cowen*, p.99; *Newcastle Courant*, 29 Oct. 1880, p.8.

121. Quoted in Aaron Watson, *A Great Labour Leader: Being a Life of the Right Honourable Thomas Burt M.P.* (London, 1908), p.265.

122. Cowen broke with Gladstone over the San Stefano Treaty in 1878.

123. Watson, *Burt*, pp.262-3.

124. In 1873 the paper reported that its daily sales had reached 35,534, considerably above its nearest competitor the *Manchester Guardian*. 'Clearly, then, the editorial standpoint of the *Chronicle* was a matter of considerable significance, locally and nationally'. Maurice Mime, *The Newspapers of Northumberland and Durham* (Newcastle, 1971), pp.69-72.

125. 21 Aug. 1873, pp.2-3.

126. 'Home Rule', editorial, *Newcastle Daily Chronicle*, 22 Aug. 1873, pp.2-3.

127. *Newcastle Daily Chronicle*, 21 Mar. 1873, p.8.

128. Quoted in *Newcastle Courant*, 10 July 1874, p.3.

129. 'Home Rule Demonstration', editorial, *Newcastle Daily Chronicle,* 9 Aug. 1880, p.2.

130. John Ferguson, quoted in *Newcastle Daily Chronicle,* 10 Aug. 1880, p.3.

131. Nossiter, 'Elections and Political Behaviour in County Durham and Newcastle, p.99.

132. Watson, *Burt,* p.262.

133. Ibid., pp.262-63.

134. At the 1881 Land League Conference in Newcastle, Crawford and Cowen were among those to declare that their aim was to 'inform English workmen as to the merits of the question [of tenant rights in Ireland]'. Quoted in Wollaston, 'The Irish Nationalist Movement in Great Britain 1886-1908', p.61.

135. *Durham Chronicle,* 4 Mar. 1881, p.7. Local branches of the Land League were meeting to protest 'against the tyrannical arrest of Mr. John Dillon, M.P. for Tipperary, by the so-called Liberal Government'. See, 'Crook Land League Meeting', *Durham Chronicle,* 20 May 1881, p.3.

136. 'Mr. Pease MP and the Coercion Bill', *Durham Chronicle,* 25 Feb. 1881, p.5.

137. 'The Irish Home Rule Cry', editorial, *Newcastle Courant,* 29 Aug. 1873, p.5.

138. 5 Jan. 1883, p.5. The Willington Land League replied to the editor of the *Durham Chronicle,* 12 Jan. 1883, p.6: 'is it fair to expect that we, as exiles, should be made to continue to pay in reality for the prodigality and extravagance of landlords ...? I daresay, sir, you have no ill-will towards the Irish, but we think you might be mistaken in your way of being charitable'.

139. For example, *A Warning Voice to the Miners of Durham and Northumberland, Being a Series of Letters Published in the Durham Chronicle on Unions and Strikes by a Durham Pitman* (Newcastle, 1864).

140. The Club at Hartlepool was established in the 1870s and boasted a membership in 1880 of 600 – 'and flourishing': *Newcastle Daily Chronicle,* 14 Dec. 1880, p.3.

141. Welbourne, *The Miners Unions of Northumberland and Durham,* pp.199-200.

142. Ibid., p.200.

143. During the O'Connell centenary celebrations. *Newcastle Daily Chronicle,* 9-10 Aug. 1875, p.3.

144. For an easily accessible depiction of the riots see, Noel Annan, 'Thoughts on Ireland', *Listener,* 23 Mar. 1973, p.369.

145. A meeting in the Town Hall, Durham, had been convened by Londonderry in response to a letter from the Lord Mayor of London. *Durham Chronicle,* 3 Feb. 1882, p.8. It is also interesting to note the support for 'Queen and Parliament' by the 'Varsity boys' of Durham University; they occupied the front row at the anti-coercion meeting in Durham City in 1881 in order to heckle O'Connor-Power. *Durham Chronicle,* 4 Mar. 1881, p.6.

146. 'T.P. O'Connor, 'Irish in Great Britain', pp.21-22.

147. Nossiter, 'Elections and Political Behaviour in County Durham and Newcastle', p.139.

148. Robert Ensor, *England:1870-1914* (Oxford, 1936), p.207.

Bibliography

Manuscript Material

Archives of the Catholic Diocese of Hexham and Newcastle
Letters and Miscellanea of the 17th, 18th and Early 19th Centuries. Transcribed by Rev. W. Vincent Smith. 10 vols.

Status Animarum, etc. for the Diocese of Hexham and Newcastle. Vol.1, 1886-1902, vol.11, 1847-1912. Transcribed and compiled by Rev. J. Lenders, January-March, 1931.

Catholic Miscellanea in the Possession of Rev. W. Vincent Smith
Transcriptions of numerous letters and pamphlets; notes and miscellaneous material collected over the last 50 years, largely in reference to the period prior to 1850.

Durham County Record Office
Londonderry Papers.

Census Enumerators' Manuscripts for the County of Durham, 1841-1861.

Durham Miners' Association
Circulars, Records and Minutes of the Executive, 1869-1885.

Newcastle Central Library
Census Enumerators' Manuscripts for the parish of All Saints, 1841-1861.

Roman Catholic Tracts: A Collection of clippings, pamphlets and miscellanea. L.282.N.563.

Newcastle City Archives
All Saints Parish: Guardians Meeting Book, 1840-48.

Borough of Newcastle Upon Tyne: Sanitary Committee Minute Book, No.1, February 1854.

Minutes of the Newcastle Board of Guardians, vol.VI, 1845-6, vol.VII, 1847.

Newcastle Union: List of Guardians and Paid Officers etc., 1866-1901.

Proceedings of the Newcastle Common Council, 1840-.1880.

Removal Warrant Papers, 1849-1853. 20/70/1249.

North of England Institute of Mining and Mechanical Engineers, Newcastle
J.G. Bell Collection: Forming a General History of Coal, Collieries, Colliery-Engineering and Mining. 20 vols.

Northumberland County Record Office
Records of the Coal Trade Office, 1844.

Public Record Office, London (now the National Archives)
Census Enumerators' Manuscripts for the parish of All Saints, 1871. R.G. 10.

Census Enumerators' Manuscripts for the County of Durham, 1871. R.G. 10.

Ushaw College Library, Durham
Crowe Collection: Pastorals, Circulars, Encyclical Letters and Miscellanea.

Ushaw Collection: Pastorals and Circulars of the Vicars Apostolic and Bishops for the Northern Division and the Diocese of Hexham and Newcastle, 1753-1869. 4 vols.

Ushaw Pamphlets Collection.

Official Publications

(a) Parliamentary Papers

1827 *Second Report from the Select Committee on Emigration from the United Kingdom*. 1826-27. V. 1.

1827 *Third Report from the Select Committee on Emigration from the United Kingdom*. 1826-27. V. 225.

1836 *Report of the Poor Inquiry (Ireland) Commission: Appendix G, Report of the State of the Irish Poor in Great Britain*. 1836. XXXIV. 427.

1842 *Children's Employment Commission, First Report of the Commissioners: Mines*. 1842. XV. 1.

1842 *Appendix to the First Report to Her Majesty, of the Commissioners for Inquiring into the Employment and Condition of Children in Mines and Manufactories, Mines, Pt.I: Report by James Mitchell on south Durham*. 1842. XX. 119.

1844 *Census of Great Britain, 1841: Ages, Civil Conditions, Occupations and Birth Place: Pt.I: England and Wales*. 1844. XXVII. 1.

Bibliography

1845 *Report of the Commissioner... to Inquire into the Operation of 5 and 6 Vict. And the State of the Population in the Mining Districts.* 1845. XXVII. 197.

1845 *Second Report of the Commissioners on the State of Large Towns and Populous Districts: Appendix II:D.B. Reid, Report on the Sanitary Conditions of Newcastle, Gateshead, North Shields, Sunderland, Durham and Carlisle.* 1845. XVIII. 427.

1846 *Report From the Select Committee on Railway Labourers.* 1846. XIII. 1.

1846 *Report of the Commissioner... to Inquire into the Operation of 5 and 6 Vict. And the State of the Population in the Mining Districts.* 1846. XXIV. 383.

1847 *Report of the Select Committee of the House of Lords on Colonization From Ireland.* 1847. VI. 1.

1852-1853 *Census of Great Britain: Religious Worship: England and Wales.* 1852-3. LXXXIX. 1.

1853 *Census of Great Britain 1851: Population Tables II: Ages, Civil Conditions, Occupations and Birth-Place of the Peoples.* 1852-3. LXXXVIII. 1.

1854 *Report of the Commissioners Appointed to Inquire into the Causes which have led to or have Aggravated the Late Outbreak of Cholera in the towns of Newcastle-Upon-Tyne, Gateshead, and Tynemouth.* 1854. XXXV. 131.

1854 *Returns of the Religious Denomination of the Poor in England and Wales for September 1852 and January 1853.* 1854. LV. 461.

1854 *Report of the Select Committee on Poor. Removals.* 1854. XVII.1.

1855 *Report of the Select Committee on Poor Removals.* 1854-5. XIII. 1.

1858 *Report of the Select Committee on the Irremovable Poor.* 1857-8. XIII. 1.

1859 *Report of the Select Committee on the Irremovable Poor.* 1859. VII. 1.

1860 *Report of the Select Committee on the Irremovable Poor.* 1860. XVII. 1. *Poor Law Removals: 25 March 1859 - 25 March 1860.* 1860. LVIII. 791.

1863 *Poor Law Removals: 1 December, 1860 - 1 December, 1862.* 1863. LII. 267.

1863 *Census of England and Wales 1861: Population Tables: Ages, Civil Conditions, Occupations and Birth-Places of the People.* 1863. LIII. Pt.I, 265.

1864 *Poor Law Removals: 31 December, 1862 - 31 December, 1863.* 1864. LII. 305.

1873 *Census of England and Wales, 1871: Population Abstracts: Ages, Civil Conditions, Occupations and Birth-Places of the People.* 1873. LXXI. Pt. 1, 1.

1883 *Census of England and Wales, 1881: Population Abstracts: Ages, Civil Conditions, Occupations and Birth-Places of the People.* 1883. LXXX. 1.

1885 *First Report of the Royal Commission of Inquiry into the Housing of the Working Classes*. 1884-5. XXXI. 1.

1886 *First Report of the Royal Commission Appointed to Inquire into the Depression of Trade and Industry*. 1886. XXI. 1.

1886 *Second Report of the Royal Commission Appointed to Inquire into the Depression of Trade and Industry*. 1886. XXI. Pt.I, 231.

1887 *Labour Statistics: Return of Wages Published between 1830 and 1886. 1887.* LXXXIX. 273.

1887 *Labour Statistics: Statistical Tables and Reports on Trade Unions by the Labour Correspondent to the Board of Trade*. 1887. LXXXIX. 715.

1894 *Royal Commission on Labour: Group 'A' (Mining Iron, Engineering, Hardware, Shipbuilding, and Cognate Trades): Volume III*. 1893-4. XXXII. 5.

(b) Reports

Artisan and Labourers Dwellings Improvement Act, 1875: Report of the Sanitary Committee presented to Council 2nd August, 1876. Newcastle, 1876.

Bell, I. Lowthian. *Report of the Sanitary Committee Presented to the Council, 5th March, 1862*. Newcastle, 1862.

Borough of Newcastle. *Criminal and Miscellaneous Statistical Returns of the Constabulary for the Year Ending 29th September, 1869*. Newcastle, 1869.

Borough of Newcastle. *Report of the Public Health During the Year 1866*. Newcastle, 1866.

Borough of Newcastle. *Reports of the Medical Officer of Health, 1878-1882*. Newcastle.

Criminal and Miscellaneous Statistical Returns of the Newcastle Police for the Year Ending 29th September, 1861. Newcastle, 1861.

Ranger, William. *Report to the General Board of Health on Darlington, 1850*. London, 1850.

Rawlinson, Robert. *Report to the General Board of Health on the Municipal Borough of Sunderland, 1851*. London, 1851.

Rawlinson, Robert. *Report to the General Board of Health on the Township of Houghton-le-Spring, 1854*. London, 1854.

Newspapers and Periodicals

British Protestant or Journal of the Religious Principles of the Reformation, 1845-64

Catholic Magazine, 1844

Catholic Schools Magazine, 1847-65

Dolman's Magazine, 1845-50

Dublin Review, 1840-80

Durham County Advertiser, 1833-50

Durham Chronicle, 1840-86

Gateshead Observer, 1852

Newcastle Chronicle, 1845-56

Newcastle Courant, 1840-85

Newcastle Daily Chronicle, 1858-88

Newcastle Journal, 1847-55

Rambler, 1840-80

Record, 1852-67

Tablet, 1840-80

The Times, 1861-67

Tyne Mercury, 1844

Directories

Durham Directory and Almanack. 1846-86.

Fordyce, T. *Local Register of Remarkable Events of Northumberland and Durham, Newcastle-Upon-Tyne and Berwick-Upon-Tweed, 1833-1875.* Newcastle, 1876. 4 vols.

Havelock's *Local Records of Northern England, 1884-1886.* Newcastle. 2 vols.

Kelly's Directory of the Northern Towns, 1886.

Newcastle and Gateshead Annual Directory. 1870-71.

Northern Catholic Calendar. 1869-1936.

Ordo and Catholic Directory. 1836-69.

Richardson, Moses A. *Local Historians Table Book Connected With the Counties of Newcastle, Northumberland and Durham, 1838-1842.* V. Newcastle, 1846.

Richmond, Thomas. *Local Records of Stockton-on-Tees and the Neighbourhood.* London, 1868.

Whellan's Directory of Durham and Newcastle, 1856.

Books, Articles, Thesis and Papers

'A Statement of the Number of Seats in the Several Churches and Chapels Within the Parish of All Saints.. In the Month of August, 1838.' *Journal of the Statistical Society of London*, I (October 1838), 379.

'An Appeal to the Catholic Laity on the Present Condition of the Poor.' *Rambler*, 2 (October 1854), 277-290.

'Catholic and Protestant Missionary, Book and Education Societies.' *Rambler*, new series, X (October 1858), 268-279.

'Conditions of our Chief Towns–Newcastle-upon-Tyne.' *Builder*, 13 April 1861, 241-244.

'How to Convert Protestants.' *Rambler*, new series, I (January 1854), 1-19.

'Our Picture in the Census.' *Rambler*, new series, I (March and April 1854), 257-280, and 356-375.

'The Irish in England.' 16 letters by a 'special correspondent' appearing weekly. *Nation*, 6 July-9 November 1872.

'The Religious Census of England.' *Rambler*, new series, I (February 1854), 183-190.

'The Work and Wants of the Catholic Church in England.' *Dublin Review*, new series, 1 (July 1863), 139-166.

'Where Does Our Strength Lie?' *Rambler*, XIV (May 1849), 1-7.

'Who's Who of the Tyneside Irish Movement and Associates (Past and Present).' Ed. F. Lavery. *Irish Heroes in the War*. London, 1917, 321-335.

A Few Brief Observations, Illustrations and Anecdotes Respecting Pitmen in a Northern Colliery Village by an Incumbent in the Diocese of Durham. Sunderland, 1862.

A Full Report of the Proceedings at the Meeting of the British Reformation Society Held at North Shields Thursday, July 6, 1831. North Shields.

A View of the Pitmen's Strike in Answer to a Letter in the Durham Chronicle, of June 14th, signed 'an overman.' By The Miners of Framwellgate Moor Colliery. Newcastle, 1844.

A Warning Voice to the Miners of Durham and Northumberland, Being a Series of Letters Published in the Durham Chronicle on Unions and Strikes by a Durham Pitman, 1864. Newcastle, 1864

Albion, Rev. Gordon. '"Papal Aggression" on England.' *Irish Ecclesiastical Record,* LXXII (October 1950), 350-357.

Allen, E. *The Durham Miners' Association, a Commemoration.* Pamphlet. Durham, 1969.

Allen, E., J.F. Clarke, N. McCord, D.J. Rowe. *The North-East Engineers' Strikes of 1871: The Nine Hours' League.* Newcastle, 1971.

Altholz, Josef. 'The Political Behaviour of the English Catholics, 1850-1867.' *Journal of British Studies,* IV (1964-5), 89-103.

An Account of the Great Fire and Explosion Which Occurred in Newcastle-Upon-Tyne and Gateshead on the 6th of October, 1854. Newcastle and London, 1854.

Baring-Gould, S. *The Church Revival: Thoughts Thereon and Reminiscences.* London, 1914.

Barrett, D.W. *Life and Work Among the Navvies.* 3rd ed. London, 1883.

Beck, G. (ed.) *The English Catholics, 1850-1950.* London, 1950.

Belaney, Rev. Robert. *The Reign of Sin and the Reign of Grace: A Sermon Preached at St. Wilfrid's Church, Bishop Auckland. 13th December, 1863.* Bishop Auckland, 1863.

Best, G.F.A. 'Popular Protestantism in Victorian Britain.' Robert Robson ed. *Ideas and Institutions of Victorian Britain.* London, 1967, 115-142.

Bickersteth, M.C. *A Sketch of the Life and Episcopate of the Right Reverend Robert Bickersteth D.D.* London, 1887.

Bishop, M.C. 'The Social Methods of Roman Catholicism in England.' *Contemporary Review,* XXXIX (March 1877), 603-634.

Blair, C.H. Hunter. *The Mayors and Lord Mayors of Newcastle Upon Tyne 1216-1940.* Newcastle, 1940.

Bossy, John. 'Four Catholic Congregations in Rural Northumberland 1750-1850.' *Recusant History,* IX (April, 1967), 88-119.

Bossy, John. 'More Northumbrian Congregations.' *Recusant History,* X (January 1969), 11-34.

Boyle, J.R. *The County of Durham.* London, 1892.

Boyle, K. 'The Irish Immigrant in Britain.' *Northern Ireland Legal Quarterly,* XIX (December 1968), 418-445.

Brady, W. Maziere. *Annals of the Catholic Hierarchy in England and Scotland, 1585-1876.* London, 1877.

British Society for the Promoting of the Religious Principles of the Reformation. *Short Tracts Nos. I-XXXIV*. London, 1843-51.

Bryson, Thomas. *Remarks by the Town Surveyor and Inspector Nuisances [T. Bryson] On An Article In the 'Builder,' headed 'Conditions of Our Chief Towns – Newcastle-On-Tyne.'* Newcastle, 1861.

Burt, Thomas. *From Pitman to Privy Councilor: An Autobiography*. London, 1924.

Cahill, Gilbert A. 'Irish Catholicism and English Toryism.' *Review of Politics*, XIX (January 1957), 62-76.

Capes, J.M. 'The Progress of Catholic Poverty.' *Rambler*, V (March 1850), 187-216.

Cargill, William and a Committee of the Educational Society of Newcastle. 'Educational, Criminal, and Social Statistics of Newcastle-upon-Tyne.' *Journal of the Statistical Society of London*, I (October 1838), 355-361.

Catholic Institute of Great Britain. *Annual Reports for 1840-1847*.

Catholic Poor School Committee. *Annual Reports for 1848-60*.

Chadwick, Edwin. *Report on the Sanitary Condition of the Labouring Population, 1842*. Ed. M.W. Flinn. Edinburgh, 1965.

Challinor, Raymond, and Brian Ripley. *The Miners' Association: A Trade Union in the Age of the Chartists*. London, 1968.

Charlton, L.E.O. *Recollections of a Northumbrian Lady [Barbara Charlton] 1815-1866*. London, 1949.

Cheney, R.H. 'Papal Pretensions.' *Quarterly Review*, LXXXIX (September 1851), 452-491.

Clapham, Sir John. *An Economic History of Modern Britain*. Cambridge, 1926-38. 3 vols.

Clarke, J.F. 'Labour Relations in Engineering and Shipbuilding on the North East Coast in the Second Half of the 19th Century'. MA thesis, Newcastle University, 1966.

Clarke, J.F. 'Labour in Shipbuilding on the North East Coast, 1850-1900.' *North East Group for the Study of Labour History*, Bulletin No.2 (October 1968), 4-7.

Coleman, Terry. *The Railway Navvies*. London, 1965.

Conference of the Newcastle-On-Tyne Brotherhood of St. Vincent De Paul, Report of. Newcastle, 1849.

Connell, Kenneth Hugh. *Population of Ireland, 1750-1845*. Oxford, 1950.

Consett Iron Co. Ltd. *Description of the Works*. Newcastle, 1893.

Cooper, W. Donald. *The Teetotal Movement with Particular Reference to the North-East of England: 1835-1860*. Honours Paper. Durham University. 1968.

Cooter, Roger. 'Lady Londonderry and the Irish Catholics of Seaham Harbour: "No Popery" Out of Context'. *Recusant History*, 16 (1976), 288-98.

Cooter, Roger. 'Hibernians and Geordies in the Nineteenth Century'. *Northern Catholic History*, No.4 (1976), 20-9.

Cooter, Roger. 'On Calculating the Nineteenth Century Irish Catholic Population of Durham and Newcastle'. *Northern Catholic History*, No.2 (1975), 16-25.

Cowen, Joseph. *Speeches on the Near Eastern Question: Foreign and Imperial Affairs: and on the British Empire*. Revised by his Daughter. Newcastle and London, 1909.

Curtis, Lewis Perry Jr. *Anglo-Saxons and Celts: A Study of Anti-Irish Prejudice in Victorian England*. New York, 1968.

Davies, Rev. J. *Sermon on Behalf of the Church Building Society preached at St. Mary's Church, Gateshead, Sunday March 12, 1843*. Gateshead, 1843.

Davies, Rev. J. *Sermon on Public Thanksgiving day October 27, 1853*. Gateshead, 1853.

Denvir, John. *The Brandons: A Story of Irish Life in England*. London, 1903.

Denvir, John. *The Irish in Britain from the Earliest Times to the Fall and Death of Parnell*. London, 1892.

Devyr, Thomas Ainge. *The Odd Book of the Nineteenth Century or 'Chivalry' in Modern Days: A Personal Record of Reform—Chiefly Land Reform for the Last Fifty Years*. New York, 1882.

Dewdney, J.C. 'Population: Growth, Distribution and Structure.' J.C. Dewdney (ed.) *Durham County and City with Teesside*. Durham, 1970, 353-368.

Dougan, David. *The History of North East Shipbuilding*. London, 1968.

Dunn, Matthias. *Coal Trade of the North of England*. Newcastle, 1844.

Durham County Council. *The Londonderry Papers: Catalogue of the Documents Deposited in the Durham County Record Office by the 9th Marquess of Londonderry*. Durham, 1969.

Ecclesiastical Developments in the Churches of Rome and England and Missionary Efforts by the Protestant Reformation Society. London, 1872.

Eden, Sir Timothy. *Durham*. London, 1952. 2 vols.

Engels, Frederick. *The Condition of the Working Class in England*. Leipzig, 1845. Panther ed. introduced by E.J. Hobsbawm, London, 1969.

Ensor, R.C.K. *England, 1870-1914*. Oxford, 1936.

Etherington, Henry French. *Full Report of the Proceedings of A Public Meeting Held in the Wesleyan Chapel, Hartlepool, On Monday Evening, March 9th, 1840, To Establish An Auxiliary In Aid of the British Reformation Society*. Sunderland, 1840.

Evennett, H.O. *The Catholic Schools of England and Wales*. Cambridge, 1944.

Fordyce, William. *History of Coal, Coke, Coal Fields [and] Iron*. London, 1860.

Forster, Ann M.C. 'Catholicism in the Diocese of Durham in 1767.' *Ushaw Magazine*, LXXII (March 1962), 68-91.

Freeman, T.W. 'The Irish in Great Britain.' *Geographical Journal*, CXXIII (June 1957), 274-275.

Fynes, Richard. *The Miners of Northumberland and Durham: a History of Their Social and Political Progress*. Blyth, 1873.

Gard, R.M. 'Labour History of the Railways in Durham and Northumberland to 1900: An Introduction to Sources and Bibliography.' *North East Group for the Study of Labour History*, Bulletin No.3 (October 1969), 17-23.

Gay, John D. *The Geography of Religion in England*. London, 1971.

Gilley, S.W. 'Heretic London, Holy Poverty and the Irish Poor, 1830-1870.' *Downside Review*, LXXXIX (January 1971), 64-89.

Gilley, S.W. 'Protestant London, No-Popery and the Irish Poor, 1830-1860,' *Recusant History*, X and XI (January 1970; January 1971), 210-30, and 21-46.

Gilley, S.W. 'The Roman Catholic Mission to the Irish in London, 1840-1860.' *Recusant History*, X (October 1969), 123-145.

Gilley, Sheridan Wayne. 'Evangelical and Roman Catholic Missions to the Irish in London 1830-1870'. PhD thesis, Cambridge, 1970.

Gillow, J. *Bibliographical Dictionary of English Catholics*. London, 1885-1898. 5 vols.

Gleave, J.T. 'The Tees-side Iron and Steel Industry.' *Geographical Journal*, XCI (May 1938), 454-467.

Gorman, W. Gordon. *Converts to Rome, 1850-1900*. London, 1910.

Greenall, R.L. 'The Rise of Popular Conservatism in Salford, 1868 to 1874.' Presented to the Urban History Conference, University of Canterbury, April 1972.

Halevy, Elie. *A History of the English People in the Nineteenth Century,* Vol.4: *1841-1895.* London, 1951.

Handley, James Edmund. *The Irish in Modern Scotland.* Cork, 1947.

Harmon, Maurice ed. *Fenians and Fenianism.* Dublin, 1968.

Hart, Father Charles. *The Early Story of St. Cuthbert's Grammar School, Newcastle.* London, 1941.

Healy, T.M. *Letters and Leaders of My Day.* London, 1929. 2 vols.

Heesom, Allan J. The Third Marquis of Londonderry as an Employer Paper presentation pesented to the North-Eastern Group for the Study of Labour History, 20 May, 1972.

Heyes, John Francis. 'Roman Catholic Education in County Durham, 1580-1870'. MEd thesis, Durham University, 1969.

Hickey, J. *Urban Catholics.* London, 1967.

Hobsbawm, E.J. *Labouring Men: Studies in the History of Labour.* London, 1964.

Hodgson, George B. *The Borough of South Shields.* Newcastle,1903.

House, J.W. *North Eastern England Population Movements and the Landscape since the early 19th Century.* Newcastle, 1954.

Howard, C.H.D. 'The Parnell Manifesto of 21 November, 1885, and the Schools Question.' *English Historical Review,* LXII (January 1947), 42-51.

Hughes, W.M. 'Economic Development in the Eighteenth and Nineteenth Centuries.' J.C. Dewdney ed. *Durham County and City with Teesside.* Durham, 1970, 227-234.

Inglis, K.S. 'Patterns of Religious Worship in 1851.' *Journal of Ecclesiastical History,* XI (1960), 74-86.

Inglis, K.S. *Churches and the Working Classes in Victorian England.* London, 1963.

Inquiry into the Condition of the Poor of Newcastle-Upon-Tyne. Reprinted from the *Newcastle Weekly Chronicle.* Newcastle, 1850.

Jackson, John Archer. *The Irish in Britain.* London, 1963.

Jones, Evan Rowland. *The Life and Speeches of Joseph Cowen,* M.P. London, 1885.

Keating, Joseph. 'Tyneside Irish Brigade, History of its Origin and Development.' Felix Lavery ed. *Irish Heroes in the War.* London, 1917, 37-128.

Kelly, Bernard W. *Historical Notes on English Catholic Missions.* London, 1907.

Kirk, John C. 'The History of Thornley.' *Northern Daily Mail,* 27 January-21 April 1970.

Kitching, J. 'The Catholic Poor Schools 1800 to 1845: The Catholic Poor: Relief, Welfare and Schools.' *Journal of Educational Administration and History,* I (June 1969), 1-8.

Kitching, J. 'The Catholic Poor Schools 1800 to 1845: The Schools: Development and Distribution.' *Journal of Educational Administration and History,* II (December 1969), 1-12.

Knight, Rev. W. *Reply to the Rev. Brabazon Ellis: A Sermon on True Christian Charity.* Hartlepool, 1840.

Kohl, J.G. *Ireland: Dublin, The Shannon, Limerick... O'Connell and the Repeal Association.* London, 1844.

Large, David. 'The Third Marquess of Londonderry And the End of the Regulation 1844-45.' *Durham University Journal,* LI (1958.59), 1-9.

Lawton, R. 'Irish Immigration to England and Wales in the Mid-Nineteenth Century.' *Irish Geography,* IV (1959-63), 35-54.

Lenders, Rev. J. *History of the Parish of Sacriston.* Minsteracres, 1930.

Lenders, Rev. J. *The History of the Parish of Prudhoe on Tyne.* c.1930.

Letters Respecting the Suffering Irish Clergy the Persecuting Romish Priesthood, Daniel O'Connell and the Present Administration by Clericus Anglicanus to the Editor of the Newcastle Journal. Newcastle, 1836.

Longstaffe, William H.D. *History of Darlington.* Darlington, 1854.

Losh, James. *Diaries and Correspondence.* Ed. Edward Hughes, Vol.II: Diary 1824-1833 and Letters to Charles, 2nd Earl Grey and Henry Brougham. Durham and London, 1963. (Surtees Society Publication, vol.174, 1959.)

Lumley, W.G. 'The Statistics of the Roman Catholic Church in England and Wales.' *Journal of the Statistical Society of London,* XXVII (September 1864), 303-23.

Mann, Horace. 'On the Statistical Position of Religious Bodies in England and Wales.' *Journal of the Statistical Society of London,* XVIII (June 1855), 141-159.

Manning, Archbishop. *Ireland: A Letter to Earl Grey.* London, 1868.

Manning, Henry Edward. *Truth Before Peace: A Sermon Preached At the Opening of S. Godric, in Durham, November 15th, 1864.* Dublin, London and Durham, 1865.

McClelland, Vincent Alan. *Cardinal Manning, His Public Life and Influence, 1865-1892*. London, 1962.

McCord, Norman. 'Some Aspects of Mid-Nineteenth Century Newcastle.' Presented to the Urban History Conference, University of Canterbury, April 1972.

McFaul, James A. 'Hibernians', *Catholic Encyclopedia*. New York, 1910, vol.VII, pp.320-21.

Metcalf, G.H. 'A History of the Durham Miners' Association 1869-1915'. MA thesis, Durham University, 1947.

Mewburn, Francis. *The Larchfield Diary: Extracts from the Diary of the late Mr. Mewburn, First Railway Solicitor*. London, 1876.

Middlebrook, S. *Newcastle Upon Tyne, Its Growth and Achievement*. Newcastle, 1950.

Milburn, David. *History of Ushaw College*. Ushaw, 1964.

Milne, Maurice. *Newspapers of Northumberland and Durham: A Study of Their Progress During the 'Golden Age' of the Provincial Press*. Newcastle, 1971.

Moody, T.W. ed. *The Fenian Movement*. Cork, 1968.

Morley, John Viscount. *Recollections*, vol II. London, 1918.

Morris, J.H., Williams, L.J. *The South Wales Coal Industry 1841-1875*. Cardiff, 1958.

Morris, Rev, John. *The English Poor Laws and the Catholic Poor*. London, 1860.

Morris, Rev. John. *Catholic England in Modern Times*. London, 1892.

National Association for the Promotion of Social Science. *Transactions, 1861*. Ed. George Hastings. London, 1862.

Neasham, George. *History and Biography of West Durham*. 1881.

Neasham, George. *The Progress of Consett: A Sketch*. Consett, 1892.

Nicholson, T. Cooke. *The Catholic Churches and Chapels of Newcastle-.Upon-Tyne: Being an Historical Sketch... down to the Present Day*. Newcastle, 1871.

Norman, E.R. *Anti-Catholicism in Victorian England*. London, 1968.

Nossiter, T.J. 'Elections and Political Behaviour in County Durham and Newcastle 1832-74'. D.Phil. thesis, Oxford, 1968.

O'Brien, George. *The Economic History of Ireland from the Union to the Famine*. London, 1921.

O'Connor, D.M. 'The Irish in Countries Other Than Ireland: IV: In Great Britain and Wales.' *Catholic Encyclopedia*. New York, 1910, vol.VIII, pp.151-4.

O'Connor, T.P. 'The Irish in Great Britain.' Ed. F. Lavery. *Irish Heroes in the War*. London, 1917, 13-34.

O'Higgins, Rachel. 'The Irish Influence in the Chartist Movement.' *Past and Present*, XX (November 1961), 83-96.

O'Leary, John. *Recollections of Fenians and Fenianism*. London, 1896. 2 vols.

Our Coal and Our Coalpits: the People in Them and the Scenes Around Them by a Traveler Underground. London, 1853.

Page, William ed. *The Victorian History of the County of Durham*, Vol.11. London, 1907.

Pickering, W.S.F. 'The 1851 Religious Census - A Useless Experiment?' *British Journal of Sociology*, XVIII (December 1967), 382-407.

Protestant Aggression: Remarks on the Bishop of Durham's letter to the Archdeacon of Lindisfarne by a Catholic Clergyman Resident Within the Diocese of Durham, January 20th, 1851. Newcastle, 1851.

Protestant Alliance. *Second Annual Report*. London, 1853.

Purcell, Edmund S. *Life of Cardinal Manning*. London, 1895. 2 vols.

Read, Donald, Glasgow, Eric. *Fergus O'Connor, Irishman and Chartist*. London, 1961.

Redford, Arthur. *Labour Migrations in England, 1800-1850*. Manchester, 1926.

Richardson, C. 'Irish Settlement in Mid-Nineteenth Century Bradford.' *Yorkshire Bulletin of Economic and Social Research*, XX (May 1968), 40-57.

Richardson, C. 'The Irish in Victorian Bradford.' Presented to the History Conference, University of Durham, September, 1969.

Richardson, William. *History of the Parish of Wallsend*. Newcastle, 1923.

Robertson, Isobel M.L. 'The Census and Research: Ideals and Realities.' *Transactions of the Institute of British Geographers*, XLVIII (1969), 173-187.

Robinson, George. *Lecture on the Sanitary Condition of Newcastle delivered before the Literary and Philosophical Society 10th February, 1847*. Newcastle, 1847.

Rogers, Rev. Patrick. *Father Theobald Mathew: Apostle of Temperance*. Dublin, 1943.

Russell, Charles A. *The Catholic in the Workhouse*. London, 1859.

Russell, Charles E.B. *Social Problems of the North*. London, 1913.

Samuel, Raphael. 'The Catholic Church and the Irish Poor.' Presented to the Past and Present Conference July 1966.

Sharratt, Rev. Bernard C. *Catholic Church in Hartlepool and West Hartlepool: 1834-1964*. West Hartlepool, 1960.

Simpson, John Bell. *Capital and Labour in Coal Mining During the Past 200 Years*. Newcastle, 1900.

Smailes, Arthur E. 'Population Changes in the Colliery Districts of Northumberland and Durham.' *Geographical Journal*, XCI (January 1938), 220-232.

Smith, John ed. *Public Health Act Report to the General Board of Health on Darlington, 1850*. Durham Local History Society, 1967.

Smith, W. Vincent. *Catholic Tyneside 1534-1850*. Newcastle, 1931.

Stephens, John. 'Abstract of a Return of Prisoners Coming Under the Cognizance of the Police of Newcastle-upon-Tyne, During the Ten Months from the 2nd of October, 1837, to the 2nd of August, 1838.' *Journal of the Statistical Society of London*, I (October 1838), 324-326.

Strauss, Eric. *Irish Nationalism and British Democracy*. London, 1951.

Street, James C. *The Night-side of Newcastle: A Lecture Delivered in the Church of the Divine Unity*. Newcastle, 1865.

Surtees, Robert. *History and Antiquities of the County Palatine of Durham*. London, 1816-1840. 4 vols.

The Church and Our Lady of Mercy and Saint Godric, Durham, to Commemorate the Centenary. Pamphlet. 1964.

The League of the Cross and Crusade Against Intemperance: Official Report of the Conventions of London, July 12 1875 and of Manchester, October 11 1876. Manchester, 1877.

The Life of Joseph Cowen, Esq., M.P. Newcastle, 1874. Reprinted from the *Newcastle Critic*, January 24, 1874.

The Moral Condition of Newcastle: Sabbath Profanation in a Letter to the Rev, the Vicar of Newcastle by a Layman, April 2nd, 1846. Newcastle, 1846.

The Nine Hours Movement Conference between CM. Palmer, Esq. and the Workmen of Jarrow, on Thursday Evening, February 22nd, 1866. Newcastle, 1866.

The Report of the Commissioners Appointed by the Right Reverend The Lord Bishop of Newcastle to Examine into the Spiritual Wants and Requirements of Certain Parishes in the Diocese of Newcastle. Newcastle, 1883.

Thompson, E.P. *The Making of the English Working Class.* London, 1963.

Thornley, David. *Isaac Butt and Home Rule.* London, 1964.

Todd, William G. *The Irish in England.* Reprinted with additions from the *Dublin Review*, LXXXI (December 1856), 470-521. London, 1857.

Torregiani, Father Elzear. *Franciscan Missions Among the Colliers and Ironworkers of Monmouthshire.* London, 1876.

Treble, J.H. 'The Attitude of the Roman Catholic Church Towards Trade Unionism in the North of England 1833-1842.' *Northern History*, V (1970), 93-113.

Treble, J.H. 'The Place of the Irish Catholics in the Social Life of the North of England, 1829-51'. PhD thesis, Leeds University, 1969.

Urban, Miriam Belle. *British Opinion and Policy on the Unification of Italy, 1856-1861.* Pennsylvania, 1938.

Ward, Mgr. Bernard. *The Sequel to Catholic Emancipation,* Vol.2: *1840-1850.* London, 1915.

Watson, Aaron. *A Great Labour Leader: Being a Life of the Right Hon. Thomas Burt, M.P.* London, 1908.

Watson, Archdeacon. 'Our Churches and Our Schools.' *Durham Diocesan Magazine*, (October 1884), 109-118.

Watson, Robert Spence. *Labour: Past, Present, and Future, A Lecture Delivered to the Tyneside Sunday Lecture Society, March 9th, 1890.* Newcastle, 1890.

Wearmouth, R.F. *Methodism and the Struggle of the Working Classes, 1850-1900.* Leicester, 1954.

Webb, Sidney and Beatrice. *The History of Trade Unionism.* London, 1896.

Webb, Sidney. *The Story of the Durham Miners 1662-1921.* London, 1921.

Welbourne, E. *The Miners Unions of Northumberland and Durham.* Cambridge, 1923.

Weston, W.J. *The County of Durham.* Cambridge, 1914.

Wilkinson, Ellen. *The Town That Was Murdered: The Life-Story of Jarrow.* London, 1939.

Wilson, John. *History of the Durham Miners Association 1870-1904.* Durham, 1907.

Wilson, John. *Memories of a Labour Leader: The Autobiography of John Wilson J.P., M.P.* London, 1910.

Wollaston, E.P.M. 'The Irish Nationalist Movement in Great Britain, 1886-1908'. MA thesis, London University, 1958.

Wood, Robert. *West Hartlepool: The Rise and Development of a Victorian New Town*. West Hartlepool, 1967.

Woodward, Sir Llewellyn. *The Age of Reform, 1815-1870*. 2nd edn. Oxford, 1962.

Young, W. *Public Health in Newcastle 1845-54 With Special Reference to the Cholera Epidemic of 1853*. Honours Paper. Newcastle University, 1965.

Index

A
Adventure Colliery 131
agricultural labour 13, 117, 123
Alison, Sir Archibald 104
All Saints parish, Newcastle *see* Sandgate
American Civil War 120
Amnesty Demo, Newcastle 143, 160
Anderson, Michael xii
Anderson, Robert 107, 108
Anglicans 97-98
anti-clericalism 64
anti-sacredotalism 74
Auricular Confession 83, 213n50

B
Bamber, Rev. J. 49, 81
Baring, Charles 219n142
Barke, Mike xiii
Barn Close, Gateshead 24
Barry, John, MP 162
Barry, Lewis 162
Battle of Boyne Day 101
Beckwith, Priscilla 109
Belaney, Rev. Robert 58, 68, 104-6, 120, 121
Benedictines 48
Benfieldside 102
Berwick 149
Betham, Rev. F. 80, 91, 200n91
Bewick, Bishop 36, 54, 110

Bible Society 84
Biggar, Benjamin 163-65
Biggar, Joseph 162, 163-65
Birtley 48, 51, 113
Bishop Auckland 16, 51, 58, 62, 68, 79
Bishopric Bill 1878, 99
Bishopwearmouth 46
Blackhill 49, 51, 68
blacklegs 126-27
Blake, Robert 104
Blandford St., Sandgate 37
Blue Bell, Sandgate 27
Board of Health *Report*, (1854) 39
Booth, Charles 147
Bossy, John 46
Bourke, Rev. M. 66
Bradford 28
Briggs, Asa 4
Briggs, Vicar Apostolic 35, 54
Bright, John, MP 241n112
British Protestant 83, 88
British Reformation Society (BRS) 84, 85-89, 92
British Society for Promoting the Principles of the Reformation, *see* British Reformation Society
Brooms 49
Brougham, Lord 14
Bruce, Dr. 82
Bryson, John 167, 169
Builder 23
building trades 115
Bunting, Jabez 101
Burt, Thomas 101, 167, 168, 172
Bute, Marquis 105
Butt, Isaac, MP 160, 163, 167
Byermoor 49, 51, 68
Byers Green 25

C

Callaly Castle 68
Campbell, Henry 162
Candlish, John 163
Cardiff 105
Carlyle, Thomas 14, 28
Carstairs, Mr. 82, 83
cathedrals
  Durham 70
  St. Mary's, Newcastle 47, 48, 55, 80
  St. Nicholas', Newcastle 48
Catholic Association for the Propagation of the Faith 91
Catholic Church
  on trade unions 136
  on secret societies 34-36
  and politics 146, 156-57
Catholic Defence Association 91
Catholic Diocesan Archives 2
Catholic Friendly Societies 36, 136
Catholic Institute 36, 207n77, 216n94
Catholic Orders of Odd Fellows 36
Catholic Poor-school Committee, 56
Catholic Relief Act (1778), 74
Catholic Rent 56
Catholic Schools 60, 69, 117, 120
Catholic Stafford Club 160
Catholic Young Men's Societies 36
Catholicism, 'social' 136
Catholics
  converts 45-46, 73
  Easter Communicants 59, 65
  English 54-56
  population 46
  priests 62
  urban 51
  recusant 46

census *xii-xiii*
  Enumerators 27, 114, 115, 117
  Religious (1851) 93-94, 99
  'Sunday' (1851) 61, 94
Chadwick, Bishop 66, 110, 162
Charlton, Barbara 55, 61
Charlton, family 54
Chartism 144
chemical works 115
Cheshire 12
Chester-le-Street 68
cholera 39-40, 64
Christian Brothers 69
church building 47-48
Church of England 98, 99-101
churches
  Presbyterian Church, Sandgate 29
  St. Andrew's, Newcastle 35, 80
  St. Cuthbert's, Durham City 53
  St. Dominic's, Newcastle 65
  St. Godric's, Durham City 71, 89, 92, 107, 117, 120
  St. John's, Newcastle 120
  SS. John and Patrick's, Felling 162
  St. Joseph's, Gateshead 60, 91
  St. Joseph's, Sunderland 49, 115
  St. Mary Magdalen, Seaham Harbour 110
  St. Mary's, Gateshead 39
  St. Mary's, Newcastle 35
  St. Mary's, Sunderland 47, 70, 147
  St. Patrick's, Felling, Gateshead 47, 53
  St. Patrick's, Sunderland 49, 53, 70
  St. Patrick's, Wall Knoll St, Newcastle 62, 78
  St. Wilfrid's, Bishop Auckland 68
  St. William's, Darlington 60
  see also cathedrals

Index   265

Clerkenwell explosion 148, 150, 152, 155-56
Clifton Tracts 218n95
coal mining 112; *see also* strikes
Coal Owners' Association 128, 129
Coals pits, *see* collieries
Coal Trade Office 121, 133
Coal Vend 129
Coercion Bill 166, 167, 170
Coleman, Terry 117
collieries, *see* Adventure; New Silksworth; Pensher; Rainton; Seaham; Seaton
Colonial Church and School Society 84
Committee on Emigration (1827) 7, 122
Confraternity of the Holy Cross 33
Congregationalists 98-99
Conservative Party 159
Consett Iron Works 139
Consett 8, 26, 33, 49, 92, 101, 114, 120, 126, 157
Consitt, Very Rev. 64, 67, 71
Conventu Ecclesiastico 67
Cornforth 60
Cornish miners, 42, 113, 134
Cowen, Joseph *xiv*, 99, 100, 165, 167-68, 169, 172
Craig-alley Stairs, Sandgate 196n39
Cramlington 129
Crawford, William 101, 137, 138, 140-41, 169, 172
crime 32-33
Crimean War 120
Crook 53, 56, 102, 153
Croxdale 54
Cumberland *xi*, 13
Cummings, Rev. John 87

D
Dan's Castle 10
Darlington 24, 31, 37, 46, 68, 80, 81, 117, 122, 126; *see also* churches
Davitt, Michael 144, 162
Dearness Valley 138
Denvir, John 114, 137
Deptford 115
Derwent-Consett Iron Works 25
discrimination 124-25
Disraeli, Benjamin 104, 107, 146
docks 114
Doherty, S. *xiii*
domestic service 118
Dougan, David 7
Drummond, H. 76
drunkenness 30, 60
Dublin Monitor 132
Dublin Review 92
Dunn, Thomas 41, 48, 54, 79
Dunston 60, 68
Durham, Bishops of 74, 84, 90, 102, 239n142
Durham Chronicle 170
Durham City 4, 24, 51, 53, 78, 85, 87-88, 92, 116, 151, 165
  see also, cathedrals; churches
Durham Directory 24
Durham, Lord 79, 123, 129, 165
Durham Miners' Association (DMA) 2, 18, 137, 138, 141, 171

E
Easington 53, 60, 62, 68, 113
Ecclesiastical Titles Bill, 198n133
Ellis, Brabazon 86
Emancipation Bill 199n108
emigration, Irish 17
Engels, F. 28
English Church Missions 85, 87

epidemics 38
Errington family 54
Evangelical missions 83

F

family employment 118-20
Felling 51, 62, 82, 164,
  see also, churches
female labour 118
Fenian Brotherhood 155
Fenianism 146, 148-49
Ferry Hill 116
Foran, James 67
Foran, Jeremiah 68
Foran, Rev. Robert 66, 67
Fortin, Rev. Philip 138-40
Framwellgate 19, 30
Franco-Prussian War 113, 120
Freemasons 146
Furniss, Father 89

G

Gaelic 29, 67
Garibaldi 146-47, 153
Gateshead, 113, 115
  Catholics 53, 62
  Irish National Foresters 157
  Irish population 12, 13, 21, 56
  Methodists 101
  municipal election 163-65
  workhouse 91
  see also, churches; Pipewellgate
Gilley, Sheridan *x*
Gilligan, Father 68
Gillow, Rev. C. 81, 138
Gladstone 159, 166, 167, 168, 172
Glasgow 15, 21, 110, 172
glass and bottle works 115, 121
Gloucestershire miners 133
Grainger, Mr. 118
Grey, George 22, 27
Grey, Lord 102, 165

H

Hammond, Charles 163
Hanson family 54
Harcourt, Sir William 76
Hardcastle, Rev. 19
Harivel, Father 53
Hartlepool 51, 80, 86, 116, 119, 149
  chapel building 100
  drink 30
  Fenian recruiting 150
  Irish National Foresters 158
  riots 14
  see also churches
hawking 14
Headlam, Dr. Thomas 39-40
Headlam, M. 90
Healy, Timothy 162-63, 164, 166
Hebburn *xi*, 20, 68
Hedley Hill 42
Heleyside 54
Hibernians 34-36, 101, 128, 136, 146
Highwardens 54
Hindhaugh, Nathaniel 130
Hogarth, Vicar Apostolic 31, 35-36, 52, 56, 57, 81, 109
Holy Guilds 36
'holy poverty' 63-65, 67
Home Missionary and Irish
  Evangelical Society 84, 87
Home Rule *xiv*, 159, 169, 162, 163, 166, 172
  Association 161, 162
  Confederacy 160, 162
  Conference (1880) 168
Houghton-le-Spring 48, 75, 131
housing 122
Howdon *xi*
Hull 117

Hull Advertiser 107, 109
Hunter, George 131, 133, 134
Hylton 127

I

Independent Irish Party 146, 159
Irish Church Bill 166
Irish Church Missions in Ireland 85
Irish Distress meeting 170
'Irish fever' *see* typhus
Irish immigrants, origins 22
Irish Institutes 157, 162
Irish National Foresters 157
Irish People 155
Irish priests 31, 66-69
Irish Republican Brotherhood (IRB) 155
Irish Revolutionary Brotherhood 150
Irish Tribune 236n32
iron trade, 121-22

J

Jackson, Ralph Ward 163
Jarrow *xi*, 20, 25, 26, 114, 115, 120, 147, 164
Jocelyn, Lady 110, 221n175
John Holland 24

K

Kearney, Father P. 47, 48
Kelly, Colonel 148, 151
Kelly, Michael J. 239n79
Kelly, Rev. John 82, 91
Knaresborough Viaduct 117
Knight, Cannon 53
Knights of Labour 231n144

L

Labouchere, Henry, MP 241n114
Lambeths family 102
Lancashire *ix, x,* 12, 98
Land Bill 167

Land League *see*, Northern Land League
Langley Moor 51
Larkin, Charles 91
League of the Cross 33
leakage of faithful 19, 58-60
Leeds 38
Lenders, Rev. John 79
Lescher, Father 33
Lewis, George Cornewall *xi*, 15
Liberal Party 159, 163, 165-66
Liberal Registration Association 163
Lightfoot, Joseph 102
Liverpool *x*, 12, 15, 28, 58, 117
lockouts *see strikes*
Londonderry Papers 2
Londonderry, Earl Vane (5th Marquis) 109, 220n160
Londonderry, Lady (Dowager Marchioness, Frances Anne Vane) 104-9
Londonderry, Lord (3rd Marquis) 8, 105, 113, 129-34, 138, 172, 220n160, 243n145
Longley, Charles Thomas 219n142
Losh, James 14, 40

M

Major, Rev. 103
Maltby, Bishop of Durham 74, 102
Manchester 12, 28, 33, 144, 151
Manchester Martyrs 148, 156
Mann, Horace 94
Manning, Cardinal Henry Edward 33, 45, 55, 66, 69, 71, 136, 161
Marries, Rev. Howel 212n27
Mathew, Theobald 31
Matthews, Father Patrick 68
Mayhew, Henry 20, 28
Maynooth 73, 74, 75, 78, 82, 87
Mayo Co. 22

McAnulty, Bernard 145, 158, 162, 166, 168
McCord, Norman 154
McEvoy, Father J.A. 48, 52, 54
Methodists 75, 98-99, 100
Mewburn, Francis 81, 103, 117, 123
Middlesbrough 3, 52, 119, 127, 151; Fenians in, 150, 154,
Millfield 115
Miners' Advocate 129
Minsteracres 54, 90
Monkwearmouth 46, 49
Moravian Mission 84
Morpeth 123
Morris, Rev. 61
Morton, Henry 79, 123
Mostyn, Francis (Vicar Apostolic) 16, 55, 62
Mount Pleasant, Sandgate 196n39
Murphy, William *xxi*, 76, 152, 211n12
music 30

N
Nags Head, Sandgate 196n39
Napoleonic Wars 123
Nation 112, 155, 158
National Amalgamated Union of Labourers 137
National Brotherhood of St. Patrick 155, 235n14
National League 162
Neal, Frank *xiii, xv*
New Silksworth Colliery 137
New Tunstall 49
New Unionism 136
Newcastle
 Amnesty demonstration 143, 160
 Anglican Bishop 100,
 Armoury, Nelson St.149

Board of Commerce 121
 explosions 23, 152
 health officer 121
 Home Rulers 161
 immigrant population 9
 Infirmary 35
 Irish Institute 157, 162
 Poor Law Guardians 41, 42
 Precursor Society 145
 Racecourse 147
 rents 122
 St. Cuthbert's Grammar School 236n32
 Town Moor rioters 147, 154
 see also cathedrals; churches; Sandgate
Newcastle Daily Chronicle xiv, 153, 160, 167-68
Newhouses 138, 141
Nolan, John 160
Nonconformist 99
Nonconformists 98-99, 101
No-Popery 74-78, 87
North of England Institute of Mining 2
North of England Iron Trade 119
North of England Protestant Alliance *see* Protestant Alliance
North Shields 97
Northern Catholic Calendar 62, 81
Northern Crusade 33
Northern District Fund 54, 55
Northern Land League 163, 165, 167, 242n138
Northern Star 128
Northumberland Miners' Association 167
Northumberland 3
Nugent, Father 33
Nunneries Inspection Bill 91

O

O'Connell, Daniel 56, 74, 144
O'Connell, Ellen 69
O'Connor, Feargus 144
O'Connor, T.P. 172
O'Connor-Power, J. 137, 141, 162, 169, 243n145
O'Donnell, John Francis 162
O'Leary, John 145
Operative Jewish Converts' Society 84
Orange lodges *xv*, 101
Owen, Robert 144
Oxford Movement 45, 74

P

Pall Mall Gazette 148
Pallion 115
Palmer, Charles M. *xiv*, 8, 25, 100, 114, 120, 136
Parnell, Charles S. 143, 162, 165
Parnell Leadership Committee 162
Parnell Manifesto 160
Pastoral-Aid Society (C of E) 84, 87
Pease, J.W., MP 153, 170
Peel, Sir Robert 122
Pemberton, R.L. 108
Pensher Colliery 134
Perrin, Rev. 161
piece work 121, 135
pigs 23, 24, 26, 38, 139
Piper, Stephen Edward (MOH) 37
Pipewellgate, Gateshead 24
Platt, Provost 53, 67
Pontypool, Wales 68
Poor Law removals 15, 18, 40-42
Pope Leo XIII 136
Pope Pius X 87, 205n49
Port Clarence 115
Portract 172
potato blight 10

Prayer-Book and Homily Society 84
Precursor Society 145, 235n14
Preston 12
Primitive Methodists 101
prostitutes 40, 119
Protestant Aggression 90
Protestant Alliance 76, 78, 85, 87, 91
Pudlers 120

Q

Quarries 16

R

Railways construction 14, 115, 116-17
Rainton Colliery 131, 134
Rambler 55, 65, 96
Ranter Dick 76-77
Ravenshaw, J.H. 104
Ravensworth family 102, 130
Record 84, 106
Redhills Viaduct, Durham 117
Reid, Dr. 23
Religious Tract Society 84
Removal Warrants *see* Poor Law Removals
Repeal Associations 145, 235n14
Repeal Club 235n14
Report ... on Irish Poor (1836) 111, 123, 145
Report on ... Population ... Mining Districts (1846) 133
revisionism *ix*
Rex, John *ix*
Rhondda Valley 124
Ribbonmen 34-35, 101, 144, 146
Riddell, William (Bishop) 39, 54, 55, 62, 64, 80, 81
riots, 30-31, 76-77, 147, 150, 154
Ripon, Bishop 84
Robinson, Dr. 38

Robinson, Thomas 138-41
Robson, Mr. 163-65
Roscommon Co. 22
Rosedale and Ferry Hill Iron Works 60
Rowntree, Seebohm 26, 27
Royal Commission on the Health of Town, 24
Russell, Lord John 74
Rutherford, Dr. 100

S

Sacriston 33, 51, 68
St. Cuthbert's Grammar School, Newcastle 236n32
St. Mary's Street, Sandgate 192n35, 196n34, 196n39
St. Patrick *see* National Brotherhood
St. Patrick's Day 31-32, 35, 141, 162
  Jarrow 164
  Newcastle 79, 102, 148
  South Shields 161
St. Vincent de Paul, Brotherhood 28, 63-64, 91
Salford 154
Salvation Army 103
Salvin, W.T. 54, 79
Samuel, Raphael 19
Sandgate St., Sandgate 22
Sandgate, 22, 28, 29, 37, 38, 40, 41-42, 61, 118
  Catholic population 47
  Riot 76-77
  see also Blandford St.; Blue Bell; churches; Craig-alley Stairs; Mount Pleasant; Nags Head; St. Mary's St.; Sandgate St.; Trolley; Young's Entry
Savage, Edward 162
Scotch Presbyterians 125
Scotland *x*

Scott, Caroline *xiii*
Scott, Rev. W.A. 107
Scriptual Reader's Association 84
Seaham Colliery 108
Seaham Harbour 8, 51, 104-10 116, 124, 137
Seaham Weekly News 106
Seaham, Viscount Henry 90, 220n160
Seaton Colliery 107, 170
Seaton Delaval 129, 151
Sedgefield 51, 113
Select Committee on Emigration (1841) 117
Select Committee on Railway Labourer (1846) 119
Shaftesbury, Earl 84
Sheffield Independent 133
Sheridan, J.J. 48
shipbuilding 114
shipping 115-17
Silvertop family 54
Sisters of Mercy 69, 89
Sligo Co. 22
Small Tenements Act 145
Society of the Holy Family 33
South Shields 17-18, 20, 25, 56, 75, 91, 97, 116
  Irish row 153
  Fenian recruiting 150
  Temperance 33
  Hibernians, 35;
  St. Patrick's Day 161
  see also churches
Southwick-on-Wear 31, 115
Stanley 49, 53, 68
Status Animarum 45
Stella 60, 68, 67
Stockport 12, 110

Stockton-upon-Tees 16, 18, 86, 103, 150
Storey, Samuel 165
Strauss, Eric 127
strike pay 140
strikes 121
  iron trade (1865) 120, 126
  miners (1832), 129; (1844) *xv*; 112, 127-35; (1865), 119; Ushaw Moor, (1882) 137-41
  shipwrights 127
  engineers (1871) 121, 127
  Seaham Colliery 170
Suffield, Father 146
Sullivan, T.D. 137, 162
Sunderland 7, 18, 48, 49, 75, 81, 113, 114, 115, 116, 149
  BRS 85
  Catholic population 46
  Fenianism 150, 151
  Methodists 101
  mortality 24
  prostitution 119
  town council 12
  see also churches
Swift, Roger *x*

T

Tablet 2, 52, 53
Tadini, John 83
Talbot case 76
Taylor-Smith family 54
Temperance movement 33-34
Tenant League 235n14
Thompson, E.P. *ix*, 126
Thompson, Thomas 165
Thornley 10, 13, 29, 31, 45, 51, 56, 68, 103, 113, 129
Tolpuddle Martyrs 136
Torregiani, Father 68
Tory press 48

Tow Law 8, 10, 29, 30, 54, 115
Town Moor Rioters 147, 150, 154
Townsend, Rev. 87, 89
trade unions 25, 135
Treble, John *xi*, 115
Tremenheere, Seymour 133
Trimdon 60
Trolley, Sandgate 27
Tudhoe 51
Tyne Dock 115
Tyne Mercury 127, 128
Tynemouth 119, 150
Tyneside and National Labour Union 137
Tyneside Catholic News 196n32
typhus 38-39

U

Ultramontanism 63, 168
United Kingdom Alliance 33
Ushaw College 2, 66, 140
Ushaw Moor 19, 25, 92, 138-41

V

Vane, Earl Adolphous 106, 108, 220n160
Villiers, Henry 199n142

W

Wages 118-20, 122-23
Wales
  Irish 124, 134, 144
  see also Cardiff; Pontypool; Rhondda Valley; Welsh
Walker *xi*
Wall Knoll St, Sandgate 10, 13, 29, 40, 62, 192n35
Wallsend *xi*
Walsh, John 155
Waterton, Father 161
Weardale 113, 151
Welsh 20, 129, 134

West Cornforth 32
West Hartlepool 8, 53, 126, 150
Wilkinson, Rev. G. Howard 105, 106
Williamson, Sir Hedworth 102
Willington 170, 242n138
Wilson, John 101, 169, 171
Wiseman, Cardinal 66, 70, 146
Witton Park 113
Witton-le-Wear 116

Wolsingham 29, 51, 56
working men's clubs 135-36, 171

Y
Yorkshire 81
Young Ireland Confederate Club 235n14
Young Ireland 145
Young's Entry, Sangate 196n39

Z
Zavier, Rev. Mother 69

University of Sunderland Press Publications

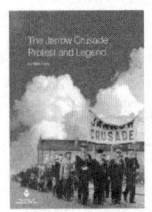

The Jarrow Crusade: Protest and Legend by Matt Perry
ISBN 1 873757 60 3   Pages: 280   **Price: £12.95**
Plus postage and packing on single copies - £1.50

The Jarrow Crusade is hailed as a defining moment of the hungry thirties. It was the protest of the people of a Tyneside town against the closure of their shipyard and the blocking of their new steelworks. More than any other protest, it is held up as a model for others to follow. Its rejection of politics and its courting of respectable opinion are seen as the reason for its success; this at least is the version of events that many will be familiar. However, the Crusade did not win jobs for Jarrow and a series of myths and folklore have come to surround the event. This book is an attempt to get to grips with the real history of the Crusade. It is a history that offers insights into the character of British society and into the nature of protest then and now.

Tom Hadaway The Prison Plays
Including Long Shadows co-written with Pauline Hadaway, Edited and with an introduction by Val McLane
ISBN 1 873757 10 7   Pages: 280   **Price: £12.95**
Plus postage and packing on single copies - £1.50

Tom Hadaway is one of North East England's leading playwrights. He has written more than twenty plays, films and television scripts, including The Filleting Machine, God Bless Thee Jackie Maddison, Seafarers and The Long Line, all performed by The Live Theatre in Newcastle. The Prison Plays is a collection of two full-length and two short plays written after his term as writer in residence at Durham and Frankland prisons in 1986.

Sir Tom Cowie A True Entrepreneur – A Biography
by Denise Robertson – Foreword by Wilbur Smith
Hardback – ISBN 1 873757 30 1   Pages: 240   **Price: £16.99**
Paperback – ISBN 1 873757 84 0   Pages: 240   **Price: £8.99**
Plus postage and packing on single copies - £2.50

This is the storey of a young man from Sunderland who was discharged from the RAF in 1946 with a gratuity and went on to build one of the fastest-growing companies in the United Kingdom. The story moves from the small backyard where Tom Cowie's motor-cycle business started, through his days as manager and director of a successful lease-hire car company, to his accolades for political and other services.

The Whaling Trade of North-East England 1750-1850
by Tony Barrow   ISBN 1 873757 83 2   Pages: 192   **Price: £14.95**
Plus postage and packing on single copies - £1.50

North East England was one of the most important centres of British whaling enterprise. From Berwick in the north to Whitby in the south, stoutly built whaling ships sailed annually to the Arctic grounds in search of the Greenland whale. The Whaling Trade of North-East England 1750-1850, is the first comprehensive, academic account of this fascinating aspect of the maritime heritage of the region.

Art & the Spiritual Edited by Bill Hall and David Jasper
ISBN 1 873757 78 6   Pages: 104   **Price: £14.95**
Plus postage and packing on single copies - £1.00

A collection of essays and responses; this book is challenging without retreating into the arcane world of academic debate and discussion. Written by artists, each essay is given a response by a professional theologian.

Reform and Reformers in Nineteenth Century Britain
Edited by Michael J Turner
ISBN 1 873757 94 8   Pages: 184   **Price: £11.95**
Plus postage and packing on single copies - £1.50

This volume of essays carries forward some of the most interesting recent debates about the nature and scope of reform, the identity, motives and goals of reformers, and the place of reform in the political, social and economic development of nineteenth-century Britain.

A Concentration of Moral Force – The Temperance Movement in Sunderland, 1830 to 1853 by Allan Harty
ISBN 1 873757 93 X   Pages: 64   **Price: £7.95**
Plus postage and packing on single copies - £1.00

This study examines the evolution of the Temperance cause in Sunderland from its inception until the demand for parliamentary intervention heralded a new phase in the town's crusade against intemperance. Set against the prevailing culture of drink, the author discusses the conflict within the temperance movement as its objectives changed from 'moral suasion' to 'legislative suppression'.

Britain and the Baltic Studies in Commercial, Political and Cultural Relations 1500-2000 Edited by Tony Barrow and Patrick Salmon
ISBN 1873757 49 2   Pages: 384   **Price: £17.95**
Plus postage and packing on single copies - £2.50

Political, commercial and cultural connections between Britain and the Baltic are amongst the oldest and most enduring in the historical record. And yet, paradoxically, they are also amongst the least known and poorly understood. The essays contained within this volume demonstrate that scholarly study of Britain's historical relationship with the countries of Scandinavia and the Baltic region is both varied and dynamic.

Merchants and Gentry in North-East England 1650-1830
The Carrs and the Ellisons by A W Purdue
ISBN 1 873757 08 5   Pages: 304   ~~RRP £16.95~~ **Now £12.95**
Plus postage and packing on single copies - £2.50

This book follows the progress of the Ellisons of Hebburn Hall and the Carrs of Dunston Hill from their mercantile success in the seventeenth century to their solid gentry and land-owning status in the nineteenth century. The aim of this book is to set the history of the Carrs and Ellisons against the development of the region on which they made such an influence.

To order any of the above publications you can either Fax, Telephone or contact: Business Education Publishers Limited, The Teleport, Doxford International, Sunderland, SR3 3XD, Tel: +44(0) 191 5252410, Fax: +44(0) 191 5201815, email: info@bepl.com